ENJOYING ENGLISH

Books featured

Brown, Christy *My Left Foot*
Charlwood, Don *All the Green Year*
Dahl, Roald *The Wonderful Story of Henry Sugar*
Evans, Russell *Survival*
Golding, William *Lord of the Flies*
Hemingway, Ernest *The Old Man and the Sea*
Herriot, James *The Lord God Made Them All*
Hinton, S. E. *Tex*
Hinton, S. E. *That Was Then, This Is Now*
Huxley, Aldous *Brave New World*
Jennings, Paul *Round the Twist*
Lee, Harper *To Kill a Mockingbird*
Lucas, Jeremy *Whale*
Morgan, Sally *My Place*
Orwell, George *Animal Farm*
Peyton, K. M. *Pennington's Seventeenth Summer*
Remarque, Erich Maria *All Quiet on the Western Front*
Richter, Hans Peter *Friedrich*
Steinbeck, John *The Pearl*
Zindel, Paul *The Pigman's Legacy*

ENJOYING ENGLISH

BOOK 4

SADLER/HAYLLAR/POWELL

MACMILLAN

First published 1991 by
MACMILLAN EDUCATION AUSTRALIA PTY LTD
107 Moray Street, South Melbourne 3205
Reprinted 1993 (twice), 1994, 1995

Associated companies and representatives
throughout the world.

National Library of Australia
cataloguing in publication data.

Sadler, R.K. (Rex Kevin).
Enjoying English. Book 4.

ISBN 0 7329 0299 1.

1. English language – Rhetoric – Juvenile literature.
2. English language – Composition and exercises –
Juvenile literature. I. Hayllar, T. A. S. (Thomas Albert S.).
II. Powell, C. J. (Clifford J.). III. Title.

808'.042

Typeset in Palatino by
Superskill Graphics, Singapore
Printed in Malaysia

CONTENTS

PREFACE

The *Enjoying English* series is a literature-based course for secondary students. It features an extensive selection of passages drawn from high-interest, contemporary novels and non-fiction books. These constitute a base for the development of comprehension skills and additional work on language and writing skills. Because of the quality of these passages, we anticipate that students will be encouraged to read more widely by seeking out these and other similar books from libraries.

The course gives considerable emphasis to poetry and drama. The wide range of poems presented offers an opportunity for students to explore and appreciate the richness of this strand of literature. Many drama extracts and complete scripts are included, as well as creative drama projects and tasks.

The creative writing sections encourage the development of writing skills by the use of writing models and stimulus photographs. Practical language work is incorporated in each unit to reinforce and develop the students' understanding of essential language concepts.

All the material in *Enjoying English* has been thoroughly tested in the classroom to ensure that it offers rich possibilities for valuable learning and enjoyment.

1

STARTLING STORIES

STORIES

Lucky Lips

Marcus was sixteen years old and had never been kissed. His determination to change this embarrassing state of affairs led to some painful encounters.

The lighthouse slumbered in the sun. Inside, however, Pete's room was gloomy. Pete lay half awake looking at a poster of his favourite rock star — Zan. She sat, dressed in leather, on the seat of a motorbike. Her full lips were slightly parted. A sultry youth leaned against a wall and looked at her in a bored, assured manner.

Pete's eyes closed. His imagination wandered. He was the one looking at Zan. She beckoned him with a crooked finger and pouting mouth. Pete sauntered over and bent down. 'Kiss me,' she whispered.

Peter moistened his lips and bent down. Zan's arm pulled his head forward.

'Pete,' came a loud shout.

The daydream cracked and tinkled to the floor. Linda stood there grinning and brandishing a copy of *Dolly* magazine. 'Did you buy this?' she said.

'Sure,' said Pete sarcastically. 'I was just checking the latest shades of lipstick and eyeshadow.'

'That's funny,' said Linda. 'There's a letter to the agony column and someone's put a pencil mark next to it.'

'So?'

'The letter's from someone in Port Niranda. Someone with the initials PT . . . Peter Twist?'

'There's probably millions of PTs in Port Niranda,' said Pete lamely.

Linda smelt victory. She started to read. 'Dear Never Been Kissed. Here is my advice. One — take her to a disco. Two — dance wildly for the first hour. Three — dance slow and close for the next hour. Four — walk her home. Five — look into her eyes and if they say "yes" — kisssssss.'

Pete went red as Linda tossed the magazine onto the bed.

'Good luck, Never Been Kissed,' said Linda. 'And if her name's Fiona you're going to need it. She wouldn't even look at you.'

Pete gave a cocky grin. 'Well, she's going to the disco with me. That must mean something.'

Music blared. Disco lights splashed the dancers' faces with colour. Pete couldn't believe his luck. Fiona, the most beautiful girl in the school, was dancing with him. And tonight he was going to walk her home. He couldn't stop thinking about Step Five. 'Look into her eyes. And if they say "yes" — kisssssss.' He had the five steps written down on the back of his hand.

Pete was already well into Step Two. He danced crazily, pumping his hands up and down like a wild thing. Fiona wore an amused smile as she tried to keep up.

Over against the wall, Gribble and Rabbit watched the dancers. Gribble stared at Linda who was dancing with Jill Henderson. 'Think I'll do that Twist sheila a favour,' smirked Gribble. He wandered out onto the dance floor. 'G'day, desperate,' he said. 'Wanna dance?'

'I'd have to be desperate to dance with you,' snorted Linda.

Tiger Gleeson looked down from the DJ's booth. 'Here's something with a bit more pace for all you rockers,' he said. He turned down the lights and played a smooth, slow number. A few boos came up from the floor. Pete pulled Fiona towards him gently. Step Three. It was working.

Gribble returned to Rabbit. 'Changed me mind about the Twist sheila,' he said.

Rabbit was watching Pete. 'Why would Fiona come with a jerk like Twist?' he said.

Gribble watched jealously. 'Felt sorry for him,' he said. Then he added. 'Twist has had it.'

Pete's big moment finally came. The disco was over. He walked with Fiona through the dark, lonely streets. Neither of them spoke. Pete was nervous. All he could think about was Step Five. He'd never kissed a girl before.

He was so nervous that he didn't see Gribble, Rabbit and Tiger sneaking along behind. They ran from car to car and bush to bush. 'This is it,' said Tiger in an excited whisper. 'He's wetting his lips.'

Fiona looked at Pete and smiled. 'Thank you for a lovely . . .'

'I'll walk you up to the door,' said Pete nervously.

Tiger dug Gribble in the ribs. 'He's trying the old "walk-her-to-the-door tactic",' he said.

Gribble frowned.

'They've reached the door,' said Tiger. 'He's limbering those lips. Puckering in preparation.'

Rabbit punched his hands together gleefully. 'He's going to kiss her, Gribs.'

'Shut up,' growled Gribble.

Fiona opened the front door. 'It was a great night, Pete,' she said. 'Thanks.'

Pete closed his eyes and leaned gently forward. He pursed his moist lips and kissed the closed front door.

Loud hooting and laughing split the darkness. The gang mocked mercilessly from the road. 'Splinter mouth,' yelled Gribble.

'Kissed off,' shouted Rabbit.

'Give up, Twist,' called Gribble. 'No one'd kiss a maggot mouth like you.'

Pete hung his head. He blushed with shame. There was nothing he could say.

Pete felt miserable for days afterwards. He didn't want to be with anyone. On Sunday he went to the local show, all on his own. He didn't feel like going to the sideshows. He didn't look at the animals. He walked around the fairground kicking stones and ignoring the laughing kids on the merry-go-rounds and rides.

He wandered between the tents and trucks not looking where he was going. Suddenly he found himself in front of an old caravan. On the side was written:

There was a drawing of a hand with an eye in the middle of the palm.

And sitting on the step was the most beautiful girl Pete had ever seen. Her smile was the promise of a gentle spring. It warmed him like the summer sun. Her teeth were as white as the winter snow. Her hair shone with the sheen of spiders' webs on an autumn morning. Pete looked behind him. The smile was for him. She beckoned with a crooked finger and then, drawing a coloured shawl over her head, turned and walked into the caravan.

Pete followed in a daze and peered into the shadowy silences where cobwebs joined hands. At the far end of the van a cooking pot shimmered with a silver liquid. The figure in the shawl turned.

Pete gasped. She had changed. The beautiful girl was now a wrinkled old woman wearing garish red lipstick. She cackled like a monkey squealing in the treetops.

Fear grabbed Pete by the throat. 'Er, I think I'd better be going,' he stammered. 'I forgot to put the cat out.'

Madame Fortune pushed him down onto a velvet seat.

'Not yet,' she chuckled. 'You haven't got what you want.'

'What do I want?'

Madame Fortune puckered her wrinkled lips. 'A kiss,' she said.

Pete stood up. 'Thanks, but no thanks,' he said.

'Not from me, you silly boy. From the girl of your dreams.'

Madame Fortune stirred the silver liquid. Pete's eyes were drawn to it. He couldn't look away. It shimmered and glimmered and then a ghostly figure formed and stared at him as if from the bottom of a pool.

'Fiona,' gasped Pete. 'How did you know about . . .'

'A kiss,' shrieked Madame Fortune. 'A kiss from the girl of your dreams.'

She stirred the liquid again and the image faded.

'In this bath,' she said, 'are washed all the world's grubby longings. I know all. Never Been Kissed,' she hooted. 'Never Been Kissed.'

Pete hung his head again. He didn't need reminding.

Madame Fortune put a gnarled hand into a string bag and drew out a small tube.

'What's that?' said Pete as she waved it under his nose.

'Lipstick. Special lipstick. Invisible lipstick.'

'No way,' said Pete. 'I'm not wearing lipstick.'

Madame Fortune gently pushed him back into the chair. 'It will make Fiona kiss you. It will make any girl kiss you. Just smear it on your lips when you're near a girl and she won't be able to stop herself kissing you.'

Pete shook his head. 'Don't you want a kiss?' asked Madame Fortune. She pointed to the silver liquid. An image formed. Pete saw himself at Fiona's door. He saw the door close in his face. He saw himself with his lips pressed against the cold glass. He shivered as the image faded.

'You can run away from the past,' said the old woman. 'But you can't avoid the future.' She put the lipstick in Pete's hand.

'For nothing?' asked Pete.

'For nothing. It's a loan. I'll come for it and get it back at five o'clock on Wednesday. Wherever the lipstick is, I'll find it. If you can't get a kiss by then you miss out.'

Pete took the lipstick doubtfully. 'It won't make the boys kiss me, will it?' he said.

'No. But it will work on any female. Only once though. You'll only get one kiss from each girl with this lipstick.'

Pete put it in his pocket. 'One kiss from Fiona,' he said. 'Will last forever.'

Bronson sat in his little lighthouse room and played with his computer. Outside the sun was setting across the sea. He looked up as Pete came into the room.

'You know that wonderful watch of yours,' said Pete. 'Can you make it beep at exactly 5pm on Friday?'

Bronson picked up the watch. 'Yeah. Why?'

'I have to do something by then,' said Pete. 'Can you lend it to me?'

Bronson fiddled with the watch and handed it over. 'Two dollars,' he said holding out his hand. 'And it'll beep at exactly 5pm.'

Much later Fiona and Linda jogged towards Fiona's house. They stopped outside the gate, puffing. Neither of them knew that Pete was hiding some distance away. As Linda jogged off he took out the lipstick and stared at it. 'Fiona. This is it,' he said to himself. 'Tonight all my dreams come true.' He wound out the lipstick and smeared some of it over his lips. Then he ran across the road. Fiona had gone in.

Pete pursed his lips. 'Fiona,' he whispered. He knocked loudly on the door.

There was a sound of footsteps and the door was thrown open. There stood Fiona's mother.

'Is Fiona home?' began Pete.

He stopped. Fiona's mother was staring. Her lips were twitching. She trembled and then tottered forward pulled by an unseen force. She threw her arms around Pete and lowered him in a wild embrace. Their lips met as Pete struggled furiously.

Fiona's father gaped from the door.

The poor woman suddenly stopped kissing. She looked up. 'I'm sorry,' she said. 'I don't know what got into . . .'

Pete furiously wiped away the lipstick. He saw Fiona staring at him accusingly. Fiona's father charged out. Pete ran for it.

'Hey, come back here,' yelled the enraged husband. He turned around to his wife. 'Is there something you want to tell me, dear?' he said.

Things weren't working out well for Pete. But he wasn't about to give up.

The next day at school, the students all filed into a Human Development class. 'Twist kissed Fiona Richmond's mum,' yelled Gribble.

'Desperate,' said Rabbit. 'She must be a least forty years old. No one else would kiss him.'

Pete was embarrassed. He tried to joke his way out of it. 'Women can't resist me,' he said.

Some of the girls groaned. Fiona hadn't come in yet.

'He tried to kiss Fiona and ended up kissing the doorknob,' smirked Gribble.

'Yeah,' added Rabbit.

'You'll see. I've got animal magnetism,' said Pete. He tapered off as Fiona came in and sat down across the aisle. She looked at Pete with a curious expression.

Ms James came in and put her books down. Pete was desperate for a kiss from Fiona. If she kissed him in class those fools would have to stop mocking him. He bent down under the desk and smeared on the lipstick.

'Fiona,' said Ms James. 'Would you take this note to Mr Snapper, please?' Fiona took the note and left the room.

Pete looked up. 'Fee oh nah,' he said. His face fell as he saw her empty seat.

The nearest girl was Jill Henderson. She stared at Pete with wide open eyes. Her lips started to twitch. Her fingers trembled. With a look of horror she threw herself onto Pete and kissed him passionately.

Ms James was shocked. 'Jill,' she said. 'What are you doing?'

Tiger grinned. He started to call the action. 'Twist has had a big breakthrough here,' he yelled. 'Jill has jumped him.'

An epidemic swept through the room. All the girls started to twitch and stare. Suddenly in one movement they jumped out of their desks and scrambled for Pete. Like wild, uncaged animals they shrieked and piled on top of him in a wriggling mass. They tore his clothes. They scratched and scrabbled for Pete, wrestling him to the floor.

Each girl kissed him and then staggered away and slumped in her desk. They were stunned. Unbelieving. They didn't know what was happening. The boys stared in amazement.

'The girls are going crazy,' yelled Tiger. 'They're twisted.'

Ms James clung to the edge of her desk. 'Girls. Please,' she yelled.

'Ms James doesn't like this,' yelled Tiger.

Pete struggled to his feet. His clothes were torn. He was cut and bruised. He looked up and saw Linda bearing down on him. 'No,' he yelled.

'His own sister is going for it,' shouted Tiger. 'Yes. His own sister is kissing him.'

Linda kissed Pete wildly and then leapt back and wiped her mouth.

Ms James stared at Pete with wide open eyes. Her lips trembled. She clung to the edge of the desk. But it was no good. The power of the lipstick was too strong. Her fingers slipped from the desk and she lunged forward.

'Ms James does like it,' shrieked Tiger. 'She's going for it. Ms James is sucking face with Twist.'

Ms James kissed Pete long and wildly. Then she jumped back, shocked and upset. Pete furiously wiped his lips and looked up — to see Fiona staring at him through the corridor window. She shook her head in puzzlement.

Jill put her hand up to her throat and screamed. 'I kissed Pete Twist,' she groaned.

She rushed out of the room. All the other girls followed, wiping their mouths as if they had just eaten something awful.

'Talk about lucky,' said Rabbit.

'Lucky lips,' yelled Tiger.

Everyone laughed. Except Gribble. He was looking at the lipstick which Pete still held in his hand. 'I want that lipstick,' he said to himself.

The lipstick was spooky.

So was the music that kept coming from Nell's room at the top of the lighthouse. No one could ever find out who was playing it.

Later that night, Dad, Bronson, Pete and Linda stood outside the door at the top of the lighthouse. Dad opened it a fraction. The music grew louder. They burst through the door. Nothing. Silence. The music had stopped. The old clarinet, saxophone and violin lay there covered in dust. They looked at each other and shrugged. The mystery of the music had them stumped.

Linda peered out of the window as Ms James' little Volkswagen pulled up at the foot of the lighthouse.

'Dad, look,' said Linda. 'It's Ms James. You'd better make your move soon. She's a good catch.'

'I'm not interested in her,' said Dad.

'Not much,' scoffed Linda as they walked down the spiral staircase. 'You blush every time we mention her name.'

Pete looked gloomy. He thought he knew why Ms James was coming.

'She danced with Mr Snapper at the disco the other night,' said Linda.

Dad looked up sharply. 'He's too old for her,' he snapped. He rushed down to the front door with a red face.

'Hello,' said Dad as he opened the door. 'This is a pleasant surprise.'

'We've had some complaints about Pete,' said Ms James. 'Fiona's father says that Pete kissed his wife.'

'No,' said Pete. 'She kissed me.'

'This morning he kissed every girl in the class.'

'They kissed me,' said Pete.

'He kissed Ms James too,' added Linda.

Dad was shocked. 'What?' he gasped. 'What's going on here, Pete?'

Pete slowly pulled the lipstick out of his pocket. 'It's this stuff,' he said. 'You put it on and the girls kiss you.'

'Yuck,' said Bronson. 'Who'd want a rotten old girl kissing them?'

'Stay out of this, son,' said Dad.

'He's after Fiona,' said Linda.

Dad took the lipstick from Pete. Pete didn't want to lose it.

'But, Dad,' he said. 'It has to go back tomorrow.'

'I think I'd better keep this,' Dad said thoughtfully. 'To be on the safe side.' He took Ms James' arm and led her outside. The kids trailed behind.

Dad looked into Ms James' eyes earnestly. 'It's hard bringing them up on my own,' he said. 'Pete's getting a bit wild.'

'You don't think there's anything in his story about the lipstick then? Something happened at school. Even Linda kissed him.'

'Of course not,' said Dad. 'Look.' He smeared some of the lipstick on his lips.

'Oh no,' yelled Linda. She bolted into the lighthouse and shut the door.

Ms James twitched. Her eyes stared. She tried to resist but she was drawn forward by the power of the lipstick. She threw her arms around Dad and kissed him wildly.

Dad just stood there with his arms hanging down limply. Then he took her in his arms, making the best of it. The kiss went on and on. It was a very long kiss indeed. Nell wandered by carrying a fishing rod. She shook her head. 'In my day,' she grumbled, 'teachers taught reading and writing.'

Dad and Ms James sprung apart.

'Sorry,' trembled Ms James. She stared at Dad with puzzled eyes. 'I, I, didn't mean that.'

'Didn't you?' said Dad. He sounded disappointed.

Ms James turned and rushed off to her car. Dad stared at the lipstick with a devilish smile. He pushed it into the pocket of his overalls.

'What about my lipstick?' complained Pete. 'You've had your kiss.'

'This is too powerful for children to handle,' he said. 'I'll look after it.'

'But, Dad . . .' protested Pete. He was wasting his breath. Dad was already walking off.

That night, when everyone was asleep, Pete crept down the spiral staircase into the kitchen. Dad's overalls lay across a chair. Pete put his hand into the pocket and pulled out the lipstick.

The next morning he left for school before Dad was up. This was his last chance to get a kiss from Fiona.

Poor Pete sat alone at the back of the class. All the girls shuffled away from him. Ms James spoke in a loud voice to get their attention.

'You've got the whole afternoon at the agricultural show,' she said. 'Don't even look at a sideshow until you've answered all the questions on your sheet. I want you to pair up. One girl and one boy.'

'I'm not going with Pete Twist,' said Jill.

'Me neither,' said Bessie.

Gribble grinned. 'No girl'll ever go near Twist again,' he leered.

'Not even his own sister,' said Rabbit.

'I'll go with Pete,' said a voice from the back. It was Fiona.

Gribble frowned. 'We'll follow em,' he said to Rabbit.

Pete and Fiona didn't say much as they walked around the showground. Pete noticed that Madame Fortune's caravan was nowhere to be seen. They stopped at a booth where a pretty girl was selling kisses.

Gribble, Rabbit and Tiger were in the queue. 'I'm having fifty kisses,' said Gribble.

Rabbit's mouth fell open. 'That's a hundred bucks, Gribs,' he said.

'Nah,' said Gribble. 'After the first one, she'll be paying me.'

Gribble reached the front of the line. The girl took one look at him and turned over a sign with a smile. It said,

Fiona looked at Pete. 'It's not right,' she said. 'Buying kisses. Kisses should be free. I wouldn't want to be kissed by someone who didn't really like me.'

Pete hung his head. He felt ashamed. 'You're right,' he said. 'Fiona, there's something I want to tell you.' He took out the lipstick.

Gribble and Rabbit approached. 'Hand over that lipstick,' said Gribble. 'If anyone's going to show Fiona how it works it's going to be me.'

'No way,' yelled Pete. He turned and ran for it. The gang charged after him.

Pete raced through the dodgem cars and ducked behind a fairy-floss stall. The gang pelted after him. Pete looked around for escape. He darted between two tents and into the animal pavilion. The gang stuck to his tail. He couldn't shake them off.

Rabbit leapt forward in a rugby tackle and brought Pete to the ground. Gribble and Tiger piled on top. Pete clutched the lipstick in his fingers. Gribble grabbed his wrist and tried to pull his arm down. The lipstick, like a loaded gun, came closer to Pete's face. Their hands quivered. And then slowly, Pete's arm collapsed. The lipstick smeared across his face and lips.

Pete struggled out and looked around desperately. They were next to the pig pen. He jumped up onto the railings and walked along the pens. The gang followed. Pete looked down at the horrible pigs below. Their green teeth slobbered with slime. Their teats swung like water-filled rubber gloves.

A keeper yelled out in a loud voice. 'Hey, you kids. Get out of there.' The gang jumped down and ran off. Suddenly Pete slipped. He fell headlong into a stall with three enormous sows. He looked at their drooling faces and remembered Madame Fortune's words. 'It works on any female, female, female . . .'

The pigs charged over for their kiss.

Later that afternoon, Gribble, Rabbit and Tiger hid behind a bush on the clifftop. They were waiting for someone. 'Here he comes,' whispered Tiger.

A dejected Pete trudged along the track. He was covered in pig dirt and his clothes were torn. He approached the bush not knowing that it hid the waiting gang.

He looked up startled as the gang jumped out. Rabbit thumped his hand into his palm. 'Hand over that lipstick,' he said. 'Or you're a dead duck.'

'If you don't we'll rip your ears off,' said Gribble.

'Pulverise your brains,' added Rabbit.

The gang moved in. Pete tossed the lipstick over to them. 'You can have it,' he said. 'I've learned my lesson. It's nothing but trouble.'

'Don't give me that,' sneered Gribble. He caught the lipstick. 'Girls, your luck has changed. Gorgeous Gribble is coming for a kiss.'

The three of them ran off along the cliff. They didn't stop until they reached the road. 'Look, Gribs,' said Rabbit.

In the distance a beautiful girl with a shawl around her shoulders walked towards them.

'You're onto a winner here, Gribs,' said Tiger. 'She's beautiful.'

Gribble smeared on some of the lipstick. The girl put the shawl over her head and turned back the other way. The boys ran after her. They tapped her on the shoulder. Gribble puckered up for a kiss. The girl turned around.

She had a gnarled face that carried the wrinkles of a thousand years. It was Madame Fortune. The boys froze. Then they screamed. They turned and ran. Madame Fortune went after them. She shrieked and chuckled. The gang fled for their lives.

Pete walked down to the beach and sat on a rock. He threw stones into the sea. He was miserable, ashamed and lonely. At first he didn't even notice the quiet figure that approached. It was Fiona. She sat down next to him without saying anything. Pete looked at her. His heart thumped. He hoped she couldn't hear it.

'I'm sorry about your mum,' Pete said at last. 'You won't believe this but it wasn't me. It was the lipstick.'

Fiona smiled. A warm smile with the promise of spring. 'I do believe you,' she said. 'Linda told me all about it. Look, you idiot. You're never going to have trouble getting kisses. You don't need to steal them. Not you. And anyway, a stolen kiss isn't a kiss at all.'

She gently lifted up Pete's chin and kissed him tenderly on the lips. Pete's head filled with music. It was a long, gentle kiss like winter and spring, autumn and summer all rolled into one.

Suddenly Bronson's watch beeped on Pete's wrist. But he didn't hear it. Nor did he see the gang running for their lives on the cliffs above.

from *Round the Twist* by Paul Jennings

Reading for Meaning

1. What evidence can you find to show that Pete has a vivid imagination?
2. What caused Pete's daydream to end abruptly?
3. What comments would you make about the relationship between Pete and his sister?
4. How did Linda react to Gribble's offer to dance with her?
5. 'Pete was nervous.' Why was this so?
6. How did Pete's attempt to kiss Fiona end in failure?
7. How did Rabbit and Gribble react to Pete's failure to kiss Fiona?
8. How did Pete feel after he failed to kiss Fiona?
9. What contrast in appearance was there between the girl sitting on the step and the woman in the shawl?
10. How did Madame Fortune reveal that she had supernatural powers?
11. What magical powers did the lipstick possess?
12. How did Fiona's mother react to Pete's appearance at the door?
13. Why do you think Fiona's father asked his wife, 'Is there something you want to tell me dear'?
14. How did Pete react when the students mocked him for kissing Fiona's mother?
15. What effect did the magic lipstick have on Ms James?
16. Using Rabbit's and Tiger's comments, explain why the story is called 'Lucky Lips'?
17. Why did Ms James come to the lighthouse?
18. 'Dad stared at the lipstick with a devilish smile.' Why do you think Pete's father's smile was 'devilish'?
19. 'All the girls shuffled away from him.' Why did the girls keep away from Pete?
20. What happened to Pete when he fell into the pig pen?
21. Why did Pete hand over the lipstick without a fight to Rabbit, Gribble and Tiger?
22. 'Gribble smeared on some of the lipstick.' How did the lipstick lead Gribble to trouble?
23. Do you think the ending to 'Lucky Lips' is a good one or not?
24. What did you learn about Pete's character from the story?
25. What comments would you make about Fiona's character?
26. Do you think 'Lucky Lips' is a good title for the story? Why or why not?

The Hitch-hiker

A car driver picks up a mysterious hitch-hiker. However, the driver is both surprised and delighted when he discovers the hitch-hiker's secret.

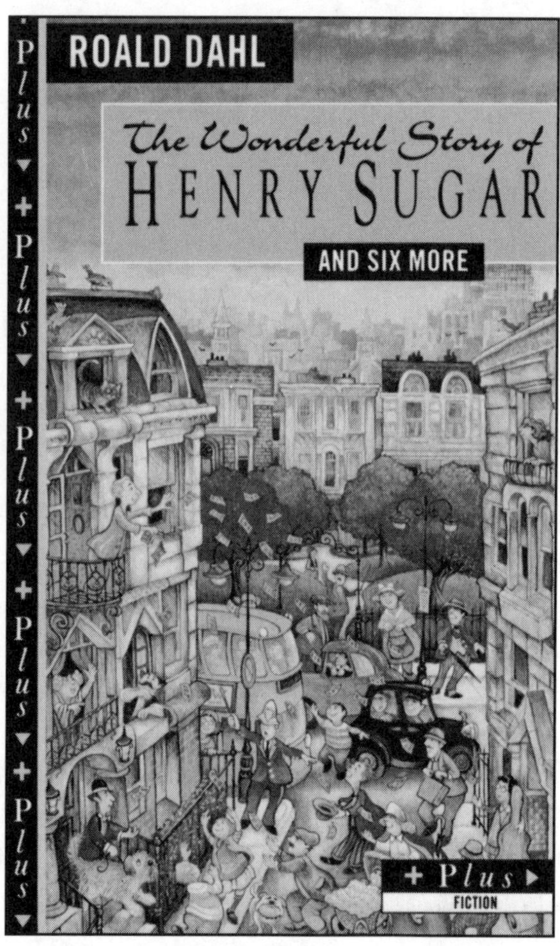

I had a new car. It was an exciting toy, a big BMW 3.3 Li, which means 3.3 litre, long wheelbase, fuel injection. It had a top speed of 129 mph and terrific acceleration. The body was pale blue. The seats inside were darker blue and they were made of leather, genuine soft leather of the finest quality. The windows were electrically operated and so was the sunroof. The radio aerial popped up when I switched on the radio, and disappeared when I switched it off. The powerful engine growled and grunted impatiently at slow speeds, but at sixty miles an hour the growling stopped and the motor began to purr with pleasure.

I was driving up to London by myself. It was a lovely June day. They were haymaking in the fields and there were buttercups along both sides of the road. I was whispering along

at seventy miles an hour, leaning back comfortably in my seat, with no more than a couple of fingers resting lightly on the wheel to keep her steady. Ahead of me I saw a man thumbing a lift. I touched the footbrake and brought the car to a stop beside him. I always stopped for hitch-hikers. I knew just how it used to feel to be standing on the side of a country road watching the cars go by. I hated the drivers for pretending they didn't see me, especially the ones in big cars with three empty seats. The large expensive cars seldom stopped. It was always the smaller ones that offered you a lift, or the old rusty ones, or the ones that were already crammed full of children and the driver would say, 'I think we can squeeze in one more.'

The hitch-hiker poked his head through the open window and said, 'Going to London, guv'nor?'

'Yes,' I said. 'Jump in.'

He got in and I drove on.

He was a small ratty-faced man with grey teeth. His eyes were dark and quick and clever, like a rat's eyes, and his ears were slightly pointed at the top. He had a cloth cap on his head and he was wearing a greyish-coloured jacket with enormous pockets. The grey jacket, together with the quick eyes and the pointed ears, made him look more than anything like some sort of a huge human rat.

'What part of London are you headed for?' I asked him.

'I'm goin' right through London and out the other side,' he said. 'I'm goin' to Epsom, for the races. It's Derby Day today.'

'So it is,' I said. 'I wish I were going with you. I love betting on horses.'

'I never bet on horses,' he said. 'I don't even watch 'em run. That's a stupid silly business.'

'Then why do you go?' I asked.

He didn't seem to like that question. His little ratty face went absolutely blank and he sat there staring straight ahead at the road, saying nothing.

'I expect you help to work the betting machines or something like that,' I said.

'That's even sillier,' he answered. 'There's no fun working them lousy machines and selling tickets to mugs. Any fool could do that.'

There was a long silence. I decided not to question him any more. I remembered how irritated I used to get in my hitch-hiking days when drivers kept asking *me* questions. Where are you going? Why are you going there? What's your job? Are you married? Do you have a girl-friend? What's her name? How old are you? And so on and so forth. I used to hate it.

'I'm sorry,' I said. 'It's none of my business what you do. The trouble is, I'm a writer, and most writers are terrible nosey parkers.'

'You write books?' he asked.

'Yes.'

'Writin' books is okay,' he said. 'It's what I call a skilled trade. I'm in a skilled trade too.

The folks I despise is them that spend all their lives doin' crummy old routine jobs with no skill in 'em at all. You see what I mean?'

'Yes.'

'The secret of life,' he said, 'is to become very very good at somethin' that's very very 'ard to do.'

'Like you,' I said.

'Exactly. You and me both.'

'What makes you think that *I'm* any good at my job?' I asked. 'There's an awful lot of bad writers around.'

'You wouldn't be drivin' about in a car like this if you weren't no good at it,' he answered. 'It must've cost a tidy packet, this little job.'

'It wasn't cheap.'

'What can she do flat out?' he asked.

'One hundred and twenty-nine miles an hour,' I told him.

'I'll bet she won't do it.'

'I'll bet she will.'

'All car makers is liars,' he said. 'You can buy any car you like and it'll never do what the makers say it will in the ads.

'This one will.'

'Open 'er up then and prove it,' he said. 'Go on, guv'nor, open 'er right up and let's see what she'll do.'

There is a roundabout at Chalfont St Peter and immediately beyond it there's a long straight section of dual carriageway. We came out of the roundabout on to the carriageway and I pressed my foot down on the accelerator. The big car leaped forward as though she'd been stung. In ten seconds or so, we were doing ninety.

'Lovely!' he cried. 'Beautiful! Keep goin'!'

I had the accelerator jammed right down against the floor and I held it there.

'One hundred!' he shouted . . . 'A hundred and five! . . . A hundred and ten! . . . A hundred and fifteen! Go on! Don't slack off!'

I was in the outside lane and we flashed past several cars as though they were standing still — a green Mini, a big cream-coloured Citroën, a white Land-Rover, a huge truck with a container on the back, an orange-coloured Volkswagen Minibus . . .

'A hundred and twenty!' my passenger shouted, jumping up and down. 'Go on! Go on! Get 'er up to one-two-nine!'

At that moment, I heard the scream of a police siren. It was so loud it seemed to be right inside the car, and then a policeman on a motor-cycle loomed up alongside us on the inside lane and went past us and raised a hand for us to stop.

'Oh, my sainted aunt!' I said. 'That's torn it!'

The policeman must have been doing about a hundred and thirty when he passed us, and he took plenty of time slowing down. Finally, he pulled into the side of the road and I pulled in behind him. 'I didn't know police motor-cycles could go as fast as that,' I said rather lamely.

'That one can,' my passenger said. 'It's the same make as yours. It's a BMW R90S. Fastest bike on the road. That's what they're usin' nowadays.'

The policeman got off his motor-cycle and leaned the machine sideways on to its prop-stand. Then he took off his gloves and placed them carefully on the seat. He was in no hurry now. He had us where he wanted us and he knew it.

'This is real trouble,' I said. 'I don't like it one bit.'

'Don't talk to 'im any more than is necessary, you understand,' my companion said. 'Just sit tight and keep mum.'

Like an executioner approaching his victim, the policeman came strolling slowly towards us. He was a big meaty man with a belly, and his blue breeches were skintight around his enormous thighs. His goggles were pulled up on the helmet, showing a smouldering red face with wide cheeks.

We sat there like guilty schoolboys, waiting for him to arrive.

'Watch out for this man,' my passenger whispered. ''Ee looks mean as the devil.'

The policeman came round to my open window and placed one meaty hand on the sill. 'What's the hurry?' he said.

'No hurry, officer,' I answered.

'Perhaps there's a woman in the back having a baby and you're rushing her to hospital? Is that it?'

'No, officer.'

'Or perhaps your house is on fire and you're dashing home to rescue the family from upstairs?' His voice was dangerously soft and mocking.

'My house isn't on fire, officer.'

'In that case,' he said, 'you've got yourself into a nasty mess, haven't you? Do you know what the speed limit is in this country?'

'Seventy,' I said.

'And do you mind telling me exactly what speed you were doing just now?'

I shrugged and didn't say anything.

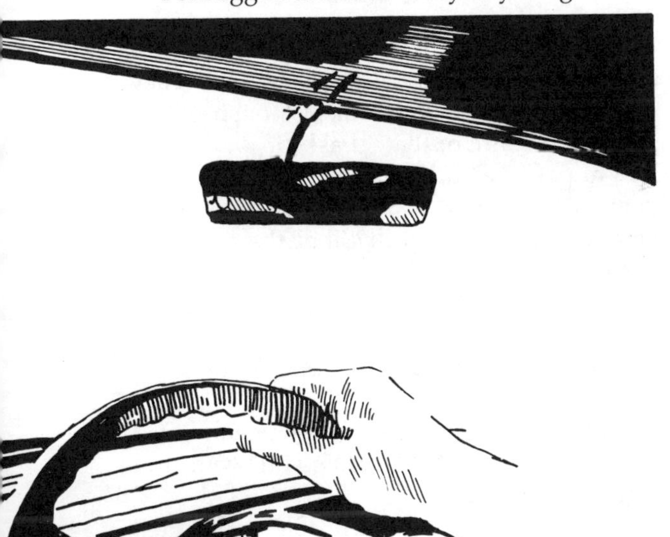

When he spoke next, he raised his voice so loud that I jumped. *'One hundred and twenty miles per hour!'* he barked. 'That's *fifty* miles an hour over the limit!'

He turned his head and spat out a big gob of spit. It landed on the wing of my car and started sliding down over my beautiful blue paint. Then he turned back again and stared hard at my passenger. 'And who are you?' he asked sharply.

'He's a hitch-hiker,' I said. 'I'm giving him a lift.'

'I didn't ask you,' he said. 'I asked him.'

''Ave I done somethin' wrong?' my passenger asked. His voice was as soft and oily as haircream.

'That's more than likely,' the policeman answered. 'Anyway, you're a witness. I'll deal with you in a minute. Driving-licence,' he snapped, holding out his hand.

I gave him my driving-licence.

He unbuttoned the left-hand breast-pocket of his tunic and brought out the dreaded books of tickets. Carefully, he copied the name and address from my licence. Then he gave it back to me. He strolled round to the front of the car and read the number from the number-plate and wrote that down as well. He filled in the date, the time and the details of my offence. Then he tore out the top copy of the ticket. But before handing it to me, he checked that all the information had come through clearly on his own carbon copy. Finally, he replaced the book in his tunic pocket and fastened the button.

'Now you,' he said to my passenger, and he walked around to the other side of the car. From the other breast-pocket he produced a small black notebook. 'Name?' he snapped.

'Michael Fish,' my passenger said.

'Address?'

'Fourteen, Windsor Lane, Luton.'

'Show me something to prove this is your real name and address,' the policeman said.

My passenger fished in his pockets and came out with a driving-licence of his own. The policeman checked the name and address and handed it back to him. 'What's your job?' he asked sharply.

'I'm an 'od carrier.'

'A *what?*'

'An 'od carrier.'

'Spell it.'

'H-O-D C-A-. . .'

'That'll do. And what's a hod carrier, may I ask?'

'An 'od carrier, officer, is a person 'oo carries the cement up the ladder to the bricklayer. And the 'od is what 'ee carries it in. It's got a long 'andle, and on the top you've got two bits of wood set at an angle . . .'

'All right, all right. Who's your employer?'

'Don't 'ave one. I'm unemployed.'

The policeman wrote all this down in the black notebook. Then he returned the book to its pocket and did up the button.

'When I get back to the station I'm going to do a little checking up on you,' he said to my passenger.

'Me? What've I done wrong?' the rat-faced man asked.

'I don't like your face, that's all,' the policeman said. 'And we just might have a picture of it somewhere in our files.' He strolled round the car and returned to my window.

'I suppose you know you're in serious trouble,' he said to me.

'Yes, officer.'

'You won't be driving this fancy car of yours again for a very long time, not after *we've* finished with you. You won't be driving *any* car again come to that for several years. And a good thing, too. I hope they lock you up for a spell into the bargain.'

'You mean prison?' I asked, alarmed.

'Absolutely,' he said, smacking his lips. 'In the clink. Behind the bars. Along with all the other criminals who break the law. *And* a hefty fine into the bargain. Nobody will be more pleased about that than me. I'll see you in court, both of you. You'll be getting a summons to appear.'

He turned away and walked over to his motor-cycle. He flipped the prop-stand back into position with his foot and swung his leg over the saddle. Then he kicked the starter and roared off up the road out of sight.

'Phew!' I gasped. 'That's done it.'

'We was caught,' my passenger said. 'We was caught good and proper.'

'I was caught, you mean.'

'That's right,' he said. 'What you goin' to do now, guv'nor?'

'I'm going straight up to London to talk to my solicitor,' I said. I started the car and drove on.

'You mustn't believe what 'ee said to you about goin' to prison,' my passenger said. 'They don't put nobody in the clink just for speedin'.'

'Are you sure of that?' I asked.

'I'm positive,' he answered. 'They can take your licence away and they can give you a whoppin' big fine, but that'll be the end of it.'

I felt tremendously relieved.

'By the way,' I said, 'why did you lie to him?'

'Who, me?' he said. 'What makes you think I lied?'

'You told him you were an unemployed hod carrier. But you told *me* you were in a highly skilled trade.'

'So I am,' he said. 'But it don't pay to tell everythin' to a copper.'

'So what *do* you do?' I asked him.

'Ah,' he said slyly. 'That'd be tellin', wouldn't it?'

'Is it something you're ashamed of?'

'Ashamed?' he cried. 'Me, ashamed of my job? I'm about as proud of it as anybody could be in the entire world!'

'Then why won't you tell me?'

'You writers really is nosey parkers, aren't you?' he said. 'And you ain't goin' to be 'appy, I don't think, until you've found out exactly what the answer is?'

'I don't really care one way or the other,' I told him, lying.

He gave me a crafty little ratty look out of the sides of his eyes. 'I think you do care,' he said. 'I can see it in your face that you think I'm in some kind of a very peculiar trade and you're just achin' to know what it is.'

I didn't like the way he read my thoughts. I kept quiet and stared at the road ahead.

'You'd be right, too,' he went on. 'I *am* in a very peculiar trade. I'm in the queerest peculiar trade of 'em all.'

I waited for him to go on.

'That's why I 'as to be extra careful 'oo I'm talkin' to, you see. 'Ow am I to know, for instance, you're not another copper in plain clothes?'

'Do I look like a copper?'

'No,' he said. 'You don't. And you ain't. Any fool could tell that.'

He took from his pocket a tin of tobacco and a packet of cigarette papers and started to roll a cigarette. I was watching him out of the corner of one eye, and the speed with which he performed this rather difficult operation was incredible. The cigarette was rolled and ready in about five seconds. He ran his tongue along the edge of the paper, stuck it down and popped the cigarette between his lips. Then, as if from nowhere, a lighter appeared in his hand. The lighter flamed. The cigarette was lit. The lighter disappeared. It was altogether a remarkable performance.

'I've never seen anyone roll a cigarette as fast as that,' I said.

'Ah,' he said, taking a deep suck of smoke. 'So you noticed.'

'Of course I noticed. It was quite fantastic.'

He sat back and smiled. It pleased him very much that I had noticed how quickly he could roll a cigarette. 'You want to know what makes me able to do it?' he asked.

'Go on then.'

'It's because I've got fantastic fingers. These fingers of mine,' he said, holding up both hands high in front of him, 'are quicker and cleverer than the fingers of the best piano player in the world!'

'Are you a piano player?'

'Don't be daft,' he said. 'Do I look like a piano player.'

I glanced at his fingers. They were so beautifully shaped, so slim and long and elegant, they didn't seem to belong to the rest of him at all. They looked more like the fingers of a brain surgeon or a watchmaker.

'My job,' he went on, 'is a hundred times more difficult than playin' the piano. Any twerp can learn to do that. There's titchy little kids learnin' to play the piano in almost any 'ouse you go into these days. That's right, ain't it?'

'More or less,' I said.

'Of course it's right. But there's not one person in ten million can learn to do what I do. Not one in ten million! 'Ow about that?'

'Amazing,' I said.

'You're darn right it's amazin',' he said.

'I think I know what you do,' I said. 'You do conjuring tricks. You're a conjurer.'

'Me?' he snorted. 'A conjurer? Can you picture me goin' round crummy kids' parties makin' rabbits come out of top 'ats?'

'Then you're a card player. You get people into card games and deal yourself marvellous hands.'

'Me! A rotten card-sharper!' he cried. 'That's a miserable racket if ever there was one.'

'All right. I give up.'

I was taking the car along slowly now, at no more than forty miles an hour, to make quite sure I wasn't stopped again. We had come to the main London–Oxford road and were running down the hill towards Denham.

Suddenly, my passenger was holding up a black leather belt in his hand. 'Ever seen this before?' he asked. The belt had a brass buckle of unusual design.

'Hey!' I said. 'That's mine, isn't it? It *is* mine! Where did you get it?'

He grinned and waved the belt gently from side to side. 'Where d'you think I got it?' he said. 'Off the top of your trousers, of course.'

I reached down and felt for my belt. It was gone.

'You mean you took it off me while we've been driving along?' I asked, flabbergasted.

He nodded, watching me all the time with those little black ratty eyes.

'That's impossible,' I said. 'You'd have to undo the buckle and slide the whole thing out through the loops all the way round. I'd have seen you doing it. And even if I hadn't seen you, I'd have felt it.'

'Ah, but you didn't, did you?' he said, triumphant. He dropped the belt on his lap, and now all at once there was a brown shoelace dangling from his fingers. 'And what about this, then?' he exclaimed, waving the shoelace.

'What about it?' I said.

'Anyone round 'ere missin' a shoelace?' he asked, grinning.

I glanced down at my shoes. The lace of one of them was missing. 'Good grief!' I said. 'How did you do that? I never saw you bending down.'

'You never saw nothin',' he said proudly. 'You never even saw me move an inch. And you know why?'

'Yes,' I said. 'Because you've got fantastic fingers.'

'Exactly right!' he cried. 'You catch on pretty quick, don't you?' He sat back and sucked away at his home-made cigarette, blowing the smoke out in a thin stream against the windshield. He knew he had impressed me greatly with those two tricks, and this made him very happy. 'I don't want to be late,' he said. 'What time is it?'

'There's a clock in front of you,' I told him.

'I don't trust car clocks,' he said. 'What does your watch say?'

I hitched up my sleeve to look at the watch on my wrist. It wasn't there. I looked at the man. He looked back at me, grinning.

'You've taken that, too,' I said.

He held out his hand and there was my watch lying in his palm. 'Nice bit of stuff, this,' he said. 'Superior quality. Eighteen-carat gold. Easy to flog, too. It's never any trouble gettin' rid of quality goods.'

'I'd like it back, if you don't mind,' I said rather huffily.

He placed the watch carefully on the leather tray in front of him. 'I wouldn't nick anything from you, guv'nor,' he said. 'You're my pal. You're giving me a lift.'

'I'm glad to hear it,' I said.

'All I'm doin' is answerin' your questions,' he went on. 'You asked me what I did for a livin' and I'm showin' you.'

'What else have you got of mine?'

He smiled again, and now he started to take from the pocket of his jacket one thing after another that belonged to me — my driving-licence, a key-ring with four keys on it, some pound notes, a few coins, a letter from my publishers, my diary, a stubby old pencil, a cigarette-lighter, and last of all, a beautiful old sapphire ring with pearls around it belonging to my wife. I was taking the ring up to the jeweller in London because one of the pearls was missing.

'Now *there's* another lovely piece of goods,' he said, turning the ring over in his fingers. 'That's eighteenth century, if I'm not mistaken, from the reign of King George the Third.'

'You're right,' I said, impressed. 'You're absolutely right.'

He put the ring on the leather tray with the other items.

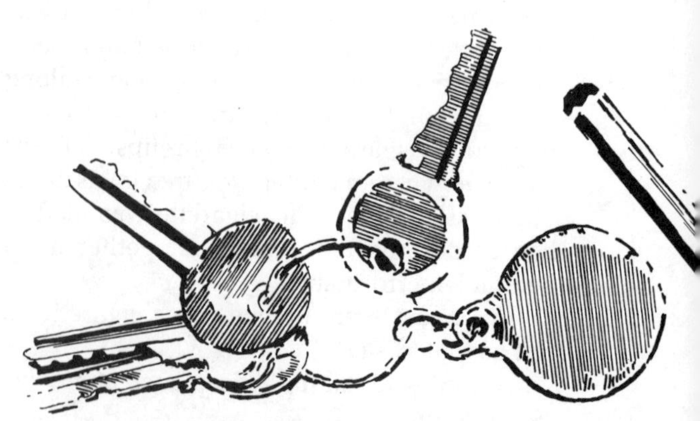

'So you're a pickpocket,' I said.

'I don't like that word,' he answered. 'It's a coarse and vulgar word. Pickpockets is coarse and vulgar people who only do easy little amateur jobs. They lift money from blind old ladies.'

'What do you call yourself, then?'

'Me? I'm a fingersmith. I'm a professional fingersmith.' He spoke the words solemnly and proudly, as though he were telling me he was the President of the Royal College of Surgeons or the Archbishop of Canterbury.

'I've never heard that word before,' I said. 'Did you invent it?'

'Of course I didn't invent it,' he replied. 'It's the name given to them who's risen to the very top of the profession. You've 'eard of a goldsmith and a silversmith, for instance. They're experts with gold and silver. I'm an expert with my fingers, so I'm a fingersmith.'

'It must be an interesting job.'

'It's a marvellous job,' he answered. 'It's lovely.'

'And that's why you go to the races?'

'Race meetings is easy meat,' he said. 'You just stand around after the race, watchin' for the lucky ones to queue up and draw their money. And when you see someone collectin' a big bundle of notes, you simply follows after 'im and 'elps yourself. But don't get me wrong, guv'nor. I never takes nothin' from a loser. Nor from poor people neither. I only go after them as can afford it, the winners and the rich.'

'That's very thoughtful of you,' I said, 'How often do you get caught?'

'Caught?' he cried, disgusted. '*Me* get caught! It's only pickpockets get caught. Fingersmiths never. Listen, I could take the false teeth out of your mouth if I wanted to and you wouldn't even catch me!'

'I don't have false teeth,' I said.

'I know you don't,' he answered. 'Otherwise I'd 'ave 'ad 'em out long ago!'

I believed him. Those long slim fingers of his seemed able to do anything.

We drove on for a while without talking.

'That policeman's going to check up on you pretty thoroughly,' I said. 'Doesn't that worry you a bit?'

'Nobody's checkin' up on me,' he said.

'Of course they are. He's got your name and address written down most carefully in his black book.'

The man gave me another of his sly, ratty little smiles. 'Ah,' he said. 'So 'ee 'as. But I'll bet 'ee ain't got it all written down in 'is memory as well. I've never known a copper yet with a decent memory. Some of 'em can't even remember their own names.'

'What's memory got to do with it?' I asked. 'It's written down in his book, isn't it?'

'Yes, guv'nor, it is. But the trouble is, 'ee's lost the book. 'Ee's lost both books, the one with my name in it *and* the one with yours.'

In the long delicate fingers of his right hand, the man was holding up in triumph the two books he had taken from the policeman's pockets. 'Easiest job I ever done,' he announced proudly.

I nearly swerved the car into a milk-truck, I was so excited.

'That copper's got nothin' on either of us now,' he said.

'You're a genius!' I cried.

'Ee's got no names, no addresses, no car number, no nothin',' he said.

'You're brilliant!'

'I think you'd better pull in off this main road as soon as possible,' he said. 'Then we'd better build a little bonfire and burn these books.'

'You're a fantastic fellow,' I exclaimed.

'Thank you, guv'nor,' he said. 'It's always nice to be appreciated.'

from *The Wonderful Story of Henry Sugar* by Roald Dahl

Reading for Meaning

1 The first paragraph of the story describes the storyteller's new car. What feelings does he reveal towards his new car?

2 Why did the driver stop for the hitch-hiker?

3 Why did the driver think the hitch-hiker looked 'like some sort of a huge human rat'?

4 What is the hint of mystery in the conversation between the two men over the Epsom Derby?

5 For the hitch-hiker, what is the secret of life?

6 Why did the hitch-hiker encourage the driver to increase the speed of his car?

7 What happened as the car reached a speed of one hundred and twenty miles per hour?

8 Explain how the policeman is sarcastic as he questions the driver about his excessive speed?

9 What evidence is there to show that the policeman was a careful and methodical man?

10 'When I get back to the station I'm going to do a little checking up on you.' What do you think caused the policeman to make this statement?

11 What threats did the policeman make to the car driver?

12 What comments would you make about the policeman's character?

13 After the policeman had left, what did the hitch-hiker say to comfort and reassure the driver?

14 'It was altogether a remarkable performance.' Why did the driver make this comment about the hitch-hiker?

15 What claim did the hitch-hiker make about his fingers?

16 How did the hitch-hiker demonstrate the special skill of his fingers to the driver?

17 Why didn't the hitch-hiker like to be called a pickpocket?

18 What did the hitch-hiker mean by 'Race meetings is easy meat'?

19 What comment did the hitch-hiker make about the driver's teeth?

20 Explain how the story ends with a surprise for the reader.

21 Why, in your opinion, is this short story such an absorbing one?

22 What did you learn about the character of the hitch-hiker from your reading of this story?

POETRY

PEOPLE WHO ARE DIFFERENT

How to Treat House-plants

All she ever thinks about are house-plants.
She talks to them and tends them every day.
And she says, 'Don't hurt their feelings. Give them
Love. In all your dealings with them,
Treat them in a tender, *human* way.'

'Certainly my dear,' he says, 'O.K.
Human, eh?'

But the house-plants do not seem to want to play.

They are stooping, they are drooping,
They are kneeling in their clay:
They are flaking, they are moulting,
Turning yellow, turning grey,
And they look . . . well, quite revolting
As they sigh, and fade away.

So after she has left the house he gets them
And he sets them in a line against the wall,
And I cannot say he cossets them or pets them —
No, he doesn't sympathise with them at all.
Is he tender? Is he human? Not a bit.
No, to each of them in turn he says: 'You *twit*!

You're a
Rotten little skiver,
Cost a fiver,
Earn your keep!

You're a
Dirty little drop-out!
You're a cop-out!
You're a creep!

You're a
Mangy little whinger!
You're a cringer!
Son, it's true —

I have justbin
To the dustbin
Where there's *better men than you*!

Get that stem back!

Pull your weight!

Stick your leaves out!

STAND UP STRAIGHT!'

And, strange to say, the plants co-operate.
So when she comes back home and finds them glowing,
Green and healthy, every one a king,
She says, 'It's *tenderness* that gets them growing!
How strange, the change a little *love* can bring!'

'Oh yes,' he says. 'Not half. Right. Love's the thing.'

Kit Wright

Questions

1 Who are the two people speaking in the poem?
2 According to the woman, how should the house-plants be treated?
3 What words reveal that the house-plants are in poor condition?
4 How does the man rearrange the house-plants?
5 What comments would you make about the man's treatment of the house-plants?
6 How do the plants react to his treatment of them?
7 How do the plants look to the woman when she comes back home? What does she think caused the change?
8 Why is the poem's last line amusing?
9 How has the poet made the plants seem human?
10 What contrast is there between the man's and woman's treatment of the plants?
11 Do you think this is a serious or humorous poem? Why?
12 Why do you think the poet has written this poem?

Come Another Day

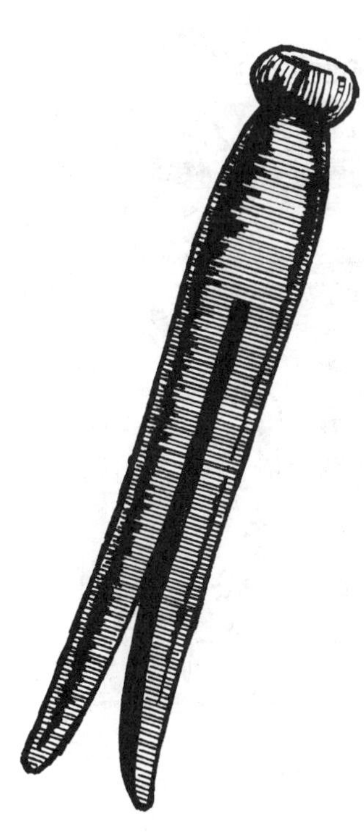

Mondays,
my mother chopped wood
and twisted newspaper
to make fire,
beneath a whitened stone
boiler, with a wooden lid
that was itself bleached
white with steam,
to imitate it seemed
an inferno, in which to work
with red hot coals
and scalding water, bubbling,
spitting, foaming, as she
drubbed at sails of linen,
fighting them with a
dolly stick, possessing
all the qualities of driftwood.
Misted in vapour, her hair
was dank and coming
in from school, dinner
was always cold meat
left from Sundays,
with potato mash
wet as the washing.
Mondays,
my mother stood
at the tin bath
and a rubbing board,
with brick hard yellow soap,
battering her knuckles
against zinc, raw
fingers wringing, squeezing
twisting the dirt of life
away, to float as scum
before the operation of
a vast machine of iron cast,
made in Doncaster,
with massive rollers
that mangled buttons
as slowly and certainly
as it mangled my mother.
Home from school,
the end of our day,

we sat upon the floor,
peering under wet clothes
to glimpse the stove,
our comics soggy, as we
munched our bread.
Mondays,
my mother sweated,
heavy black irons
heated on kitchen range,
gripped with scorching
slipping cloths, to
brand the flesh and
press and hiss the dampness
from the wearying pile,
filling wicker baskets
with sweet smooth warmth,
before she sat by mantle
light, to rummage
in a biscuit tin
matching buttons crushed,
sewing, thin cotton
edges frayed.
From the memory smell
of steam and starch,
childhood skies of Reckitts
blue. I remember,
Mondays, my mother
earned two shillings.

John Gorman

Questions

1 'My mother chopped wood'. What does this statement reveal about the poet's mother?

2 What words reveal the intense heat of the boiler?

3 'She drubbed at sails of linen'. Why did the linen look like sails?

4 What words create a picture of wetness?

5 Why did the poet's mother experience pain as she stood at the tin bath and rubbing board?

6 What impression does the poet give us of the machine made in Doncaster?

7 How were the children affected by the washing?

8 What sound-words does the poet use to describe the ironing?

9 Why do you think the word 'Mondays' is repeated throughout the poem?

10 What is the poet trying to show the reader in 'Come Another Day'?

11 What are your feelings towards the poet's mother?

12 How has the poet made this poem true to life?

Hypochondria

I'm delicate, fragile,
and highly at risk.
If I made my own bed,
I could get a slipped disc.
Me? Wash the dishes?
With my dermatitis?
Dusting? You're kidding!
I'd get sinusitis!
If spring cleaning, don't
include *me* in the action —
I might break a leg
and spend six months in traction.
I don't just get colds,
but pneumonia (protracted),
nor ordinary toothache,
but molars — impacted!
Help clear the table?
Oh, didn't I mention
I need lots of rest
for acute hypertension?
Black plague, malaria,
beriberi, jungle rot —
I'm the only one in history
who's had the whole lot!
So don't boast to me
of your migraines and flu.
Nobody suffers
the way that I do.

Robin Klein

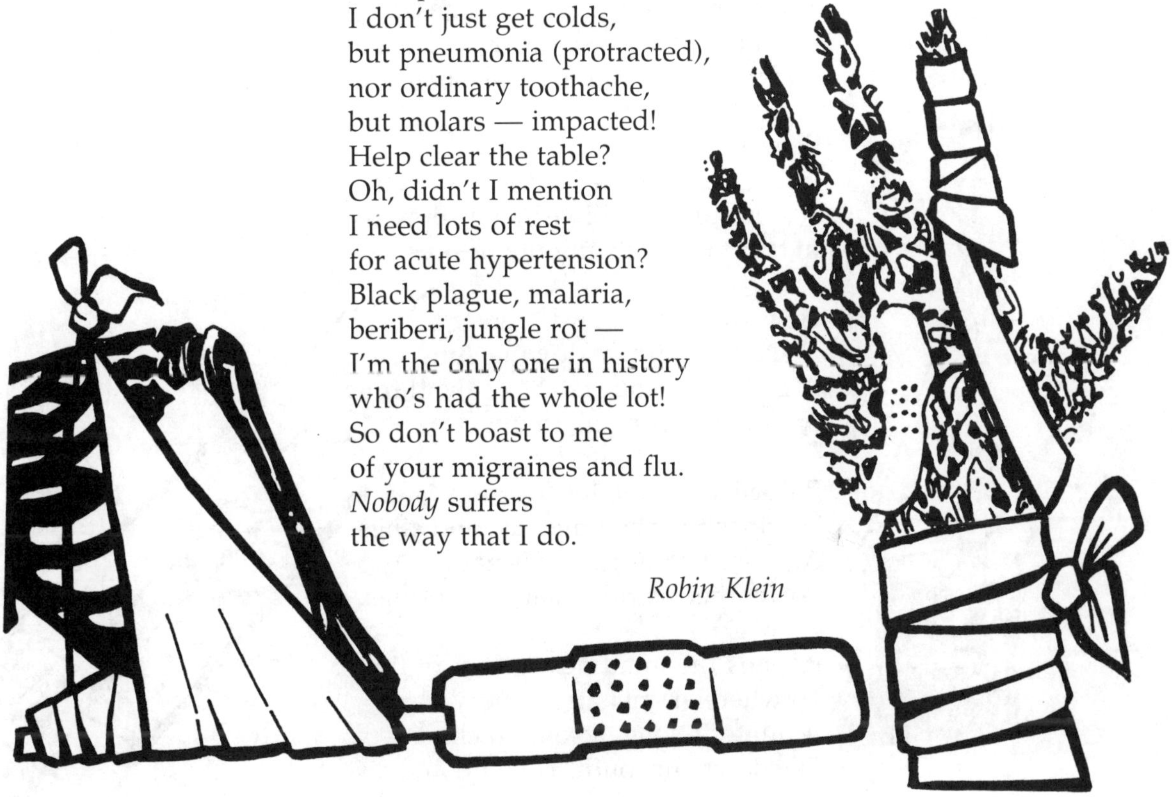

A dogman is a person who directs the operation of a crane while riding on an object it is lifting. The poet Robert Clark described how when he was walking in an Adelaide street he heard a song up in the air: 'I looked up and there was the flying dogman, astride a beam, singing as if the world were his.'

What does Robert Clark show you about the life of a dogman?

The Dogman

The dogman dangles from the clouds,
Astride a beam of swinging air,
Unrealised hero of the crowds,
Whose upturned faces dimly stare

Like daisies watching from the ground,
Arrayed in far-off random files.
Their homage rises without sound
In grave content or drifting smiles.

The earth is open to his eye,
Spreading before him like a chart,
From the blue-washed blind of sea and sky
To where the mountains lie apart.

Beneath his feet the city falls
In patterns of great blocks and spires,
A sumptuous Gulliver who sprawls
In bond to man's minute desires.

He is immune, a bird, a song,
A shaft of light, a glowing sun,
A god who ploughs above the throng,
A man reflecting all in one.

Propelled by joy, his love in spate,
He rides the climbing sky, and sings.
Another lark at heaven's gate
To another world his aubade brings.

It sends the mind down flues of time
To where all men in memory meet,
A hunter's song, a song to climb
The dawn, uncouth, yet wild and sweet.

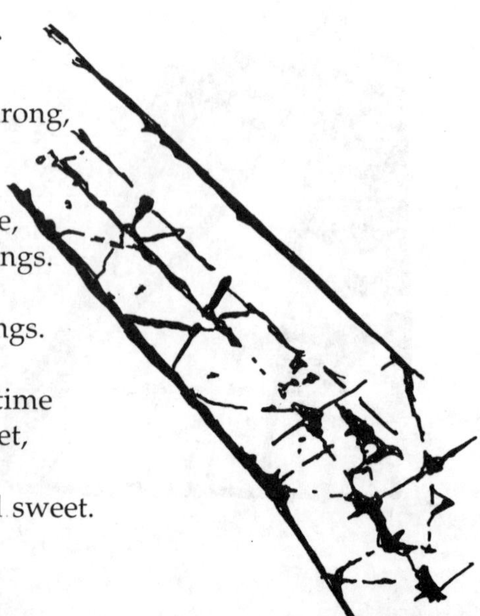

Spent eyes revive and spill delight.
Dead hearts resolve to live again.
Once more a man upon a height
Recalls their dignity to men.

Robert Clark

The Pirate

He walks the deck with swaggering gait,
(There's mischief in his eye)
Pedigree Pirate through and through,
With pistols, dirk and cutlass too;
A rollicking rip with scars to show
For every ship he's sent below.
His tongue is quick, his temper high,
And whenever he speaks they shout, 'Ay, Ay!'
To this king of a roaring crew.

His ship's as old as the sea herself,
And foggity foul is she:
But what cares he for foul or fine?
If guns don't glitter and decks don't shine?
For sailormen from East to West
Have walked the plank at his request;
But if he's caught you may depend
He'll dangle high at the business end
Of a tickly, tarry line.

Hugh Chesterman

Questions

1 What words show the pirate's arrogance?
2 What tells us that the pirate is looking for trouble?
3 How is his success as a pirate measured?
4 What do we learn of the pirate's temperament?
5 How do his 'roaring crew' show their obedience?
6 What comparison is used to show the great age of his ship?
7 How do we learn of the pirate's cruelty?
8 What fate awaits him if he is caught?
9 How is the feel of the hangman's noose suggested?
10 How has the poet used his imagination in this poem?

At the Railway Station, Upway

'There is not much that I can do,
For I've no money that's quite my own!'
Spoke up the pitying child —
A little boy with a violin
At the station before the train came in —
'But I can play my fiddle to you,
And a nice one 'tis, and good in tone!'

The man in the handcuffs smiled;
The constable looked, and he smiled, too,
As the fiddle began to twang;
And the man in the handcuffs suddenly sang
With grimful glee:
'This life so free
Is the thing for me!'
And the constable smiled and said no word,
As if unconscious of what he heard;
And so they went on till the train came in —
The convict, and boy with the violin.

Thomas Hardy

Focusing on a Feeling

1 What is this poem's setting?
2 Who is speaking in the first part of the poem?
3 What is the apology the boy with the violin makes to the man in the handcuffs?
4 What feeling causes the boy to play a tune for the man?
5 How do both the convict and the constable react to the boy's offer to play a tune?
6 What word is used by the poet to describe the sound of the fiddle?
7 What is sad about the convict's song?
8 For how long did the boy play and the convict sing?
9 What message do you think the poet has for the reader?
10 Why is this poem worth remembering?

WRITING

THE WRITER'S PURPOSE

All writing is designed to accomplish something. Its purpose may be to warn, inform, describe, persuade, entertain or a combination of some of these. Writing is successful when it gains the attention of the readers to whom it is specifically directed.

Look at the following pieces of writing and decide each one's purpose. Then decide the kind of reader each piece of writing is specifically directed towards? Here is an example.

Road sign: DO NOT OVERTAKE ON CRESTS OR CURVES
Purpose: To warn
Readers: Motorists

REEF RESORT

Reef Resort is an exotic, colourful holiday spot that operates at a relaxed tropical pace. It spreads its verdant acres beachside from one of the world's great natural wonders, the Great Barrier Reef. Offshore of your resort you snorkel amongst fabulous coloured corals with their fantastic marine life. Ashore again, you explore the natural beauty of the reef islands and discover lush rain forest, sun-soaked beaches and skies alive with multi-hued bird life. Make *Reef Resort* your holiday of a lifetime.

from a tourist brochure

Purpose: ....
Readers: ....

BASKERVILLE HALL

The avenue opened into a broad expanse of turf, and the house lay before us. In the fading light I could see that the centre was a heavy block of building from which a porch projected. The whole front was draped in ivy, with a patch clipped bare here and there where a window or a coat-of-arms broke through the dark veil. From this central block rose the twin towers, ancient, crenellated, and pierced with many loopholes. To right and left of the turrets were more modern wings of black granite. A dull light shone through heavy mullioned windows, and from the high chimneys which rose from the steep, high-angled roof there sprang a single black column of smoke.

'Welcome, Sir Henry! Welcome to Baskerville Hall!'

from *The Hound of the Baskervilles* by Arthur Conan Doyle

Purpose: ....

Readers: ....

CARTOON CHARACTER

from *Garfield* by Jim Davis

Purpose: ....

Readers: ....

EXAMINING THE WRITER'S PURPOSE

Here is a piece of writing that shows the writer's purpose. It describes a car crash which occurs after two vets, Tristan and James, leave their car at the top of a hill to stretch their legs. They forget to put the handbrake on and the car races off down the hill. The two vets can only watch in dismay as the inevitable happens.

Read through the passage carefully, then answer the questions that are designed to explore the writer's purpose in this piece of action writing.

RUNAWAY CAR

The car appeared now to be doing about 70 mph hurtling terrifyingly down the long, green hill. One by one the doors burst open till all four flapped wildly and the car swooped downwards looking like a huge, ungainly bird.

From the open doors, bottles, instruments, bandages, cotton wool cascaded out on to the turf, leaving a long, broken trail. Now and again a packet of nux vomica and bicarb stomach powder would fly out and burst like a bomb, splashing vivid white against the green.

Tristan threw up his arms. 'Look! The bloody thing's going straight for that hut.'

There was indeed only one obstruction on the bare hillside — a small building near the foot where the land levelled out and the Austin, as if drawn by a magnet, was thundering straight towards it.

I couldn't bear to watch. Just before the impact I turned away.

When I looked back down the hill the building was no longer there. It had been completely flattened and everything I had ever heard about houses of cards surged into my mind. On top of the shattered timbers the little car lay peacefully on it side, its wheels still turning lazily.

from *It Shouldn't Happen to a Vet* by James Herriot

Questions

1 How does the writer immediately gain the reader's interest in the first sentence of the passage?

2 What comparison vividly tells us how the car looked when all its doors had opened?

3 How does the writer achieve his purpose of dramatically describing the course of the car's runaway dash downhill?

4 In the fourth paragraph, what comparison warns us that the car will hit the small building?

5 What did the sight of the flattened building remind the writer of?

6 What is the writer's purpose in this passage? How has he successfully achieved his purpose?

YOUR TURN TO WRITE

1 Missing Person Poster

Below is a missing person poster. Your job is to provide a detailed description of the missing person. Use your imagination and remember that the purpose of your writing is to describe the missing person as thoroughly as you can.

MISSING PERSON

Name: ______________________ Age: __________

Address: ______________________________

Appearance: ____________________________

____

____

____

Habits: ________________________________

____

____

____

Where the person was last seen: ______________

2 House for Sale

Imagine your house is for sale. Write an ad that will sell your own home. Your purpose is to persuade. Use the headings to help you.

FOR SALE

The house: ______________________________

____

____

Its setting: ______________________________

____

____

Interior: ______________________________

____

____

Special attractive features: ______________________________

____

____

____

____

____

Priced to sell at: ______________________________

LANGUAGE

WORDS IN FOCUS

As words form the basis of the communication process, a wide vocabulary is essential for successful communication in speech and writing. The following exercises will help you extend your vocabulary.

Names and Actions

Supply the missing noun (naming word) or the missing verb (action word) in each of the following pairs. You are given the first and last letter of each missing word. The first one has been done for you as your example.

	Nouns	**Verbs**
1	*joy*	*enjoy*
2	proof	p___e
3	r____f	relieve
4	life	l__e
5	s______n	solve
6	thought	t___k
7	c_________n	circulate
8	description	d______e
9	c_______m	criticise
10	obedience	o__y
11	l____h	lengthen
12	food	f__d
13	c_____e	comparison
14	success	s_____d
15	p________n	persuade
16	collision	c_____e
17	r_____l	remove
18	education	e_____e
19	m______e	marry
20	repetition	r____t

Studies

The ending '-ology' means the 'study of'. Each of the following '-ology' words in the left-hand column has its meaning somewhere in the right-hand column. Match each word with its correct meaning. Sometimes the first letter of the word is given in brackets to help you.

	Words	**Meanings**
1	ecology	study of caves (s)
2	geology	study of musical science
3	ornithology	study of human society
4	archaeology	study of volcanoes
5	zoology	study of weather
6	technology	study of the eye (o)
7	entomology	study of women's diseases
8	sociology	study of religion (t)
9	musicology	study of poisons and treatments (t)
10	criminology	study of life forms and habitats
11	theology	study of the descent of families (g)
12	speleology	study of the human mind
13	pathology	study of practical or industrial arts
14	gynaecology	study of animal life
15	toxicology	study of the earth's crust
16	opthalmology	study of disease
17	meteorology	study of crime
18	vulcanology	study of human antiquities
19	genealogy	study of insect life (e)
20	psychology	study of birds (o)

Replace a Phrase with a Word

Choose a word from the box to replace the phrase in italics.

audience	stationary	aisle	arrogant
literate	estuary	queue	verdict
constant	obsolete	visible	dialogue
obese	leisure	temporary	duplicate
anticipate	centenary	ascent	postpone

1. The *gathering of listeners* cheered the orchestra's conductor.
2. He overheard *the conversation between the two people* in the next room.
3. Some people know how to use their *time free from work* creatively.
4. The students thought the teacher was *overbearing in manner.*

5 We always *look forward* to the pleasures of our holidays.
6 The river is *able to be seen* from the lookout.
7 The river's *wide mouth* begins one kilometre from the sea.
8 We cannot use a video recorder because our TV is *out of date.*
9 My job is only *going to last for a short time.*
10 You have to take a test to find out whether you are *able to read and write.*
11 Before he began dieting he was *very fat.*
12 Up north the temperature is *always the same* during the winter months.
13 A *line of people* formed outside the cinema.
14 The car stood *without moving* at the curb.
15 Could you make me one *exact copy* of the document?
16 A breakdown caused the railways to *delay the time of* the train's departure.
17 Our *walk up the hill* was very tiring.
18 The *decision of the jury* was delivered to a hushed court.
19 Follow the *corridor between the seats* to reach the exit.
20 The *one hundredth anniversary* of the town hall occurs tomorrow.

Match Up the Synonyms

Match each word in the left-hand column with its synonym (or word with a similar meaning) in the right-hand column. The first one has been done for you.

	Words	**Synonyms**
1	*vanish*	*disappear*
2	obtain	anticipate
3	intention	reside
4	distinguished	persuade
5	decrease	conceal
6	protect	congregate
7	persist	irrelevant
8	readable	diminish
9	expect	incredible
10	dwell	genuine
11	sincere	destitute
12	understand	legible
13	unimportant	defend
14	poor	purpose
15	gather	eminent
16	convince	comprehend
17	unbelievable	persevere
18	hide	acquire

Find the Words

1 Select the word from the box for each of these people:

a a writer for a newspaper
b a writer of plays
c a designer of buildings
d a beekeeper
e one who studies plants
f a writer of music
g one who checks accounts
h a prison guard

2 Select the antonym (or word with an opposite meaning) for:

a seldom
b forget
c ancient
d import
e superior
f innocent
g retreat
h majority

3 Select the homophone (or word having the same sound as another but a different meaning) for:

a air
b check
c aloud
d threw
e peace
f principle
g sauce
h serial

4 Select the collective word for:

a stars
b cattle
c locusts
d books
e ships
f flowers
g sailors
h singers

Words
advance
often
architect
allowed
fleet
composer
principal
warder
choir
export
playwright
constellation
piece
modern
plague
journalist
heir
minority
through
bouquet
source
apiarist
library
inferior
remember
herd
cereal
guilty
auditor
crew
cheque
botanist

GETTING IT RIGHT

OVERWORKED AND MISUSED WORDS

When we are lazy in our speech and language we tend to rely on words such as 'good', 'nice', 'terrible', 'terrific', 'awful', 'fabulous' and 'got'. We read and hear these words so often that they threaten to become meaningless. In fact, many of these words have changed their meaning over time. For example, the words 'terrific' and 'terrible' used to mean 'causing terror and dread' but now often mean no more than 'very good' or 'very bad'. The word 'awful' used to mean 'full of awe' and the word 'fabulous' meant 'of or about fables or myths'.

By thinking before we speak or write we can usually substitute a better word for overworked or misused words. For example, 'attractive', 'charming' and 'graceful' are just a few of the many words that could be substituted for 'nice'.

Selecting Expressive Words

Substitute a more precise or expressive word from the box for the word in heavy type in each of the following sentences.

comfortable	riotous	stormy	stylish
clever	dramatic	contracted	gorgeous
long	tasty	received	courteous

1 We had a **nice** Chinese meal in the city.
2 We each **got** a special present.
3 The weather in the mountains was **terrible.**
4 Is that chair **nice** to sit on?
5 There was an **awful** queue at the ticket office.
6 She **got** measles during the holidays.
7 She is **good** at working with computers.
8 There was a **terrible** noise coming from the classroom.
9 I bought a **fabulous** pair of jeans.
10 There's a **terrific** movie on the TV tonight.
11 Can't you be **nice** for a change?
12 You look **fabulous** in that dress.

DRAMA

Oh, No, Romeo

by Bill Condon

TEENAGERS	
Tasha	**Mark**
Julie	**Paul**
Stuart	**David**

SCENE 1

Julie and Tasha are on stage as the curtain opens.

Tasha Give me my Romeo. And when I shall die, take him and cut him out in little stars, and he will make the face of Heaven so fine, that all the world will be in love with night . . .
Julie You're going to tell him that?
Tasha I've planned it for weeks!
Julie Tasha . . .
Tasha That's how I feel, Julie.
Julie But it's embarrassing.
Tasha Not to me.
Julie If you tell Stuart that, you'll never see him again — he'll do the bolt for sure.
Tasha I have to let him know how I feel.
Julie Can't you just share your lunch with him or something?
Tasha Why am I bothering with you — you don't understand.
Julie All I understand is that Stuart is a jerk.
Tasha Don't say that.
Julie He's the pits! He has nothing between his ears!
Tasha He has a very good mind!
Julie It's never been used.
Tasha And he has a great heart.
Julie So does a cabbage.
Tasha He means a lot to me!

Julie He doesn't even know you're alive!
Tasha Well how come he asked me to go to the movies?
Julie He did not.
Tasha Yes he did — we're going tonight.
Julie You mean he actually came up to you and asked if you'd go to the movies with him?
Tasha Well, no, not exactly . . .
Julie You asked him?
Tasha Who cares who asked? He said yes!
Julie I knew he wouldn't ask you.
Tasha I know your problem, Julie — you're jealous!
Julie Tash, Stuart's a pest! He natters away to me all the time — but not once has he ever mentioned you.
Tasha Because he's shy. Who do you think sent me that Valentine's card?
Julie Probably your father.
Tasha It was Stuart! I'm sure it was.
Julie What makes you so sure.
Tasha When you're in love you know these things . . .
Julie In love?
Tasha Yes. Haven't you seen the way he looks at me?
Julie He looks at everyone that way. He needs glasses.
Tasha Stuart doesn't need anything — he's perfect!
Julie Then you're the one who needs glasses.
Tasha Great! I share my good news with you and I get insults.
Julie I just don't want to see you get hurt, Tash.
Tasha It's not like I've rushed into this. I've felt deeply about Stuart since the first day I saw him.
Julie Two whole months ago. You're strangers!
Tasha All that'll change after tonight.
Julie Okay, but please don't tell him that Shakespeare stuff — he'll think you're crazy.
Tasha No he won't . . . it's all going to be just fine.
Julie I hope so — good luck.

Julie exits.

SCENE 2

Later that night. Tasha is pacing nervously back and forth. Stuart enters. He is carrying some books.

Stuart Hi.
Tasha Hi, Stuart.
Stuart Almost forgot about meeting you.
Tasha Sure you did.
Stuart Then I saw an ad for the movie and that reminded me. I love horror movies.
Tasha You're kidding. Right?
Stuart No. I think they're mega!
Tasha I mean about forgetting. You didn't forget did you?
Stuart Yeah — I don't know how though — 'cause I've wanted to see this movie for ages.
Tasha Oh . . . well, we'd better go. Are we catching a taxi?
Stuart Can you afford it?
Tasha Me? Um . . . no.
Stuart We'd better take the train then. That way I'll have more time to study.
Tasha Is that why you brought those books along — to study?
Stuart Yeah. Thought I'd do my homework on the train.
Tasha Oh . . . I thought we'd just sit and talk.
Stuart You can talk if you want to — I'll put on my headphones so you won't bother me.
Tasha Stuart . . .
Stuart Yeah?
Tasha Do you like Shakespeare?
Stuart I don't think I know him.
Tasha Shakespeare! The famous writer!
Stuart Aw yeah, Shakespeare — the writer . . . what stuff's he written?
Tasha Not stuff! *Romeo and Juliet. The Merchant of Venice.*
Stuart Sure, sure — I remember now. All that stupid junk that no one can understand.
Tasha Some of it is easy to understand — 'If music be the food of love, play on . . .'
Stuart I'm real hungry too. Let's get a pie before we catch the train.
Tasha A pie?
Stuart If you're on a diet I'll eat yours for you — but I don't think you need to go on a diet.
Tasha Thanks, Stuart.
Stuart That's okay. There's nothing wrong with being fat.
Tasha Thanks a lot!
Stuart Something the matter?
Tasha Yes there is. You're spoiling everything I planned!
Stuart Oh no!
Tasha Oh yes! This isn't how I . . .
Stuart Here come my mates!
Tasha Your mates? So what?
Stuart When they come over here I'm going to tell them you're my cousin — all right?

Tasha What?!
Stuart You don't want them to make fun of me do you?
Tasha That's an insult!
Stuart Go on — I'd do the same for you. Please!
Tasha . . . Oh, all right.

(David, Paul and Mark enter.)

David Hi, Stuart. Me and the guys are going bowling, you want to come?
Tasha We've already got something planned.
Stuart This is my cousin — Natasha. She's from the country and I'm just showing her around.
Paul You're Francesca's sister — Tasha.
Tasha That's right —
David She's not from the country.
Mark She goes to the same school as you, Stu.
Stuart Well, yeah, but she came from the country originally — didn't you, Tasha?
Tasha . . . I suppose.
David Are you sure you two are cousins?
Stuart Of course I'm sure, David.
Mark What relation are you to Stuart, Tasha?
Tasha He's . . . he's my —
Stuart We're distant cousins. Very, very distant.
Tasha That does it!
Stuart We better get going.
Tasha He's my boyfriend!
Stuart Aw no!
Paul Good one, Stu!
Stuart She's joking. Tell them you're joking, Tasha.
Tasha He's my boyfriend. We're on a date.
Stuart We're not.
Tasha He's taking me to the movies.
Stuart See you guys later.

(Stuart starts to leave.)

Tasha Where are you going?
Stuart To the movies — alone!
Tasha Wait, Stuart! I'm sorry.
Paul Oh, Stuart — she's sorry!
Mark This is so romantic!
David What are you going to do, Stu?
Stuart Don't! Just don't make fun of me . . . or my . . . my girlfriend — okay?
Mark So she is your girlfriend!
David Wait 'til the gang hears this.
Paul Come on, let's leave these two love birds alone.

(They exit.)

Stuart Why did you do that? Why did you embarrass me like that in front of my friends?
Tasha You stuck up for me.
Stuart They were being stupid.
Tasha You called me your girlfriend.
Stuart You're not. I hardly know you.
Tasha But you said it.
Stuart I was trying to be nice.
Tasha Stuart, you're shy, I know that — but you can tell me how you really feel. You don't have to pretend.
Stuart What?
Tasha I've seen the way you look at me.
Stuart I've never looked at you.
Tasha You have! I've been standing there with Julie and I've seen you give this real funny look — lots of times!
Stuart I was looking at Julie!
Tasha Julie? My best friend? Why would you look at her?
Stuart Why? Everyone knows how I feel about Julie!
Tasha I don't.
Stuart I think she's mega-fantastic! Ace!
Tasha She thinks you're the pits!
Stuart I know! And it kills me!
Tasha Tell me this is a joke, Stuart.
Stuart Why would I joke about it? I just can't get her out of my mind — I don't want anyone else but Julie.
Tasha Then why did you say you'd go out with me?
Stuart Well . . .
Tasha I want an answer.
Stuart It was a good way of getting to know Julie better — I've got heaps of questions I want to ask you about her.
Tasha You creep! You . . . cane toad!
Stuart I thought you knew how I felt about her.
Tasha How could I know? She doesn't even know!
Stuart Sorry if I hurt your feelings, Tasha . . . I didn't mean to.
Tasha Did you ever wonder why I asked you out?
Stuart I thought you wanted to see the movie.

Tasha I hate horror movies! I wanted to go out with you, Stuart! Just you!
Stuart Me?! No one's ever wanted to go out with me before — how was I supposed to know?
Tasha Forget it. Just forget it.
Stuart Hey, we can still go to the movies — you'll love *The Principal With Four Hundred Heads.*
Tasha No. I don't feel like the movies now.
Stuart Tasha — we can be friends if you like.
Tasha You have no idea how much this hurts!
Stuart Yes I do.
Tasha How could you? You didn't even know who Shakespeare was!
Stuart I just forgot.
Tasha Leave me alone.
Stuart I was dumb — I'm sorry. Am I forgiven?
Tasha Maybe in a year or so when I cool down.
Stuart We did it in school — I just didn't pay attention.
Tasha What?
Stuart *Romeo and Juliet!*
Tasha Really! Well, you're no Romeo!
Stuart Yeah? Well, you're no Juliet!
Tasha Goodbye!
Stuart Aw, Tasha — I didn't mean it.
Tasha This is the worst night of my life!
Stuart Come to the horror movie with me — that'll cheer you up.
Tasha What?
Stuart When I feel depressed about Julie, I go to a horror movie.
Tasha That doesn't make sense.
Stuart It's hard to think about your problems when you've got a principal with four hundred heads coming at you.
Tasha Stuart . . . that's weird.
Stuart The movie's in 3-D — I promise you'll scream.
Tasha Maybe some other time.
Stuart Okay.
Tasha I'll see you at school.
Stuart Hey, Tasha.
Tasha What?
Stuart If we ever go out again — you're not my cousin — okay?
Tasha Well . . . at least that's a start.

Questions

1 Why do you think the playwright has titled this play 'Oh, No, Romeo'?
2 How does the playwright use conflict between characters to gain the audience's attention as the play opens?
3 Why does Julie advise Tasha not to tell Stuart the Romeo speech?
4 What is Julie's opinion of Stuart?
5 How does the playwright succeed in making Julie and Tasha two contrasting characters in the play?
6 Why does Tasha think that Stuart is in love with her?
7 At the end of Scene 1, which opinion of Stuart did you think was likely to be correct, Tasha's or Julie's? Why?
8 When does Stuart first show his indifference to Tasha?
9 As they talk about catching the train to the movies, how does Stuart shock Tasha?
10 What understanding does Stuart have about Shakespeare?
11 'If music be the food of love, play on . . .' How does Stuart respond to this quotation?
12 As his mates arrive, why does Stuart want Tasha to pretend she is his cousin?
13 'He's my boyfriend. We're on a date.' How does Stuart react to Tasha's statement?
14 'Wait, Stuart! I'm sorry.' How do Stuart's friends react when Tasha says this?
15 How do Tasha and Stuart at last begin to act honestly towards each other?
16 At what point in the play is the conflict between Tasha and Stuart resolved?
17 When does the play's climax occur?
18 Do you think this play ends on a hopeful note? Why?
19 What interesting teenage issue is the theme of this play?
20 Did you find this play humorous or serious? Explain your viewpoint.

Drama Activity

Write a play of your own that explores some of the difficulties of teenage relationships.

2

REAL-LIFE STUDIES

NOVELS

Signs of Hope

Some people didn't expect much of poor little Chris. After all, he was terribly physically handicapped and had never given any indications of intelligence. But one day everything suddenly changed . . .

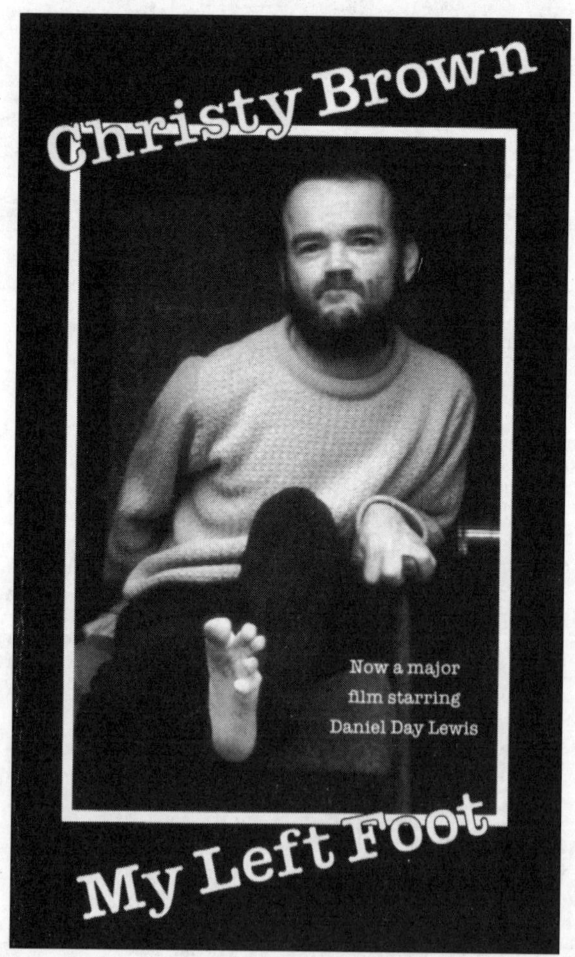

I was now five, and still I showed no real sign of intelligence. I showed no apparent interest in things except with my toes — more especially those of my left foot. Although my natural habits were clean I could not aid myself, but in this respect my father took care of me. I used to lie on my back all the time in the kitchen or, on bright warm days, out in the garden, a little bundle of crooked muscles and twisted nerves, surrounded by a family that loved me and hoped for me and that made me part of their own warmth and humanity. I was lonely, imprisoned in a world of my own, unable to communicate with others, cut off, separated from them as though a glass wall stood between my existence and theirs, thrusting me beyond the sphere of their lives and activities. I longed to run about and play with the rest, but I was unable to break loose from my bondage.

Then, suddenly, it happened! In a moment everything was changed, my future life moulded into a definite shape, my mother's faith in me rewarded and her secret fear changed into open triumph.

It happened so quickly, so simply after all the years of waiting and uncertainty that I can see and feel the whole scene as if it had happened last week. It was the afternoon of a cold, grey December day. The streets outside glistened with snow; the white sparkling flakes stuck and melted on the window-panes and hung on the boughs of the trees like molten silver. The wind howled dismally, whipping up little whirling columns of snow that rose and fell at every fresh gust. And over all, the dull, murky sky stretched like a dark canopy, a vast infinity of greyness.

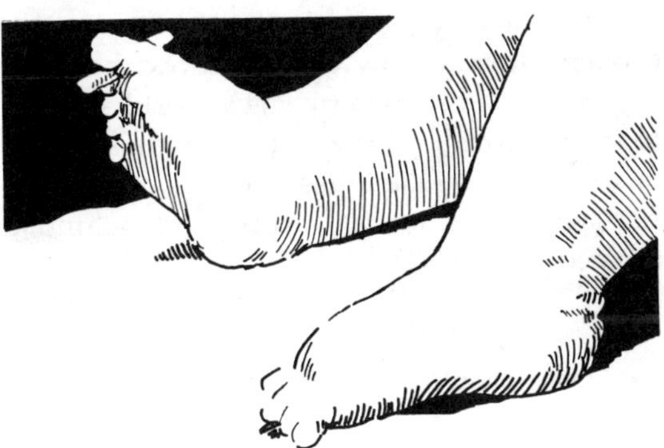

Inside, all the family were gathered round the big kitchen fire that lit up the little room with a warm glow and made giant shadows dance on the walls and ceiling.

In a corner Mona and Paddy were sitting huddled together, a few torn school primers before them. They were writing down little sums on to an old chipped slate, using a bright piece of yellow chalk. I was close to them, propped up by a few pillows against the wall, watching.

It was the chalk that attracted me so much. It was a long, slender stick of vivid yellow. I had never seen anything like it before, and it showed up so well against the black surface of the slate that I was fascinated by it as much as if it had been a stick of gold.

Suddenly I wanted desperately to do what my sister was doing. Then — without thinking or knowing exactly what I was doing, I reached out and took the stick of chalk out of my sister's hand — *with my left foot.*

I do not know why I used my left foot to do this. It is a puzzle to many people as well as to myself, for, although I had displayed a curious interest in my toes at an early age, I had never attempted before this to use either of my feet in any way. They could have been as useless to me as were my hands. That day, however, my left foot, apparently on its own volition, reached out and very impolitely took the chalk out of my sister's hand.

I held it tightly between my toes, and, acting on an impulse, made a wild sort of scribble with it on the slate. Next moment I stopped, a bit dazed, surprised, looking down at the stick of yellow chalk stuck between my toes, not knowing what to do with it next, hardly knowing how it got there. Then I looked up and became aware that everyone had stopped talking and was staring at me silently. Nobody stirred. Mona, her black curls framing her chubby little face, stared at me with great big eyes and open mouth. Across the open hearth, his face lit by flames, sat my father, leaning forward, hands outspread on his knees, his shoulders tense. I felt the sweat break out on my forehead.

My mother came in from the pantry with a steaming pot in her hand. She stopped midway between the table and the fire, feeling the tension flowing through the room. She followed their stares and saw me, in the corner. Her eyes looked from my face down to my foot, with the chalk gripped between my toes. She put down the pot.

Then she crossed over to me and knelt down beside me, as she had done so many times before.

'I'll show you what to do with it, Chris,' she said, very slowly and in a queer, jerky way, her face flushed as if with some inner excitement.

Taking another piece of chalk from Mona, she hesitated, then very deliberately drew, on the floor in front of me, *the single letter 'A'*.

'Copy that,' she said, looking steadily at me. 'Copy it, Christy.'

I couldn't.

I looked about me, looked around at the faces that were turned towards me, tense, excited faces that were at that moment frozen, immobile, eager, waiting for a miracle in their midst.

The stillness was profound. The room was full of flame and shadow that danced before my eyes and lulled my taut nerves into a sort of waking sleep. I could hear the sound of the water-tap dripping in the pantry, the loud ticking of the clock on the mantelshelf, and the soft hiss and crackle of the logs on the open hearth.

I tried again. I put out my foot and made a wild jerking stab with the chalk which produced a very crooked line and nothing more. Mother held the slate steady for me.

'Try again, Chris,' she whispered in my ear. 'Again.'

I did. I stiffened my body and put my left foot out again, for the third time. I drew one side of the letter. I drew half the other side. Then the stick of chalk broke and I was left with a stump. I wanted to fling it away and give up. Then I felt my mother's hand on my shoulder. I tried once more. Out went my foot. I shook, I sweated and strained every muscle. My hands were so tightly clenched that my fingernails bit into the flesh. I set my teeth so hard that I nearly pierced my lower lip. Everything in the room swam till the faces around me were mere patches of white. But — I drew it — *the letter 'A'*. There it was on the floor before me. Shaky, with awkward, wobbly sides and a very uneven centre line. But it *was* the letter 'A'. I looked up. I saw my mother's face for a moment, tears on her cheeks. Then my father stooped down and hoisted me on to his shoulder.

I had done it! It had started — the thing that was to give my mind its chance of expressing itself. True, I couldn't speak with my lips, but now I would speak through something more lasting than spoken words — written words.

That one letter, scrawled on the floor with a broken bit of yellow chalk gripped between my toes, was my road to a new world, my key to mental freedom. It was to provide a source of relaxation to the tense, taut thing that was me which panted for expression behind a twisted mouth.

from *My Left Foot* by Christy Brown

Reading for Meaning

1 Only one thing appeared to have attracted any interest from Chris during the first five years of his life. What was it?

2 How did the family feel about Chris?

3 Why was Chris lonely?

4 What did he long to be able to do?

5 Who had faith that Chris would be able to achieve something with his life?

6 Where was the family gathered when the incident occurred?

7 Why did the chalk capture the attention of Chris?

8 How do we know that taking the chalk with his left foot was a spontaneous action?

9 How do we know that the action stunned everyone in the room?

10 What was it that initially caused the mother to stop midway between the table and the fire?

11 Identify two pieces of evidence in the mother's behaviour, as she knelt near Chris, that suggest she was excited.

12 In the silence as the family waited for Chris to try to copy the letter 'A', what three sounds could be heard?

13 When Chris wanted to give up, what action by his mother encouraged him to try again?

14 Identify three pieces of evidence that show the intense effort that it cost Chris to keep trying.

15 When Chris's father lifted the child up onto his shoulder it was a symbolic action. What did it symbolise?

16 'That one letter . . . was my road to a new world.' Explain what the author meant by this.

17 What qualities of the mother's character are revealed in this passage? Give examples.

18 What qualities of Chris's character can you find evidence for in this passage? Refer to the passage in your answer.

The Flying Dog

When your pet has a problem and you take it to the vet for emergency treatment, it's good to know that the animal is in safe hands.

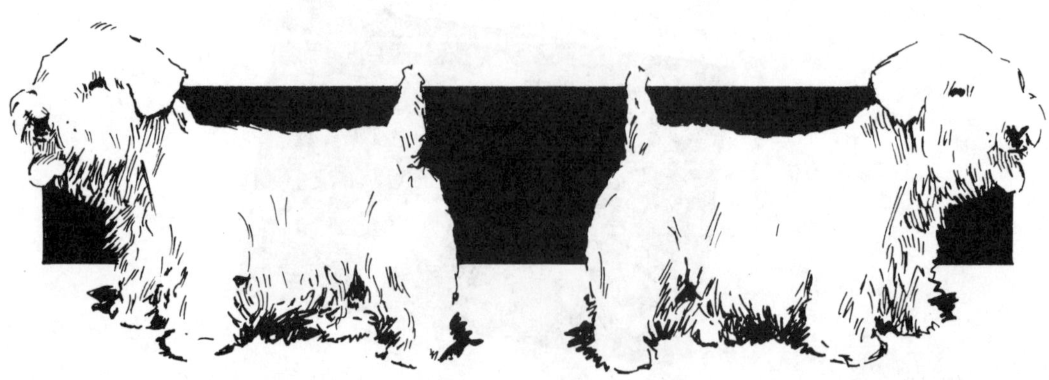

The barber was carrying Venus in his arms but she was a vastly different creature from the placid little animal I had seen in his shop. She was bubbling saliva from her mouth, retching and pawing frantically at her face.

Josh looked distraught. 'She's chokin', Mr Herriot. Look at 'er! She'll die if you don't do summat quick!'

'Wait a minute, Mr Anderson. Tell me what's happened.' Has she swallowed something?'

'Aye, she's 'ad a chicken bone.'

'A chicken bone! Don't you know you should never give a dog chicken bones?'

'Aye, ah know, ah know, everybody knows that, but we'd had a bird for our dinner and she pinched the frame out of the dustbin, the little beggar. She had a good crunch at it afore I spotted 'er and now she's goin' to choke!' He glared at me, lips quivering. He was on the verge of tears.

'Now just calm down,' I said. 'I don't think Venus is choking. By the way she's pawing I should say there's something stuck in her mouth.'

I grabbed the little animal's jaws with finger and thumb and forced them apart. And I saw with a surge of relief the sight familiar to all vets — a long spicule of bone jammed tightly between the back molars and forming a bar across the roof of the mouth.

As I say, it is a common occurrence in practice and a happy one, because it is harmless and easily relieved by a flick of the forceps. Recovery is instantaneous, skill minimal and the kudos most warming. I loved it.

I put my hand on the barber's shoulder. 'You can stop worrying, Mr Anderson, it's just a bone stuck in her teeth. Come through to the consulting-room and I'll have it out in a jiffy.'

I could see the man relaxing as we walked along the passage to the back of the house. 'Oh, thank God for that, Mr Herriot. I thought she'd had it, honest, I did. And we've grown right fond of the little thing. I couldn't bear to lose 'er.'

I gave a light laugh, put the dog on the table and reached for a strong pair of forceps. 'No question of that, I assure you. This won't take a minute.'

Jimmy, aged five, had left his tea and trailed after us. He watched with mild interest as I poised the instrument. Even at his age he had seen this sort of thing many a time and it wasn't very exciting. But you never knew in veterinary practice; it was worth hanging around because funny things could happen. He put his hands in his pockets and rocked back and forth on his heels, whistling softly as he watched me.

Usually it is simply a matter of opening the mouth, clamping the forceps on the bone and removing it. But Venus recoiled from the gleaming metal and so did the barber. The terror in the dog's eyes was reproduced fourfold in those of its owner.

I tried to be soothing. 'This is nothing, Mr Anderson. I'm not going to hurt her in the least, but you'll just have to hold her head firmly for a moment.'

The little man took a deep breath, grasped the dog's neck, screwed his eyes tight shut and turned his head as far away as he could.

'Now, little Venus,' I cooed. 'I'm going to make you better.'

Venus clearly didn't believe me. She struggled violently, pawing at my hand, to the accompaniment of strange moaning sounds from her owner. When I did get the forceps into her mouth she locked her front teeth on the instrument and hung on fiercely. And as I began to grapple with her, Mr Anderson could stand it no longer and let go.

The little dog leaped to the floor and resumed her inner battle there while Jimmy watched appreciatively.

I looked at the barber more in sorrow than in anger. This was just not his thing. He was manually ham-fisted, as his hair-dressing proved, and he seemed quite incapable of holding a wriggling dog.

'Let's have another go,' I said cheerfully. 'We'll try it on the floor this time. Maybe she's frightened of the table. It's a trifling little job, really.'

The little man, lips tight, eyes like slits, bent and extended trembling hands towards his dog, but each time he touched her she slithered away from him until with a great shuddering sigh he flopped face down on the tiles. Jimmy giggled. Things were looking up.

I helped the barber to his feet. 'I tell you what, Mr Anderson, I'll give her a short-acting anaesthetic. That will cut out all this fighting and struggling.'

Josh's face paled. 'An anaesthetic? Put her to sleep, you mean?' Anxiety flickered in his eyes. 'Will she be all right?'

'Of course, of course. Just leave her to me and come back for her in about an hour. She'll be able to walk then.' I began to steer him through the door into the passage.

'Are you sure?' He glanced back pitifully at his pet. 'We're doing the right thing?'

'Without a doubt. We'll only upset her if we go on this way.'

'Very well, then, I'll go along to me brother's for an hour.'

'Splendid.' I waited till I heard the front door close behind him then quickly made up a dose of pentothal.

Dogs do not put on such a tough front when their owners are not present and I scooped Venus easily from the floor on to the table. But her jaws were still clamped tight and her front feet at the ready. She wasn't going to stand for any messing with her mouth.

'Okay, old girl, have it your own way,' I said. I gripped her leg above the elbow and clipped an area from the raised radial vein. In those days Siegfried or myself were often left to anaesthetise dogs without assistance. It is wonderful what you can do when you have to.

Venus didn't seem to care what I was about as long as I kept away from her face. I slid the needle into the vein, depressed the plunger and within seconds her fighting pose relaxed, her head dropped and her whole body sagged on to the table. I rolled her over. She was fast asleep.

'No trouble now, Jimmy, lad,' I said. I pushed the teeth apart effortlessly with finger and thumb, gripped the bone with the forceps and lifted it from the mouth. 'Nothing left in there — lovely. All done.'

I dropped the piece of chicken bone into the waste bin. 'Yes, that's how to do it, my boy. No undignified scrambling. That's the professional way.'

My son nodded briefly. Things had gone dull again. He had been hoping for great things when Mr Anderson draped himself along the surgery floor, but this was tame stuff. He had stopped smiling.

My own satisfied smile, too, had become a little fixed. I was watching Venus carefully and she wasn't breathing. I tried to ignore the lurch in my stomach because I have always been a nervous anaesthetist and am not very proud of it. Even now when I come upon one of my younger colleagues operating I have a nasty habit of placing my hand over the patient's chest wall over the heart and standing wide-eyed and rigid for a few seconds. I know the young surgeons hate to have me spreading alarm and despondency, and one day I am going to be told to get out in sharp terms, but I can't help it.

As I watched Venus I told myself as always that there was no danger. She had received the correct dose and anyway, you often did get this period of apnoea with pentothal. Everything was normal, but just the same I wished to God she would start breathing.

The heart was still going all right. I depressed the ribs a few times — nothing. I touched the unseeing eyeball — no corneal reflex. I began to rap my fingers on the table and stared closely at the little animal and I could see that Jimmy was watching me just as keenly. His deep interest in veterinary practice was built upon a fascination for animals, farmers and the open air, but it was given extra colour by something else; he never knew when his father might do something funny or something funny might happen to him.

The unpredictable mishaps of the daily round were all good for a laugh, and my son with his unerring instinct had a feeling that something of the sort was going to happen now.

His hunch was proved right when I suddenly lifted Venus from the table, shook her vainly a few times above my head then set off at full gallop along the passage. I could hear the eager shuffle of the little slippers just behind me.

I threw open the side door and shot into the back garden. I halted at the narrow part — no, there wasn't enough room there and continued my headlong rush till I reached the big lawn.

Here I dropped the little dog on to the grass and fell down on my knees by her side in an attitude of prayer. I waited and watched as my heart hammered, but those ribs were not moving and the eyes stared sightlessly ahead.

Oh, this just couldn't happen! I seized Venus by a hind leg in either hand and began to whirl her round my head. Sometimes higher, sometimes lower, but attaining a remarkable speed as I put all my strength into the swing. This method of resuscitation seems to have gone out of fashion now, but it was very much in vogue then. It certainly met with the full approval of my son. He laughed so much that he fell down and sprawled on the grass.

When I stopped and glared at the still immobile ribs he cried, 'Again, Daddy, again.' And he didn't have to wait more than a few seconds before Daddy was in full action once more with Venus swooping through the air like a bird on the wing.

It exceeded all Jimmy's expectations. He probably had wondered about leaving his jam sandwiches to see the old man perform, but how gloriously he had been rewarded. To this day the whole thing is so vivid; my tension and misery lest my patient should die for no reason at all, and in the background the helpless, high-pitched laughter of my son.

I don't know how many times I stopped, dropped the inert form on the grass, then recommenced my whirling, but at last at one of the intervals the chest wall gave a heave and the eyes blinked.

With a gasp of relief I collapsed face down on the cool turf and peered through the green blades as the breathing became regular and Venus began to lick her lips and look around her.

I dared not get up immediately because the old brick walls of the garden were still dancing around me and I am sure I would have fallen.

Jimmy was disappointed. 'Aren't you going to do any more, Daddy?'

'No, son, no.' I sat up and dragged Venus on to my lap. 'It's all over now.'

'Well, that was funny. Why did you do it?'

'To make the dog breathe.'

'Do you always do that to make them breathe?'

'No, thank heaven, not often.' I got slowly to my feet and carried the little animal back to the consulting-room.

from *The Lord God Made Them All* by James Herriot

Reading for Meaning

1 What were the first signs of distress that the vet noticed in the dog?
2 Josh (the barber) 'was on the verge of tears'. What was he afraid of?
3 What was causing the dog so much distress?
4 Why had Jimmy followed the others into the consulting room?
5 What sentence clearly tells us that Josh was more terrified of the forceps than the dog was?
6 What did Josh do to try to avoid further agony while he held the dog?
7 Why was the vet able to feel pity rather than anger towards the ham-fisted barber?
8 What was the final indication from Josh that he would be of no further use in helping the vet?
9 What happened to Josh's face and eyes at the mention of an anaesthetic?
10 Why did the vet's 'satisfied smile' become a little fixed?
11 How did the vet show that he was a 'nervous anaesthetist' when his younger colleagues operated?
12 What effect did his father's action of swinging the dog around have on young Jimmy?
13 What impressions were left so vividly in the vet's memory of the incident?
14 What were the first signs of life returning to Venus?
15 Why didn't the vet stand up straight away?
16 What emotion did the vet feel at the end of this experience?
17 What is there about this passage that makes it humorous for the reader?
18 Identify some aspects of the vet's character that emerge in this passage. Refer to the passage for your answer.

Triumph and Disgrace

Life seems doubly cruel when a rare moment of triumph becomes a time of public humiliation.

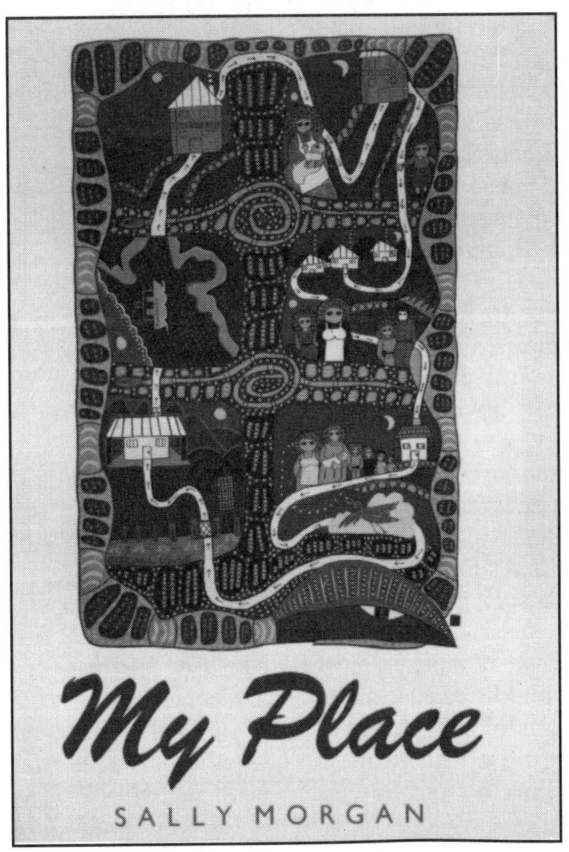

Towards the end of first term, I had an encounter with Miss Roberts that wiped out any confidence I might have had for the rest of the year.

Our school seats comprised a heavy metal frame, with jarrah slats spaced across the seat and back. This proved unfortunate for me, because one day, after what seemed hours of holding my arm in the air trying to attract Miss Roberts' attention, I was unable to avoid wetting myself.

Miss Roberts had been intent on marking our latest tests and had failed to notice my desperately flailing arm. But one of the clean, shiny-haired, no-cavity girls next to me began to chant quietly, 'You've wet ya pa-ants, you've wet ya pa-ants!'

'I have not,' I denied hotly, 'it's just water under my chair.'

'Oh yeah, well then, how come you've dumped all those hankies on it?' She had me there.

By this time, most of the surrounding children were starting to giggle.

Miss Roberts raised her horn-rimmed eyes and said firmly, '*Quiet* please!' She stared at us a few seconds longer, obviously waiting for her eagle-like gaze to have its usual effect. When the last giggle was giggled, she pushed back her solid wooden chair, breathed deeply and said: 'I . . . have an announcement to make.'

We were very impressed with Miss Roberts' use of the word 'I'. For the whole term, I had been convinced Miss Roberts was even more important than the headmistress.

'I . . . have finished marking your test papers.' There was complete silence after this statement. Under Miss Roberts' reign, our weekly tests had assumed great importance. We all waited anxiously to hear who had missed the mark this time.

'I . . . must commend you all on your efforts. All, except Rrrodney.' She always rolled her R's when she said Rodney. You'd think he was her favourite with the amount of attention she gave him. In fact, the opposite was true, Rodney could do nothing right.

'Rrrodney,' she continued, 'how many times have *I* told you bottom is spelt b-o-t-t-o-m *not* b-u-m!'

Rodney grinned, and we all snickered, but were instantly checked by Miss Roberts' look of disgust. She disliked anything even slightly earthy. I had a grudging admiration for Rodney. He'd been spelling bottom like that for three weeks now. He was my kind of person.

'Now,' she said, in a way that made us all straighten up and give full attention, 'where is Sally, hmmmn?' Resting her chin on her neck, she peered around the class in an attempt to locate my non-descript brown face amongst a sea of forty knowing smiles. 'Oh, there you are, dear.' I had been cowering behind the girl in front of me, with my hands stuffed between my legs in an attempt to prevent further trickles.

'Sally has, for the *first* time this year, managed to complete her test correctly. In fact, this week she is the only one to have done so.' Pausing, she allowed time for the greatness of

my achievement to sink in. Everyone knew what was coming next, and, mistaking the smothered raspberries and giggles for eagerness, she said: 'Well, come on Sally. Come out to the front and hold up your book. I . . . can tell the class is anxious to see your work.'

Miss Roberts waited patiently as I rose carefully to my feet. I hurriedly twisted the wet part of my dress around as far as I could, holding it tightly bunched in my left hand. With my knees locked together, and my left elbow jutting out at an unusual angle behind my back, I jerked spasmodically forward. Fortunately, Miss Roberts was gazing in amazement at my test book, and so was not confronted with the sight of my contorted body.

'I . . . want you to hold it up to the class so they can all see it. Look how eager they are to see a test that has scored one hundred per cent!'

Clutching my book in my right hand, I leant as far from Miss Roberts as possible, lest she smell my condition.

My misshapen body must have alerted her to the fact that something was wrong, because she snapped impatiently, 'Hold the book with two hands! And put your dress down, we are not interested in seeing your pants!'

A wave of giggling swept over the class. As I patted down the full skirt of my blue cotton dress, Miss Roberts' large, sensitive nostrils flared violently, and she snorted in disgust.

Grasping me by the elbow, she hauled me back to my desk and, pointing to the offending puddle, demanded, 'And *where* have all those handkerchiefs come from?' Flinging back the lid of my desk, she shrieked: 'Oh no! There are more in here!' I felt so embarrassed. It was obvious she didn't know what to attack first, my pile of dirty handkerchiefs nestled near my overflowing jar of pencil shavings, my collection of hardened orange peel, or my old apple core turned brown and on the brink of mould.

Shaking her head in disbelief, she muttered, 'You dirty, dirty girl.' She dragged me back to the front of the class and shoved me out the door.

'Out you go, you are not to enter this class again. You sit out there and dry off!'

I sat alone and wet on the hard jarrah bench.

My attitude towards school took an even more rapid downhill turn after that incident. I felt different from the other children in my class. They were the spick-and-span brigade, and I, the grubby offender.

from *My Place* by Sally Morgan

Reading for Meaning

1 What effect did this encounter with Miss Roberts have on Sally?

2 Why had Miss Roberts failed to notice Sally's hand up?

3 How did Sally try to hide the tell-tale evidence on the floor?

4 What did Miss Roberts tend to do after she said the word 'I'? How is this conveyed in the extract?

5 How much attention did Rodney usually get from Miss Roberts and why was this given to him?

6 Why did Sally have a 'grudging admiration for Rodney'?

7 Why did the class react with such eagerness when the teacher began to praise Sally?

8 What did Sally do to try to hide her wet dress as she walked to the front of the class?

9 Why did Sally lean away from her teacher?

10 What evidence was there to show that Miss Roberts *had* smelt Sally's condition?

11 What disgusted Miss Roberts about the condition of Sally's desk?

12 Why was Sally sent from the classroom?

13 How was Sally's relationship with the other school children affected by this incident?

14 How did Sally see herself as being different from the others?

15 How would you describe the character of Miss Roberts, judging from this incident?

16 Identify two important aspects of Sally's character that we see in this incident.

POETRY

SCENES FROM REAL LIFE

One Parent Family

My mum says she's clueless
not, as you'd imagine,
at wiring three pin plugs or
straightening a bicycle wheel,
but at sewing buttons
on a shirt, icing names and
dates on birthday cakes,
preparing a three course meal.

She's not like other mothers;
although she's slim and neat
she looks silly in an apron,
just great in dungarees.
She'll tackle any household job,
lay lino, fix on tiles, does
all the outside paintwork, climbs
a ladder with practised ease.

Mind you, she's good for
a cuddle when I fall and
cut my knee. She tells me
fantastic stories every night,
laughs at *my* disasters, says
that she's as bad when she
reads a recipe all wrong and
her cakes don't come out right.

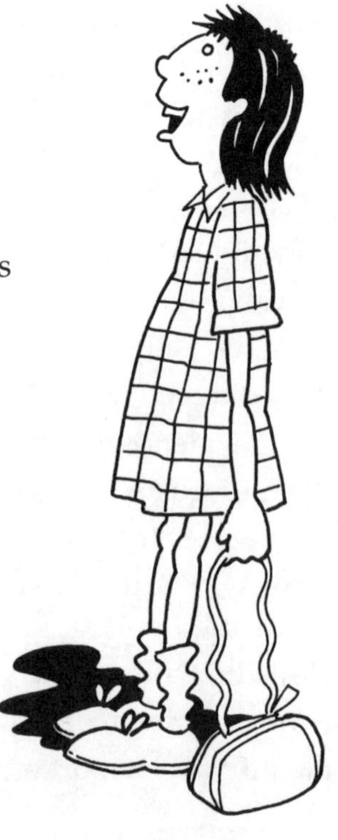

I know on open evenings
she gives a bad impression
at the school. She doesn't wear
the proper clothes. 'Too bad,'
the others sometimes say,
'You've got such a peculiar mum.'
'It's just as well,' I tell them.
'She is my mother *and* my dad!'

Moira Andrew

Questions

1 What two things might we *imagine* the writer's mother would be 'clueless' about?

2 What is she *really* 'clueless' about?

3 'She's not like other mothers'. What does the poet imply about the way other mothers look in an apron?

4 What is there about the way the poet's mother climbs a ladder that suggests she has done it before?

5 Drawing on impressions from the third verse, how old does the writer present herself as being? What evidence is there for your guess?

6 How do you think the poet's mother would react to a cup being accidentally broken?

7 What does the writer believe to be important for anyone hoping to make a good impression on a school open evening?

8 Why does the poet think it's just as well her mum is 'peculiar'?

9 From this poem, how would *you* describe the kind of person this mother seems to be?

10 Does this poem successfully present a young child's view of her mum as a single parent? Support your viewpoint.

A Striking Old Man

When grandfather first came to us
We did not know how old he was
Nor how reliable.
Regular as clockwork he wound up our day
And simply by his presence
Reminded us of things we had not done.
Not that he ever complained
And we liked him for that.
They had got tired of him at the other house,
So he arrived unceremoniously one afternoon in a van,
The few things that were his in a case.
They said he had been too much trouble,
He hardly fitted their way of life.
We came to love him.
On his face you could see what time had done
And quite a lot that had defeated time.
Sometimes his secrets were unlocked.
Then we would see right through
To the frailty and simplicity
Of something that had gone on working
Through so many changes.
His voice was occasionally sharp
But we knew he was just run down
And so we would make allowances.
Adjustment was easy.
For much of the day he was quiet
And we heard him mostly at night
Breathing throughout the house
In a satisfied old-fashioned way.
When visitors came he was good:
We saw them admiring his hands —
He had a certain veneer.
In time he was part of our lives.
The children lived by his looks.
He made us all feel at home.

Alasdair Aston

Questions

1 'Regular as clockwork he wound up our day'. What does this line tell us about the effect the old man had on the family's life?

2 What did grandfather's presence remind the family of?

3 Why had grandfather left the previous home?

4 Which short line in the poem most dramatically contrasts his reception at the new house with the way the previous family thought of him?

5 What did the old man's face reveal?

6 How did the family handle it when grandfather's voice was sharp?

7 When was grandfather most active?

8 What about the old man did visitors admire?

9 How did the family benefit from their grandfather's presence?

10 How does the poet seem to feel about the issue of having grandparents live with a family? Support your answer from the poem.

The Annual Holiday

(or Will that Old Army Suitcase Hold out Another Year Dad?)

Well, I'm off on me holidays,
It's all within me reach,
I've got myself in trim
For carting deckchairs round the beach,
With me flask of tea and cup,
I shall be pouring out the dregs,
With wasps all round me orange,
And with tar all round me legs.

All bundled up with cardigans,
(The weather's on the change)
I won't have slept the night before,
(The beds were all so strange)
I'll lay out on the beach,
Oh so remote and deeply tanned,
With me sandwiches, me knickers,
And me ears full up with sand.

At night, as we're on holiday,
It's on the town we'll go,
With sausage, chips and marrowfats,
At a couple of quid a throw,
And when we've spent our cash,
We'll wander home as best we can,
All along the Mini Golf,
To the smell of the hot dog man.

Or seeing as it's raining,
We'll pop out for a jar,
When we've fought the other tourists,
For a second at the bar,
We'll ignore those folks who've just come in,
Whose shoulders are so sore,
'Cause *last* week was so hot,
They couldn't step outside the door.

And then we'll travel home,
All sat religiously apart,
So we don't touch each other's legs,
And make the sunburn smart,
With suitcasefuls of rock,
So everybody gets a stick,
And our hearts down in our flip flops,
See you next year. Kiss me quick.

Pam Ayres

Warning

When I am an old woman I shall wear purple
With a red hat that doesn't suit me,
And I shall spend my pension on brandy and summer gloves
And satin sandals, and say we've no money for butter.
I shall sit down on the pavement when I am tired
And gobble up samples in shops and press alarm bells
And run my stick along the public railings
And make up for the sobriety of my youth.
I shall go out in my slippers in the rain
And pick the flowers in other people's gardens
And learn to spit.

You can wear terrible shirts and grow more fat
And eat three pounds of sausages at a go
Or only bread and pickles for a week
And hoard pens and pencils and beermats and things in boxes.

But now we must have clothes that keep us dry
And pay our rent and not swear in the street
And set a good example for the children.
We shall have friends to dinner and read the papers.

But maybe I ought to practise a little now?
So that people who know me are not too shocked and surprised
When suddenly I am old and start to wear purple.

Jenny Josephs

Questions

1 Why does the poem have the title 'Warning'?

2 'And make up for the sobriety of my youth'. How does the poet seem to feel about her young days?

3 What makes the line 'And learn to spit' such a strong finish to the first verse?

4 How old does the poet appear to be from this poem?

5 What idea occurs to the poet at the end of the poem? What reason does she give for considering this?

6 How does the poet seem to feel about her life up to this point?

7 What response do you think the poet hopes to draw out of her readers? Is she successful?

8 What did you like about this poem?

Blackberry-picking

(for Philip Hobsbaum)

Late August, given heavy rain and sun
For a full week, the blackberries would ripen.
At first, just one, a glossy purple clot
Among others, red, green, hard as a knot.
You ate that first one and its flesh was sweet
Like thickened wine: summer's blood was in it
Leaving stains upon the tongue and a lust for
Picking. The red ones inked up and that hunger
Sent us with milk-cans, pea-tins, jam-pots
Where briars scratched and wet grass bleached our boots.
Round hayfields, cornfields and potato-drills
We trekked and picked until the cans were full,
Until the tinkling bottoms had been covered
With green ones, and on top big dark blobs burned
Like a plate of eyes. Our hands were peppered
With thorn pricks, our palms sticky as Bluebeard's.

We hoarded the fresh berries in the byre.
But when the bath was filled we found a fur,
a rat-grey fungus, glutting on our cache.
The juice was stinking, too. Once off the bush
The fruit fermented, the sweet flesh would turn sour.
I always felt like crying. It wasn't fair
That all the lovely canfuls smelt of rot.
Each year I hoped they'd keep, knew that they would not.

Seamus Heaney

Questions

1 What are the requirements for the blackberries to ripen in late August?

2 What is the taste of the first blackberry likened to?

3 What two effects are left on the person after eating the first blackberry?

4 '. . . The red ones inked up . . .' What change in the blackberries is being described here?

5 'We trekked and picked until the cans were full'. What examples of alliteration (the repetition of consonant sounds) can you identify in this line?

6 'Until the tinkling bottoms had been covered'. What comments would you make about the word 'tinkling'?

7 The berries are 'hoarded . . . in the byre', or cowshed. What does the word 'hoarded' suggest about the way the children felt about all the berries?

8 What two things soon spoiled the berries?

9 How did the poet feel about the waste?

10 How successfully does this poem capture the events and feelings connected with childhood memories of blackberry picking? Support your answer by referring to the poem.

Kieran

Kieran can't walk like the rest of us.
He comes to school on the special bus.
He has to use crutches to get about
And he's fast, but he can't keep up when we run
When we race in the wind and fight and have fun
He can't keep up, he has to shout
'Wait for me, everyone, wait for me.'
And sometimes we wait, and sometimes we
Run off and hide, and that's when he
Sits in the yard with his sticks on the ground
Sits by himself until he's found
By Sir, or Miss, and they sit and talk
And we watch them laugh in a special way
And we'd love to know what he has to say
About the ones who ran away.
The ones who forgot that he can't walk.
And then we remember to ask him to play
And we kick the ball and he hits it back;
He's quick with those sticks, he has the knack
Of whamming the ball right into goal.
And if he falls over he doesn't fuss,
We hoist him back up and we laugh at the soil
On his hands and his face, and give him his sticks.
He's strong when he fights us, but he never kicks —
He can't use his legs like the rest of us.
He comes to school on the special bus.

Berlie Doherty

Questions

1 Whose viewpoint does this poem seem to be written from?

2 'The special bus' is not clearly defined. What kind of bus is it?

3 What two things does the writer note about the way Kieran gets about?

4 What does Kieran do when the other children run off and hide?

5 How does Kieran appear to handle it *emotionally* when he is left behind by the others? How do we know this?

6 Why do you think the children then make a special effort to include Kieran?

7 How has Kieran adjusted to his disability? What evidence is there for your view?

8 How does the poem cause you to feel about Kieran?

9 What are your thoughts and feelings about the other children in this poem, and the way they relate to Kieran?

10 How effective do you rate this poem in its attempt to give us a glimpse of Kieran and his school? Explain your answer.

Unemployment

Each Tuesday at ten o'clock I go to the
  Employment Exchange,
fill in the form they give me, tell what I have
  earned
for chopping down the neighbour's trees, feeding
  his horse,
rescuing a silly sheep from the swamp. Sometimes,
  with odd jobs,
I make as much as a pound a week, but no one
offers anything permanent. The official (whom I
  knew at school,
a bear in the back seat) gapes at me: I'm sorry we
  cannot place you.
And therefore I am not placed, not in this or that.
  I have
a fine box of tools that I keep well-oiled. I have
  experience
and knowledge tied in a waiting bundle in the corner
  of my mind
nearest the door but no one knocks and the door
  is never opened.

I collect my weekly allowance. I go home,
I cuddle my wife, feed the cat ,
and, for no purpose in no place, grow fat.

Janet Frame

WRITING

CAPTURING A DRAMATIC MOMENT

The skilled writer is able to capture the essence of a dramatic moment in his or her writing and convey this to a reader. Often this will involve being able to create suspense and build tension. Consider the following example, taken from Arthur Porges' short story 'The Ruum', in which a geologist is pursued by an alien creature.

Kill or Be Killed

Shortly after sunrise Jim Irwin reached the lake. The ruum was close enough for him to hear the dull sounds of its passage. Jim staggered, his eyes closed. He hit himself feebly on the nose, his eyes jerked open, and he saw the explosive. The sight of the greasy sticks of dynamite snapped Irwin wide awake.

He forced himself to calmness and carefully considered what to do. Fuse? No. It would be impossible to leave fused dynamite in the trail and time the detonation with the absolute precision he needed. Sweat poured down his body, his clothes were sodden with it. It was hard to think. The explosion *must* be set off from a distance and at the exact moment the ruum was passing over it. But Irwin dared not use a long fuse. The rate of burning was not constant enough. Couldn't calibrate it perfectly with the ruum's advance. Jim Irwin's body sagged all over, his chin sank toward his heaving chest. He jerked his head up, stepped back — and saw the .22 pistol where he had left it in the lean-to.

His sunken eyes flashed.

Moving with frenetic haste, he took the half-filled case, piled all the remaining percussion caps among the loose sticks in a devil's mixture. Weaving out to the trail, he carefully

placed box and contents directly on his earlier tracks some twenty yards from a rocky ledge. It was a risk — the stuff might go any time but that didn't matter. He would far rather be blown to rags than end up living but paralysed in the ruum's outdoor butcher's stall.

The exhausted Irwin had barely hunched down behind the thin ledge of rock before his inexorable pursuer appeared over a slight rise five hundred yards away. Jim scrunched deeper into the hollow, then saw a vertical gap, a narrow crack between rocks. That was it, he thought vaguely. He could sight through the gap at the dynamite and still be shielded from the blast. If it was a shield . . . when that half-case blew only twenty yards away . . .

He stretched out on his belly, watching the ruum roll forward . . . He aimed at the dynamite. And very calmly, very carefully, Jim Irwin squeezed the trigger of his pistol.

Briefly, sound first. Then giant hands lifted his body from where he lay, then let go. He came down hard, face in a patch of nettles, but he was sick, he didn't care. He remembered that the birds were quiet. Then there was a fluid thump as something massive struck the grass a few yards away. Then there was quiet.

from *The Ruum* by Arthur Porges

How does the writer create the drama in this scene? How does he successfully capture this dramatic moment?

1 His first and most important technique is his **selection of words.** We are given a vivid picture of Irwin's condition through action words and phrases such as 'Jim *staggered*', 'sweat *poured* down his body', 'his sunken eyes *flashed*', and so on. Descriptive words such as 'the *exhausted* Irwin', '*absolute* precision' and 'his *inexorable* pursuer' add to our picture of the situation, helping us to feel the tension.

2 Note the way the author **varies sentence length** to create tension. While some sentences are of moderate length and provide an important contrast, the tension is primarily created by the occasional use of short, powerful sentences. For example: 'Jim staggered, his eyes closed'; 'It was hard to think'; 'That was it, he thought vaguely'; 'He aimed at the dynamite'; 'Then there was quiet'.

Note the added dramatic effect gained by having two single-word sentences ('Fuse?' and 'No'), and also the impact of a single-sentence paragraph ('His sunken eyes flashed'). Each of these heightens the dramatic expectancy and tension in the description.

3 The author uses **distinctive sentence forms** to help us imaginatively enter the situation. We have already noticed the important use of short sentences, but notice also that much of their impact is increased because they are written in the form of thoughts by the man, Jim Irwin. For example, the sentences 'Fuse? No' and 'couldn't calibrate it perfectly with the ruum's advance' help us to feel the tension of Jim's plight as he tries frantically to work out the best tactics to use against the ruum.

Writing in the form of a person's thoughts enables the writer to omit words and, in this way, to maintain a sense of urgency.

CAPTURING A TENDER MOMENT

Marie Kuderikova was born in Moravia in March, 1921. In 1943, at the age of twenty-two, she was executed by the Nazi Secret Police because of her involvement in an anti-Nazi organisation. She wrote this last letter to her family from her prison cell, attempting to express to them her feelings — about them, about life, and about her impending death.

A Final Letter

Breslau, March 26, 1943

My dear parents, my beloved little mother and little father, my only sister, and my little brother. Dearest grandmother and aunt, my friends, dear and cherished acquaintances. My family. All of you who are precious to me in what is dearest to my heart. I take leave of you, I send you greetings, I love you. Do not weep; I am not weeping. I depart without lamentation, without trembling, without pain, and even now, yes, even now, I am attaining to that which should indeed be the goal, not the means — to parting from you and at the same time to full nearness to you and complete union with you. I can convey so little of my love, nothing but the most earnest assurance of its depth and sincerity. My sincerest thanks.

Today, the twenty-sixth of March, 1943, at half-past six in the evening, two days after having reached the twenty-second year of my life, I shall draw my last breath. And yet, up to the last moment — to live and to hope. I have always had the courage to live — moreover, I am not losing it in face of what in human speech is called death. I should like to take upon myself all your sorrow and all your pain. I feel in myself the strength to bear it for you too, and the desire to take it with me. Please, please have that strength too, do not suffer, do not weep. I love you, I cherish you so very much. Whenever I have read your words, I have grown wings. You have done everything that is within the power of human love. Do not reproach yourselves in any way. I know everything, I feel everything, I read everything that is in your hearts.

Today is a beautiful day. You are somewhere in the fields or in the little garden. Do you feel as I do that fragrance, that loveliness? It is as though I had had an intimation of it today. I was not walking, I was in the open air, which was full of the essence of spring, of warmth, the shimmer and scent of memories. The naked nerve of the soul was stirred by the poetry of the commonplace, the smell of boiled potatoes, smoke and the clatter of spoons, birds, sky, being alive — the everyday pulse beat of life. Love it, love one another, learn love, defend love, spread love. So that you may perceive the beauty of the obvious gifts of life as I do — that is my wish for myself. So that you may be able to give and to receive.

Your loving daughter,
Marie Kuderikova

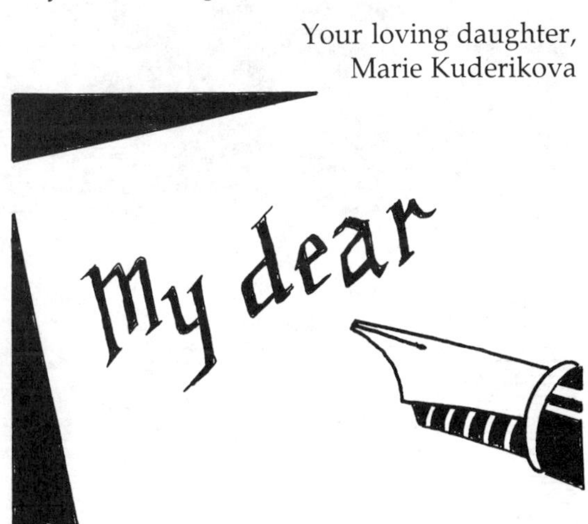

from *Dying We Live*, edited by Gollwitzer, Kuhn and Schneider

Although the language is a little dated, and also a little stilted because it is a translation from German, the writer has succeeded in conveying her tender emotions towards her family. How has this been achieved?

1 Once again, much of the impact comes through the **selection of words and phrases** — the writer's vocabulary. The writer speaks of '*cherished* acquaintances', 'all of you who are *precious* to me' and 'I can convey so little of my *love*, nothing but the *earnest* assurance of its *depth* and *sincerity*.'

2 Again, **sentence length** and the balance of short and long sentences, helps to increase the emotional impact, the tenderness of the writing. Generally the sentences are longer, more flowing and more rhythmic than in the previous example. Sentences such as 'I know everything, I feel everything, I read everything that is in your hearts', and 'Do you feel as I do that fragrance, that loveliness?' have a rhythmic balance and a gentleness that helps us to enter into the writer's tender feelings towards her family.

3 The **reality of the situation** also increases the impact in this piece of writing. We know that those words were penned by a young woman shortly before her execution. The blunt reality of that adds a potency to the feelings that she is expressing and also to our reception of them.

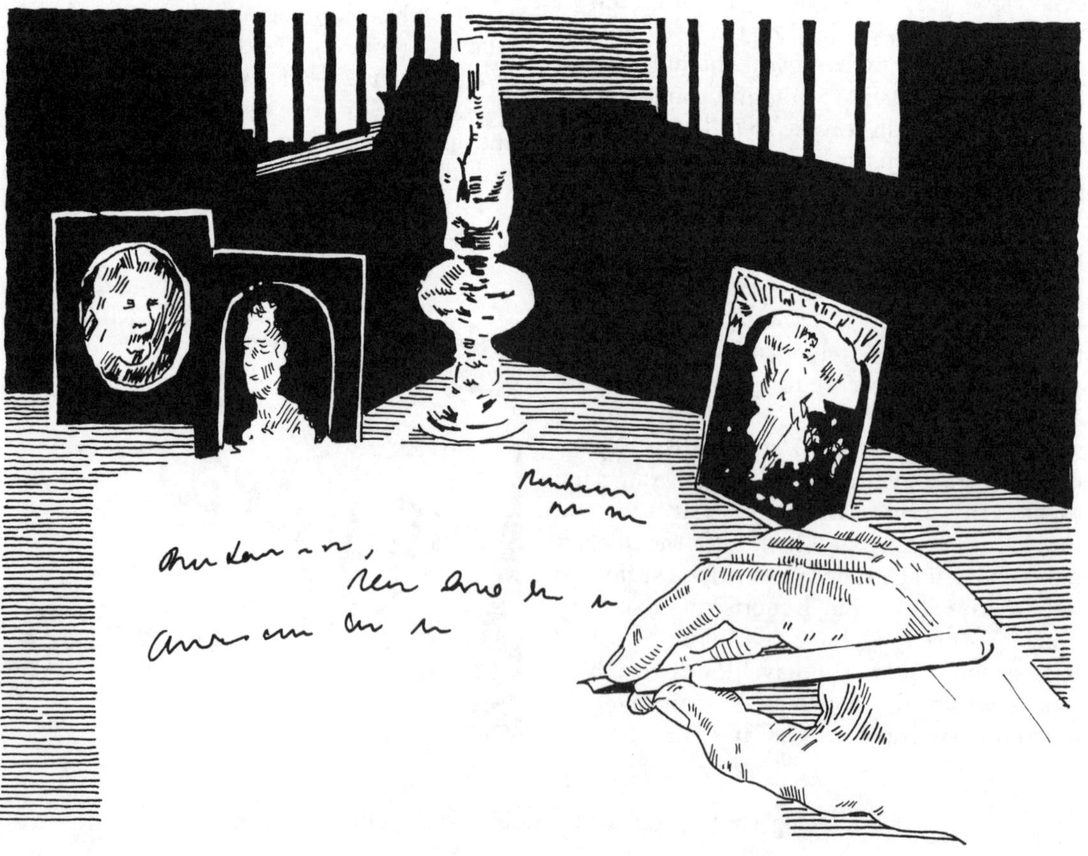

YOUR TURN TO WRITE

To successfully capture the emotions you want in a piece of writing, you will need to pay careful attention to:

- selection of words and phrases (vocabulary)
- sentence length
- rhythm and balance in sentences
- distinctive sentence forms
- the situation being written about

Try your hand at capturing either a dramatic moment or a tender moment. The situation you describe may be fictional or it may be something that you have actually experienced. Here are some suggested themes.

- Fire!
- Out of control!
- Saved from the surf
- Boating mishap
- An unexpected attack
- Father and new child — a description
- Twins!
- A lost child is found
- The new kitten
- Friends

LANGUAGE

BIAS WORDS

Writers and speakers frequently try to touch our emotions in order to achieve their desired response. To do this, they will often make use of words that already carry an emotional content. For example, if we describe a person who has a lot of sickness as a 'hypochondriac', we are using a word with a negative emotional content, a bias of disapproval. Bias words may have either favourable or unfavourable overtones.

Matching Bias Words

The words in the columns below have been jumbled. Match each word that has favourable overtones with its 'partner' that has unfavourable overtones. For example, the word 'chubby' (favourable) would match with 'fat' (unfavourable).

	Favourable	Unfavourable
1	cottage	fanatical
2	economical	skinny
3	firm	predictable
4	slim	obstinate
5	car	shack
6	aroma	cheap
7	tipsy	unattractive
8	enthusiastic	drunk
9	daring	timid
10	plain	bomb
11	reliable	smell
12	cautious	foolhardy

The Missing Word

In the following sentences, the favourable bias words are shown in heavy type. Supply the missing unfavourable bias word for each sentence by choosing the appropriate one from the box.

fussy	gullible	interrogated	insensitive	emaciated
flabby	mongrel	burden	dump	notorious

1 My dog is a **pedigree**; yours is a ....
2 I **questioned** the employee; you .... her.
3 I am a **responsibility** for my family; you are a .... for yours.
4 I am **slender** in appearance; you are ....
5 I am **particular** about tidiness; you are ....
6 Our home is **unpretentious**; yours is a ....
7 I am **famous**; you are ....
8 I am **frank** with people; you are .... to them.
9 I have **minimal muscle-tone**; you are ....
10 I am a **trusting** person; you are ....

DENOTATION AND CONNOTATION

Words have two kinds of meanings. The first is the dictionary definition, or **denotation**. The second is the personal association or the private meaning that the word has for the person hearing it. This is the **connotation**. Usually connotations have emotive overtones of goodness or badness, depending on the individual person's experience.

Thus, for example, the denotation of 'car' is 'a motor vehicle'. However, its connotations are almost limitless. They will vary greatly, for example, for a racing-car driver, a person who has just been hit by a car, a car salesman, and so on. The following diagram gives some examples.

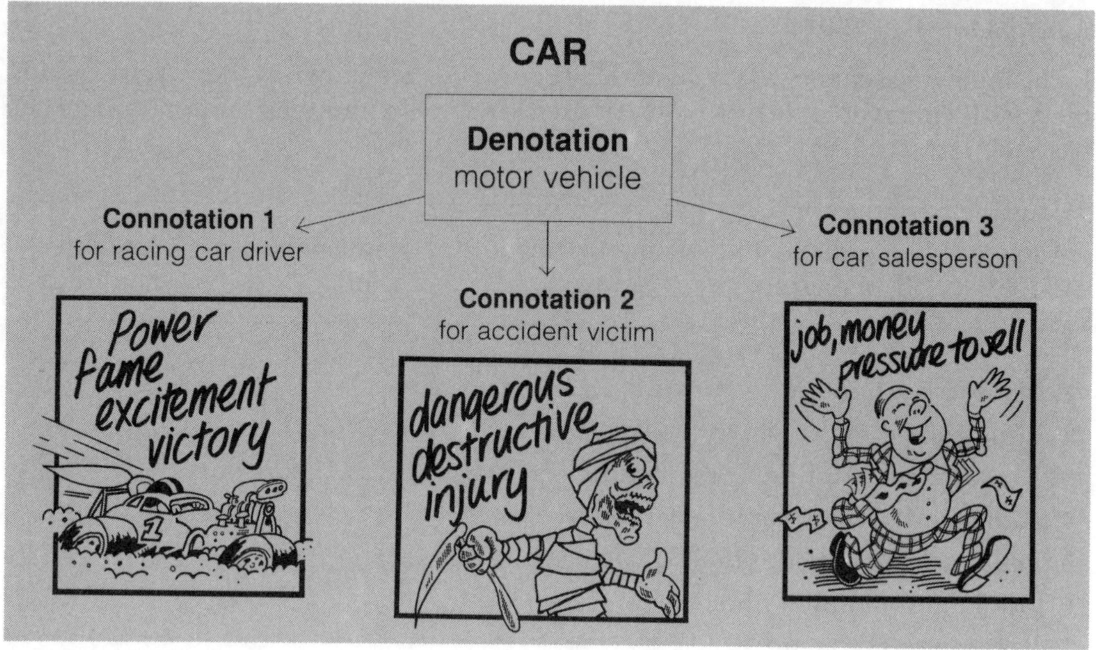

Charting Denotation and Connotation

The chart below has a number of common words listed. Copy it out and use a dictionary to find the denotation of each word, then fill out as many common connotations as you can think of. The first one has been done for you.

Word	Denotation	Connotations
green	a colour between blue and yellow on the spectrum	life, vitality, safety, inexperience, sickness, unripeness, vegetable
lion		
cigarette		
hamburger		
soldier		
homework		
politician		
chocolate		
vulture		
mouse		

Different Connotations for Different People

Each word listed below has its denotation written beside it. Think about each person listed in the third column and suggest additional connotations that the word might have for each one of them. The first one has been done for you.

Word	Denotation	People	Connotation
tree	plant with single woody stem or trunk	**conservationist**	precious, needs preserving, object of beauty, important for our world
		timber-worker	means of income; resource that we should make wise use of
mountain	natural elevation of earth's surface	**mountain-climber**	
		desert-dweller (who has never seen a mountain)	
steak	slice of beef	**cattle farmer**	
		vegetarian	
		starving person	
snail	slimy mollusc	**gardener**	
		French chef	
		pesticide company	
plane	type of aircraft	**airline executive**	
		yourself	
		trainee pilot	
rock music	loud, modern form of music	**teenager**	
		elderly person	
		classical musician	
fire	active principle in combustion	**person indoors** (on a cold night)	
		farmer (during bushfire season)	
		boy scout	

Word	Denotation	People	Connotation
gun	fire-arm	**pacifist** **soldier** **target-shooter**	
camera	photographing apparatus	**professional photographer** **tourist**	

TONE

In speech our tone is indicated by our voice. The changes in pitch level and sound indicate to the hearer whether the speaker is happy, sad, irritated or surprised. In written language we have to rely on our choice of words to indicate to the reader what our feelings and attitudes are.

Identifying Tone

In the box below are a number of words that can be used to describe the tone of a piece of writing. Match the appropriate word from the box with the tone of each of the sentences below.

arrogant	enthusiastic	depressed	intimate	angry
jovial	sarcastic	sincere	formal	threatening

1 Thank you for arranging this testimonial dinner for me. I deeply appreciate your generous comments about my work. During the twenty years that I have been with this company I feel I have gained many valued and trusted friends.

2 He felt black despair gripping his mind, sapping all his energy. His soul seemed drained. There was no hope. No hope at all.

3 This morning when I woke my first thoughts were of you. I pictured you walking, shopping, sight-seeing, riding a train. My heart was warm for you, but I missed you. Somehow I knew the day would be incomplete because you are away — my Sarah is travelling overseas.

4 Of course, you would have handled it better. You never make mistakes. After all, you are a professional, aren't you, and professionals never make mistakes!

5 It is time for you to get off your backside and take some specific action. Unless I hear from you within the next two weeks, and unless we are able to reach some compromise, my next move will be to consult my legal representative.

6 It was a magic time. The weather was perfect and the countryside was a picture. We swam and dived, soaking up every moment of fun that we could. At night we sat around our campfire and just enjoyed the chance to catch up on each other's lives again.

7 Celery raw
Develops the jaw
But celery chewed
Is more quietly chewed
Ogden Nash

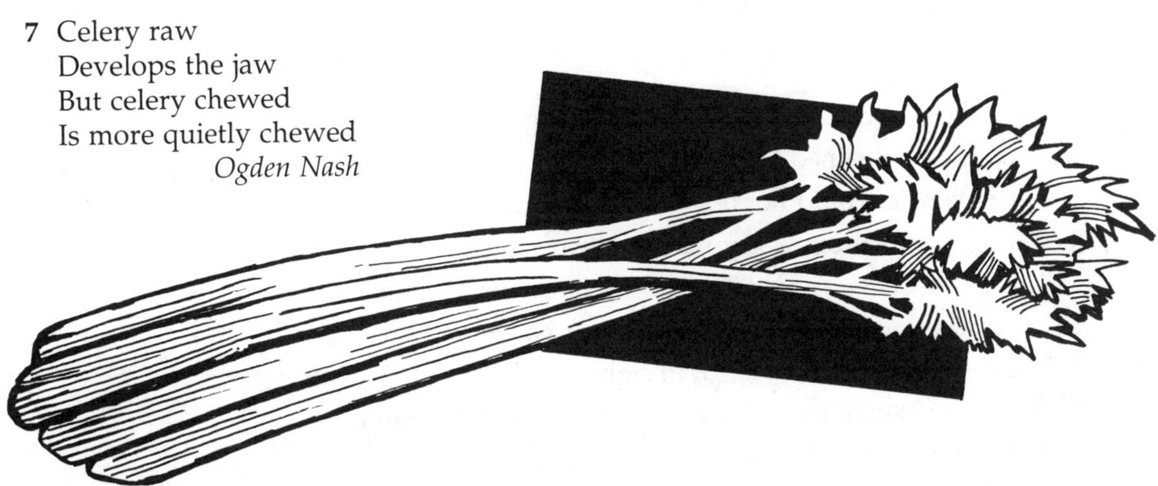

8 It was obvious that I was the best person for the job. Several people tried to advise me but I ignored them. Their ideas seemed so trivial, so boring. Who among them was as experienced or as qualified as I was? No one. Beginners, the lot of them!

9 There has been concern for a period of time in the Strata body about the deterioration of the footway leading from Smith Lane to the Laundromat. It would appear to me that the construction of this lane is appropriate to pedestrian, but not vehicular, use.

10 You have destroyed me! You have played games with my feelings and used my devotion to you! On no account are you to make any further attempt to contact me! Our friendship is over.

GETTING IT RIGHT

DOUBLE NEGATIVES

From time to time speakers or writers fall into the error of using a double negative in their communication. For example:

- I didn't tell them nothing.

Correct usage only requires a single negative. For example:

- I didn't tell them anything.

Avoiding Double Negatives

Each of the following sentences can be completed by using one of the boxed words. Use each word only once and make sure that you avoid any double negatives.

nothing	anything	nowhere	anywhere	anyone
any	nobody	no one	never	no

1 They didn't see .... signs of danger.
2 .... remained for us to eat.
3 The stolen car could not be found ....
4 .... warning was given about the storm.
5 There was .... willing to volunteer for the job.
6 We .... received an explanation for his actions.
7 The pet dog was .... in sight.
8 The car salesman never said .... about the fault.
9 They could not find .... to play goalie.
10 .... believed the man after he was shown to have lied.

DRAMA

It took author Brian Clark six years to find a theatre company courageous enough to stage his play *Whose Life Is It Anyway?*, but since that time it has been successfully performed in London and on Broadway, as well as in Australia, Japan and most of the capital cities of Europe. This dramatic extract builds on the natural tension and conflict of the courtroom. In this scene, the court case is being conducted in the hospital where Ken Harrison, the patient, is on a life-support system. It raises the difficult ethical issue of whether people should have the right to terminate their own life and, if so, under what circumstances.

Whose Life Is It Anyway?

CHARACTERS

Mr Justice Millhouse, the judge
Andrew Eden, the hospital's barrister
Dr Michael Emerson, consultant physician
Ken Harrison, the patient
Peter Kershaw, Ken's barrister
Sister Anderson, ward sister
Dr Barr, consultant psychiatrist

Dr Emerson I swear the evidence that I give shall be the truth, the whole truth and nothing but the truth.

Judge Stand over there please.

(The Judge nods to Mr Eden.)

Eden You are Dr Michael Emerson?

Dr Emerson I am.

Eden And what is your position here?

Dr Emerson I am a consultant physician and in charge of the intensive care unit.

Eden Dr Emerson, would you please give a brief account of your treatment of this patient.

Dr Emerson (*referring to notes*) Mr Harrison was admitted here on the afternoon of October 9th, as an emergency following a road accident. He was suffering from a fractured left tibia and right tibia and fibia, a fractured pelvis, four fractured ribs, one of which had punctured the lung, and a dislocated fourth vertebra, which had ruptured the spinal cord. He was extensively bruised and had minor lacerations. He was deeply unconscious and remained so for thirty hours. As a result of treatment all the broken bones and ruptured tissue have healed with the exception of a severed spinal cord and this, together with a mental trauma, is now all that remains of the initial injury.

Eden Precisely, Doctor. Let us deal with those last two points. The spinal cord. Will there be any further improvement in that?

Dr Emerson In the present state of medical knowledge, I would think not.

Eden And the mental trauma you spoke of?

Dr Emerson It's impossible to injure the body to the extent that Mr Harrison did and not affect the mind. It is common in these cases that depression and the tendency to make wrong decisions goes on for months, even years.

Eden And in your view Mr Harrison is suffering from such a depression?

Dr Emerson Yes.

Eden Thank you, Doctor.

Judge Mr Kershaw?

Kershaw Doctor. Is there any objective way you could demonstrate this trauma? Are there, for example, the results of any tests, or any measurements you can take to show it to us?

Dr Emerson No.

Kershaw Then how do you distinguish between a medical syndrome and a sane, even justified, depression?

Dr Emerson By using my thirty years' experience as a physician, dealing with both types.

Kershaw No more questions, my Lord.

Judge Mr Eden, do you wish to re-examine?

Eden No, my Lord.

Judge Thank you, Doctor. Would you ask Dr Barr if he would step in please?

(Dr Emerson goes out.)

Dr Emerson It's you now, Barr.

(Sister brings Dr Barr into Ken's room.)

Sister Dr Barr.
Judge Dr Barr, will you take the oath please.

(He does so.)

Mr Kershaw.
Kershaw You are Dr Richard Barr?
Dr Barr I am.
Kershaw And what position do you hold?
Dr Barr I am a consultant psychiatrist at Norwood Park Hospital.
Kershaw That is primarily a mental hospital is it not?
Dr Barr It is.
Kershaw Then you must see a large number of patients suffering from depressive illness.
Dr Barr I do, yes.
Kershaw You have examined Mr Harrison?
Dr Barr I have, yes.
Kershaw Would you say that he was suffering from such an illness?
Dr Barr No, I would not.
Kershaw Are you quite sure, Doctor?
Dr Barr Yes, I am.
Kershaw The court has heard evidence that Mr Harrison is depressed. Would you dispute that?
Dr Barr No, but depression is not necessarily an illness. I would say that Mr Harrison's depression is reactive rather than endogenous. That is to say, he is reacting in a perfectly rational way to a very bad situation.
Kershaw Thank you, Dr Barr.
Judge Mr Eden?
Eden Dr Barr. Are there any objective results that you could produce to prove Mr Harrison is capable?
Dr Barr There are clinical symptoms of endogenous depression, of course, disturbed sleep patterns, loss of appetite, lassitude, but, even if they were present, they would be masked by the physical condition.
Eden So how can you be sure this is in fact just a reactive depression?
Dr Barr Just by experience, that's all, and by discovering when I talk to him that he has a remarkably incisive mind and is perfectly capable of understanding his position and of deciding what to do about it.

Eden One last thing, Doctor; do you think Mr Harrison has made the right decision?
Kershaw (*quickly*) Is that really relevant, my Lord? After all . . .
Judge Not really . . .
Dr Barr I should like to answer it though.
Judge Very well.
Dr Barr No, I thought he made the wrong decision. (*to Ken*) Sorry.
Eden No more questions, my Lord.
Judge Do you wish to re-examine, Mr Kershaw?
Kershaw No thank you, my Lord.
Judge That will be all, Dr Barr.

(*Dr Barr goes out. The Judge stands.*)

Judge Do you feel like answering some questions?
Ken Of course.
Judge Thank you.
Ken You are too kind.
Judge Not at all.
Ken I mean it. I'd prefer it if you were a hanging judge.
Judge There aren't any any more.
Ken Society is now much more sensitive and humane?
Judge You could put it that way.
Ken I'll settle for that.
Judge I would like you to take the oath. Dr Scott, his right hand please.

(*Ken takes the oath.*)

The consultant physician here has given evidence that you are not capable of making a rational decision.
Ken He's wrong.
Judge When then do you think he came to that opinion?
Ken He's a good doctor and won't let a patient die if he can help it.
Judge He found that you were suffering from acute depression.
Ken Is that surprising? I am almost totally paralysed. I'd be insane if I weren't depressed.
Judge But there is a difference between being unhappy and being depressed in the medical sense.
Ken I would have thought that my psychiatrist answered that point.
Judge But, surely, wishing to die must be strong evidence that the depression has moved beyond a mere unhappiness into a medical realm?
Ken I don't wish to die.
Judge Then what is this case all about?
Ken Nor do I wish to live at any price. Of course I want to live but as far as I am concerned, I'm dead already. I merely require the doctors to recognise the fact. I cannot accept this condition constitutes life in any real sense at all.

from *Whose Life Is It Anyway?* by Brian Clark

Questions

1 Do you think the play's title is a good choice? Why?

2 Why does Eden begin by establishing who Dr Emerson is?

3 Why is Eden intent on establishing that Ken Harrison has experienced mental trauma?

4 Why are Dr Barr's credentials seemingly more impressive that Dr Emerson's?

5 Dr Barr distinguishes between 'reactive' and 'endogenous' depression. How is reactive depression defined?

6 Why do you think the judge begins his examination of the patient by asking 'Do you feel like answering some questions?'

7 How does the patient, who is on total life-support, appear to handle this interview?

8 What point is the patient trying to make in his final speech?

9 Most good drama requires some conflict. Where does the conflict lie in this extract?

10 What effect does the hospital setting for this courtroom scene have on the action?

11 What do we learn about the character of Ken Harrison from this scene?

12 What are some of the dramatic techniques used by the playwright to maximise the impact of this scene?

Ethical Issues — Class Discussion

Ethical dilemmas such as this one arise when two moral principles come into conflict. In this case the principle of autonomy, or the right of a person to make his or her own decisions, conflicts with the hospital's requirement to do good by saving life. These two principles cannot both be met in the same decision, and the dilemma lies in deciding which principle has greater weight in this case. Decisions such as these are never easy.

Hold class discussions on one or more of the following topics. In each case try to identify the principles that are in conflict.

1 A cancer patient who has to have continuous painful treatment to prolong her life requests that the treatment be discontinued. Would it make a difference to your decision if the person is 18 years old or 70? How important is the person's mental state? Why is it important?

2 A school friend tells you that he and some others are planning a major robbery. What is the ethical dilemma involved here? What action should you take?

3 The parents of a young child who is very sick have been told that he requires a blood transfusion to preserve his life. Because of religious convictions, they are unwilling to give permission. Should their decision be over-ruled by a judge?

3

PREJUDICE

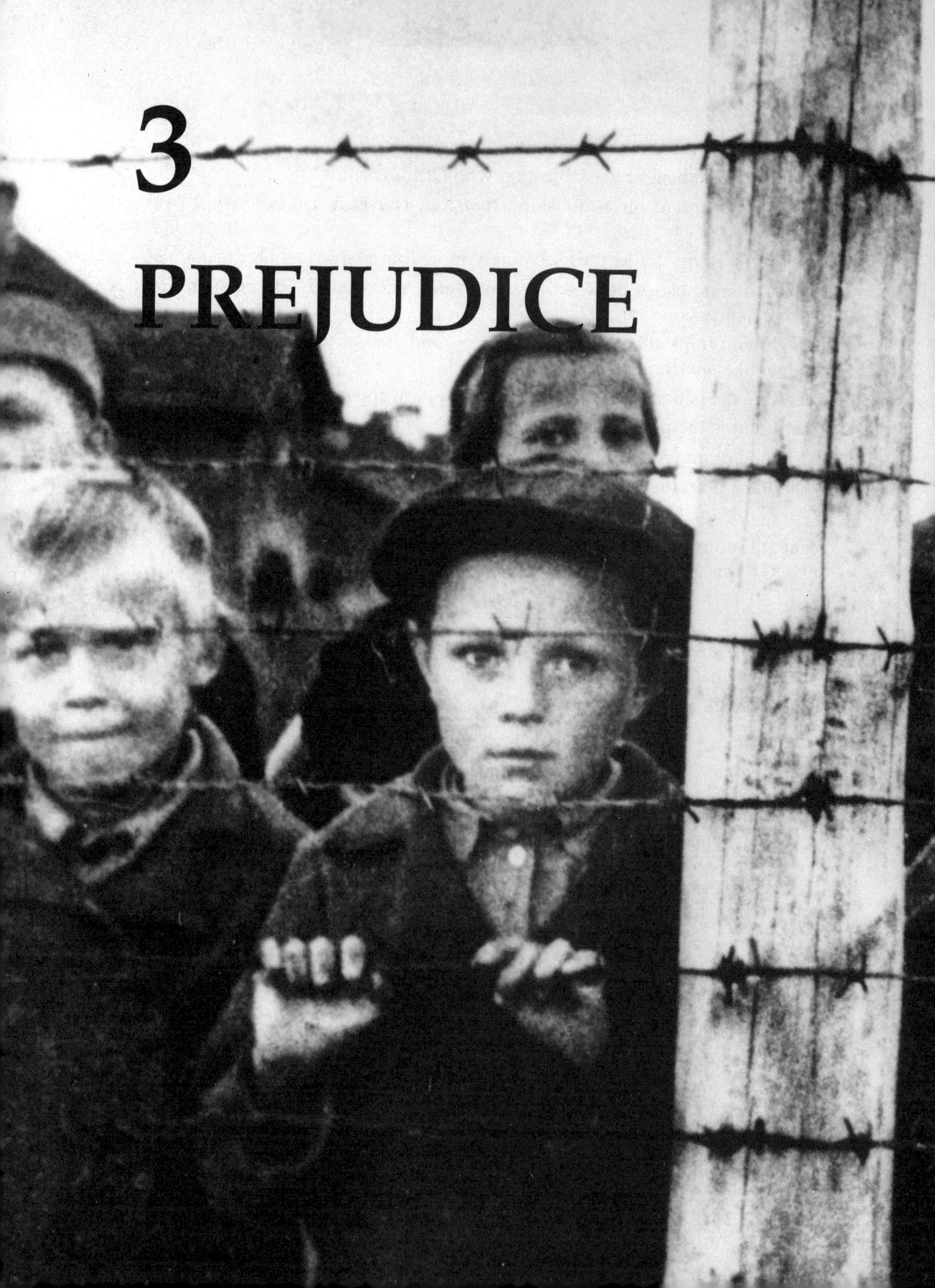

NOVELS

In the Swimming Pool

This incident at a swimming pool in Nazi Germany shows how Friedrich, a Jewish boy, was considered racially inferior to other Germans.

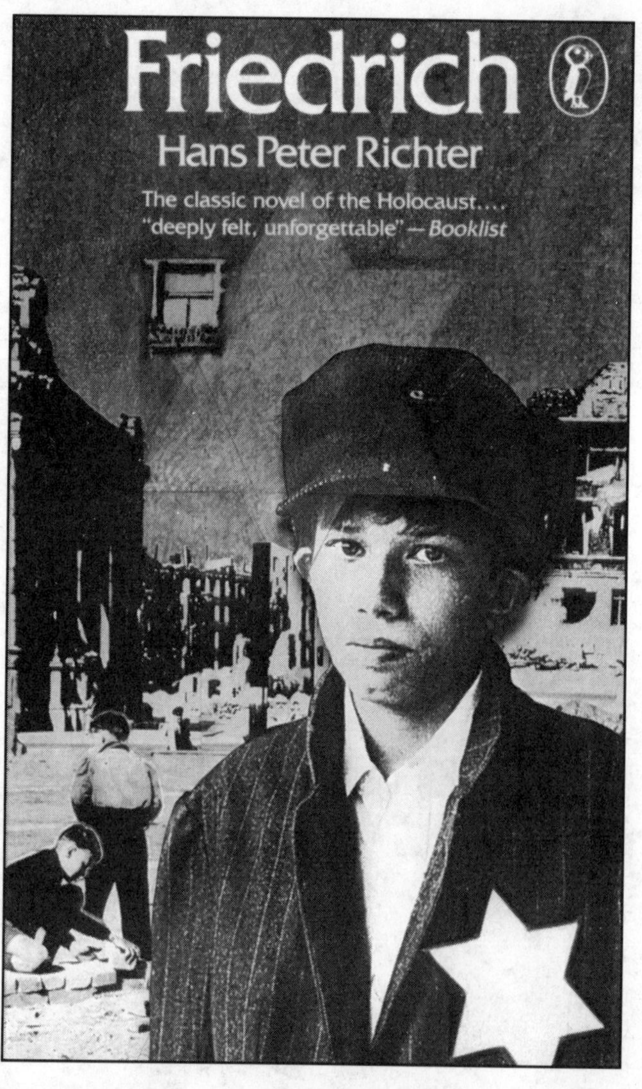

It was hot. No one who didn't have to went outside. Only a few people dragged themselves, sweating, through whatever shade they could find.

We had arranged to meet outside the town where the woods began and then cycle together to the swimming pool.

Mother had loaned me her bicycle. It didn't look beautiful any more, but it still worked very well.

Friedrich arrived on his shining new blue bicycle. Not only was the bicycle new; he had polished it as well. On the way to the forest pool we sang hiking songs like 'Waldeslust' and Friedrich let go of his handlebars. His bicycle swung from one side of the road to the other.

Suddenly a man approached on a silvery bicycle that gleamed in the sun. Even Friedrich's bike couldn't compare with that.

Despite the heat the other cyclist seemed to be in a great hurry. He rang his bell when he was still far away because Friedrich was still swinging back and forth across the road.

Friedrich gripped his handlebars but otherwise paid no attention to the man. He forced him to brake hard.

Which the stranger did, swearing loudly.

Only at the last possible moment did Friedrich clear the way. The cyclist rode on, pedalling furiously. Friedrich whistled after him through his fingers. Far from turning around, the stranger only pushed harder on the pedals and sped down the path.

A quarter of an hour later we reached the forest swimming pool. We chained our bikes to a tree. After getting undressed, we handed in our things and received tags with numbers in exchange. Friedrich tied his to his ankle and jumped into the water. He could swim much better than I, and he was an excellent diver.

I showered first. Then I carefully went down the stairs into the cold water and swam after Friedrich.

Until late afternoon we played in the water and let ourselves be broiled by the sun. When I finally looked at the big clock over the entrance, we had already stayed past our time. We were going to collect our clothes when Friedrich couldn't find his tag.

He ran back and dived to the bottom of the pool, but he didn't find the tag. Shrugging his shoulders, he joined the line of other boys waiting to get their things. They were slow at the checkout counter. The attendant was very busy.

I was ahead of Friedrich and received my hanger first. I changed quickly. When I came out of the locker room, Friedrich was still standing in line. I wrung out my bathing trunks and wrapped them in my towel.

Finally the attendant turned to Friedrich. He scolded him when he heard what had happened. But then he let Friedrich come to the

other side of the counter. Shivering with cold and accompanied by the sullen attendant, Friedrich searched for his things.

The attendant was about to let him wait until after he had tended to the waiting boys when Friedrich shouted: 'There they are!' The attendant took down the hanger he pointed to and carried it to the counter. There he hung it from a hook. 'What's your name?' he asked.

'Friedrich Schneider.'

'Where's your ID?'

'In the right back trouser pocket. The button's loose.'

The attendant looked for the pocket, unbuttoned it, and pulled out the case with the identification card. Then he took out the card and looked at it.

Friedrich still stood before the counter, his teeth chattering. He looked at the ground and seemed embarrassed.

All of a sudden the attendant whistled loudly through his teeth.

From the other side came the female attendant.

'Just take a look at this!' the attendant said. 'You won't get to see many more of them.' Everyone could hear his explanation: 'This is one of the Jewish identification cards. The scoundrel lied to me. He claims his name's Friedrich Schneider — it's Friedrich *Israel* Schneider, that's what it is — a Jew that's what he is! A Jew in our swimming pool!' He looked disgusted.

All those still waiting for their clothes stared at Friedrich.

As if he could no longer bear to touch it, the attendant threw Friedrich's identification card and its case across the counter. 'Think of it! Jewish things among the clothes of respectable human beings!' he screamed, flinging the coat hanger holding Friedrich's clothes on the ground so they scattered in all directions.

While Friedrich collected his things, the attendant announced. 'Now I'll have to wash my hands before I can go on with my work. Ugh!' He walked away from the counter, kicking one of Friedrich's shoes into a blocked-up foot bath.

He returned before Friedrich found all his things.

'It's your affair where you get dressed,' he snarled at him. 'You won't get into our changing rooms.'

Helpless and still damp, Friedrich clutched his clothes. He searched for a place where he could dry himself and get dressed. There was no protected corner, and he hastily rubbed himself with his towel and pulled his trousers on over the wet bathing trunks. Water dripping from his trouser legs, he left the swimming pool.

The attendant was still screaming, but we could no longer understand what he was saying.

I had already unlocked our bikes.

Friedrich fastened his things on the luggage carrier. He didn't dare look into my eyes. Quietly he said, 'I'll dress properly in the woods.'

Then we heard an uproar behind us. 'This is where it was!' said a big boy. 'I'm quite sure this is where I locked it. I've searched everywhere, but it's gone. It was all silver; I'd just polished it, too.'

A lot of curious boys quickly collected. They gave advice: 'Follow the trail!' 'Inform the police!'

Friedrich pricked up his ears. He left his bicycle and walked to the circle that had formed around the boy whose bike had been stolen. 'You there,' Friedrich said to him, 'I know who stole your bike. I saw the man who did it; I can describe him in detail.'

Everyone looked at Friedrich. A lane formed between him and the owner of the silver bike.

The boy stepped closer to Friedrich. 'Say,' he asked, 'aren't you the Jew from the pool a while back?' Friedrich blushed, lowered his eyes to the ground. 'You don't think the police would believe you, do you?'

from *Friedrich* by Hans Peter Richter

Reading for Meaning

1 'It was hot.' How does the author convince us of this?
2 Why had the boys arranged to meet outside the town?
3 What did the boys do as they cycled to the forest pool?
4 Why did the stranger on the silvery bicycle ring his bell when he was still far away?
5 Why did the stranger swear loudly at Friedrich?
6 'Friedrich whistled after him through his fingers.' How did the stranger react to this?
7 What words of praise does Friedrich's friend have for him?
8 Why did Friedrich run back and dive to the bottom of the pool?
9 'Friedrich searched for his things.' How was he suffering as he did so?
10 What feeling did Friedrich seem to have as he stood at the counter?
11 Why did the attendant suddenly whistle through his teeth?
12 According to the attendant, what was strange about Friedrich's ID card?
13 What feeling did the attendant show when he found out that Friedrich was a Jew?
14 What did the attendant scream out as he flung Friedrich's clothes on the ground?
15 What did the attendant claim he would have to do before he could get on with his work?
16 What final punishment did the attendant reserve for the Jewish boy?
17 Why do you think Friedrich didn't dare look into his friend's eyes?
18 'Then we heard an uproar behind us.' What caused the uproar?
19 How does the ending of the passage show us how helpless a Jew in Nazi Germany must have felt?
20 From Friedrich's experience, what do you learn of the way prejudice works?

Library Research

Look through books on the era of Nazi power in Germany to find other personal experiences of prejudice. Select the experience that makes the deepest impression on you and share it with your class.

The Lynch Mob

In a small town in the deep south of the United States, Atticus Finch, a lawyer, guards a negro who is in jail after being falsely accused of rape. In this extract, an angry lynch mob gathers outside the jail. The scene is witnessed by Atticus's children, Scout and her brother Jem, and their friend Dill. Scout tells how they soon became involved with the mob.

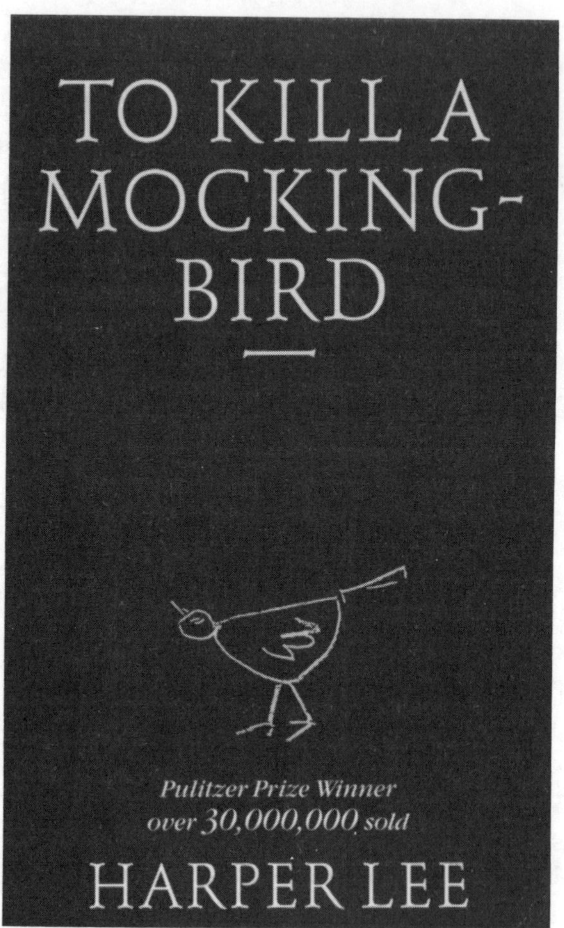

As we walked up the sidewalk, we saw a solitary light burning in the distance. 'That's funny,' said Jem, 'jail doesn't have an outside light.'

'Looks like it's over the door,' said Dill.

A long extension cord ran between the bars of a second-floor window and down the side of the building. In the light from its bare bulb, Atticus was sitting propped against the front door. He was sitting in one of his office chairs, and he was reading, oblivious of the nightbugs dancing over his head.

I made to run, but Jem caught me. 'Don't go to him,' he said, 'he might not like it. He's all right, let's go home. I just wanted to see where he was.'

We were taking a short cut across the square when four dusty cars came in from the Meridian highway, moving slowly in a line. They went around the square, passed the bank building, and stopped in front of the jail.

Nobody got out. We saw Atticus look up from his newspaper. He closed it, folded it deliberately, dropped it in his lap, and pushed his hat to the back of his head. He seemed to be expecting them.

'Come on,' whispered Jem. We streaked across the square, across the street, until we were in the shelter of the Jitney Jungle door. Jem peeked up the sidewalk. 'We can get closer,' he said. We ran to Tyndal's Hardware door — near enough, at the same time discreet.

In ones and twos, men got out of the cars. Shadows became substance as light revealed solid shapes moving towards the jail door. Atticus remained where he was. The men hid him from view.

'He in there, Mr Finch?' a man said.

'He is,' we heard Atticus answer, 'and he's asleep. Don't wake him up.'

.In obedience to my father, there followed what I later realised was a sickeningly comic aspect of an unfunny situation: the men talked in near-whispers.

'You know what we want,' another man said. 'Get aside from the door, Mr Finch.'

'You can turn around and go home again, Walter,' Atticus said pleasantly. 'Heck Tate's around somewhere.'

'The hell he is,' said another man. 'Heck's bunch's so deep in the woods they won't get out till mornin'.'

'Indeed? Why so?'

'Called 'em off on a snipe hunt,' was the succinct answer. 'Didn't you think a'that, Mr Finch?'

'Thought about it, but didn't believe it. Well then,' my father's voice was still the same, 'that changes things, doesn't it?'

'It do,' another deep voice said. Its owner was a shadow.

'Do you really think so?'

This was the second time I heard Atticus ask that question in two days, and it meant somebody's man would get jumped. This was too good to miss. I broke away from Jem and ran as fast as I could to Atticus.

Jem shrieked and tried to catch me, but I had a lead on him and Dill. I pushed my way through dark smelly bodies and burst into the circle of light.

'H-ey, Atticus?'

I thought he would have a fine surprise, but his face killed my joy. A flash of plain fear was going out of his eyes, but returned when Dill and Jem wrigggled into the light.

There was a smell of stale whisky and pigpen about, and when I glanced around I discovered that these men were strangers. They were not the people I saw last night. Hot embarrassment shot through me: I had leaped

triumphantly into a ring of people I had never seen before.

Atticus got up from his chair, but he was moving slowly, like an old man. He put the newspaper down very carefully, adjusting its creases with lingering fingers. They were trembling a little.

'Go home, Jem,' he said. 'Take Scout and Dill home.'

We were accustomed to prompt, if not always cheerful acquiescence to Atticus's instructions, but from the way he stood Jem was not thinking of budging.

'Go home, I said.'

Jem shook his head. As Atticus's fists went to his hips, so did Jem's, and as they faced each other I could see little resemblance between them: Jem's soft brown hair and eyes, his oval face and snug-fitting ears were our mother's, contrasting oddly with Atticus's greying black hair and square-cut features, but they were somehow alike. Mutual defiance made them alike.

'Son, I said go home.'

Jem shook his head.

'I'll send him home,' a burly man said, and grabbed Jem roughly by the collar. He yanked Jem nearly off his feet.

'Don't you touch him!' I kicked the man swiftly. Barefooted, I was surprised to see him fall back in real pain. I intended to kick his shin, but aimed too high.

'That'll do, Scout.' Atticus put his hand on my shoulder. 'Don't kick folks. No —' he said, as I was pleading justification.

'Ain't nobody gonna do Jem that way,' I said.

'All right, Mr Finch, get 'em outa here,' someone growled. 'You got fifteen seconds to get 'em outa here.'

A still from the 1962 film of *To Kill a Mockingbird* which starred Gregory Peck as Atticus

In the midst of this strange assembly, Atticus stood trying to make Jem mind him. 'I ain't going,' was his steady answer to Atticus's threats, requests, and finally, 'Please Jem, take them home.'

I was getting a bit tired of that, but felt Jem had his own reasons for doing as he did, in view of his prospects once Atticus did get him home. I looked around the crowd. It was a summer's night, but the men were dressed, most of them, in overalls and denim shirts buttoned up to the collars. I thought they must be cold-natured, as their sleeves were unrolled and buttoned at the cuffs. Some wore hats pulled firmly down over their ears. They were sullen-looking, sleepy-eyed men who seemed unused to late hours. I sought once more for a familiar face, and at the centre of the semi-circle I found one.

'Hey, Mr Cunningham.'

The man did not hear me, it seemed.

'Hey, Mr Cunningham. How's your entailment gettin' along?'

Mr Walter Cunningham's legal affairs were well known to me; Atticus had once described them at length. The big man blinked and hooked his thumbs in his overall straps. He seemed uncomfortable; he cleared his throat and looked away. My friendly overture had fallen flat.

Mr Cunningham wore no hat, and the top half of his forehead was white in contrast to his sun-scorched face, which led me to believe that he wore one most days. He shifted his feet, clad in heavy work shoes.

'Don't you remember me, Mr Cunningham? I'm Jean Louise Finch. You brought us some hickory nuts one time, remember?' I began to sense the futility one feels when unacknowledged by a chance acquaintance.

'I go to school with Walter,' I began again. 'He's your boy, ain't he? Ain't he, sir?'

Mr Cunningham was moved to a faint nod. He did know me, after all.

'He's in my grade,' I said, 'and he does right well. He's a good boy,' I added, 'a real nice boy. We brought him home for dinner one time. Maybe he told you about me, I beat him up one time but he was real nice about it. Tell him hey for me, won't you?'

Atticus had said it was the polite thing to talk to people about what they were interested in, not about what you were interested in. Mr Cunningham displayed no interest in his son, so I tackled his entailment once more in a last-ditch effort to make him feel at home.

'Entailments are bad,' I was advising him, when I slowly awoke to the fact that I was addressing the entire aggregation. The men were all looking at me, some had their mouths half-open. Atticus had stopped poking at Jem: they were standing together beside Dill. Their attention amounted to fascination. Atticus's mouth, even, was half-open, an attitude he had once described as uncouth. Our eyes met and he shut it.

'Well, Atticus, I was just sayin' to Mr Cunningham that entailments are bad an' all that, but you said not to worry, it takes a long time sometimes . . . that you all'd ride it out together . . .' I was slowly drying up, wondering what idiocy I had committed. Entailments seemed all right enough for living-room talk.

I began to feel sweat gathering at the edges of my hair; I could stand anything but a bunch of people looking at me. They were quite still.

'What's the matter?' I asked.

Atticus said nothing. I looked around and up at Mr Cunningham, whose face was equally impassive. Then he did a peculiar thing. He squatted down and took me by both shoulders.

'I'll tell him you said hey, little lady,' he said.

Then he straightened up and waved a big paw. 'Let's clear out,' he called. 'Let's get going, boys.'

As they had come, in ones and twos the men shuffled back to their ramshackle cars. Doors slammed, engines coughed, and they were gone.

I turned to Atticus, but Atticus had gone to the jail and was leaning against it with his face to the wall. I went to him and pulled his sleeve. 'Can we go home now?' He nodded, produced his handkerchief, gave his face a going-over and blew his nose violently.

'Mr Finch?'

A soft husky voice came from the darkness above: 'They gone?'

Atticus stepped back and looked up. 'They've gone,' he said. 'Get some sleep, Tom. They won't bother you any more.'

From a different direction, another voice cut crisply through the night: 'You're damn tootin' they won't. Had you covered all the time, Atticus.'

Mr Underwood and a double-barrelled shotgun were leaning out his window above the *Maycomb Tribune* office.

It was long past my bedtime and I was growing quite tired; it seemed that Atticus and Mr Underwood would talk for the rest of the night, Mr Underwood out of the window and Atticus up at him. Finally Atticus returned, switched off the light above the jail door, and picked up his chair.

'Can I carry it for you, Mr Finch?' asked Dill. He had not said a word the whole time.

'Why, thank you, son.'

Walking towards the office, Dill and I fell into step behind Atticus and Jem. Dill was encumbered by the chair, and his pace was slower. Atticus and Jem were well ahead of us, and I assumed that Atticus was giving him hell for not going home, but I was wrong. As they passed under a street light, Atticus reached out and massaged Jem's hair, his one gesture of affection.

from *To Kill a Mockingbird* by Harper Lee

Reading for Meaning

1 What was 'funny' about the solitary light burning over the jail door?

2 What did the children see as they were taking a short cut across the square?

3 'He seemed to be expecting them.' What movements did Atticus make when the cars stopped in front of the jail?

4 As the men got out of their cars, what did the light reveal?

5 How did 'a sickeningly comic aspect of an unfunny situation' occur outside the jail?

6 Why do you think a 'flash of plain fear' returned to Atticus's eyes 'when Dill and Jem wriggled into the light'?

7 What smell was about the crowd of men in front of the jail?

8 What signs of fear did Atticus show as he rose from his chair?

9 As Jem and Atticus faced each other, how did they contrast with each other? What made them look alike?

10 How did Scout react when the burly man grabbed Jem and yanked him 'nearly off his feet'?

11 What did Scout find at the centre of the semi-circle of men?

12 How did Mr Cunningham react to Scout's questioning?

13 How did Scout establish a personal relationship with Mr Cunningham?

14 What made Scout aware of the fact that she had captured the crowd's attention?

15 What physical sensation did Scout experience when she realised all the people were looking at her?

16 What peculiar thing did Mr Cunningham do?
17 How did Atticus show his relief at the men's departure?
18 What gesture of affection did Atticus make to Jem as they walked away?
19 What does this passage reveal about the character of Atticus?
20 What does this scene show us about the character of Jem?
21 Scout is telling the story. What are the advantages of having Scout as the narrator?
22 What lesson about prejudice can this passage teach us?

Beaten Up by a Gang

Mike, a city teenager, is recovering in hospital after getting beaten up in an alley. He tells his friend Bryon about the unexpected way he was trapped and nearly killed.

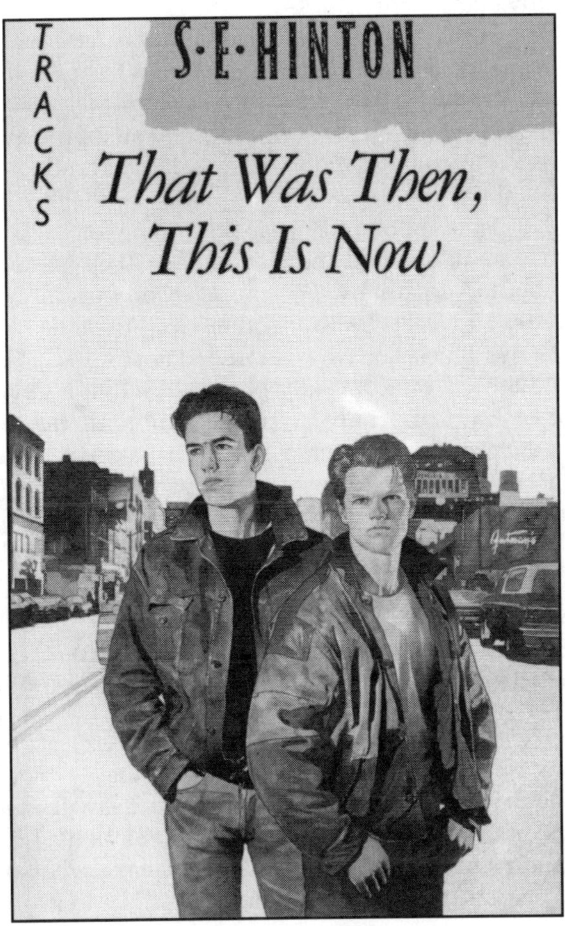

'Well,' Mike began, 'I always had this soft spot for chicks. I was always making like Sir Galahad, opening doors for them and complimenting even the homely ones, and I beat out a lot of guys better looking than me and they never could figure out why. But it wasn't just a line with me. I guess I'm a sucker — I've been taken a few times, like "loaning" money to chicks who came on with a sob story — but I'll always believe the best about a girl until I'm proved wrong, which is my own hang-up.

That explains the way I acted that night the gang and me was hanging around the drugstore and this black chick came in to buy some cigarettes. Me, I just see a nice-looking chick with really beautiful eyes, all black and inky-soft. I guess I'm a little funny that way, because Negroes just don't get me all upset. I mean, I can see a black guy and a white chick together, and it sure don't bother me, while most white guys can't stand to see that. Like the gang — the minute she walks in, they get all tensed up because black anyone, chick or otherwise, just don't happen to come around much where I live. I guess she worked downtown and got off late and just stopped in on her way to the bus stop. I think she told me that later. I don't remember too good now.

'So she gets her cigarettes and starts for the door, when a couple of guys block her way. Now the gang I hang out with is a pretty good bunch of guys — a lot of heart and only a couple of wise apples in the group — but see, nothin' much had been happenin' and they were bored so they start picking on the chick, calling her Black Beauty and some other choice things. They were really getting rude, and I was feeling sorry for the girl. She kept her eyes down and just said, "Let me by, please," real soft-like. The guys started pushing her around, not enough to hurt her but enough to scare her plenty. She just gripped her purse with both hands and tensed all over like she was trying to keep from running, which was pretty smart. Running is just an invitation to be chased, and if she got caught it wouldn't be in a lighted drugstore. The old guy who runs the drugstore

had disappeared. He was scared silly of the gang. I don't know why. We never done anything to him.

'When one of the guys grabbed hold of her and really got crude, I got fed up. I went over and said, "Let her go," like I meant it. They all looked at me for a while, like they were trying to make up their minds whether or not to jump me. We don't usually go around beating each other up, but it has happened. They finally decided not to. My big brother, he's got a pretty big rep as a tough guy in our neighbourhood. He's in jail now, that's why he don't come to see me. It was his rep and not mine that stopped them, because I ain't never been known as a tough guy.

'So they turned her loose and went back to reading comics, and I followed the girl outside. She was looking up and down the street kind of desperate-like, and I knew she'd missed her bus. I said, "Hey, uh, girl, if you've missed your bus I can give you a ride home."

'She just kept her eyes down. Finally she said something — but, brother, I'm not going to repeat it. I saw then and there she thought I had evil intentions. I don't blame her. Hell, if I'd had to take what she just did, I'd be sore and suspicious too.

I said, "Look, I don't want a pick-up or anything . . ." She gave me a funny look so I added quick, "Not that you're not real cute or anything — I mean, you'll have to stay here another hour to catch the next bus and I'll be leaving and I don't know what those other guys might do."

'She saw the logic in that, because it was getting dark. Not too many cops come around that area; it's kind of a deserted street. You know how cops are; there's a million over on the Ribbon, making sure the nice kids don't kill each other or run each other down, while we can cut each other's throats and they don't give a damn.

'Finally she said she'd let me drive her home. I had my old Ford parked in the drugstore parking lot. It was really my brother's car but he said I could drive it any time he got busted, which is often. He's a pretty good guy, but if you've got a rep for fighting, somebody's always trying to take you on. The last time that happened, my brother busted a bottle over the guy's head and got charged with assault with a dangerous weapon. He never used weapons before, but he had finally got fed up with the whole routine. It wasn't his first offence, so they sat on him kind of hard.

'Anyway, we get into my Ford, and I can see the poor kid is still scared — she sits hugging the door on her side like she's going to jump out any second. I got a couple of good looks at her; she was real slender, looked like she'd sort of sway in the wind, and her hair was down to her shoulders and it must have been straightened. She had on a yellow dress and yellow shoes and she had her straw purse sitting on her lap. She held on to it with one hand and the door handle with the other. She really was cute.

'I started talking to her about just everything. Would her old lady chew her out because she was late? My old lady did. Man, they never liked anything you did, did they? But still, sometimes you couldn't get along without them. Did she go to school? I did but, boy, it was really a hell of a place to spend all day. I wanted to drop out but the old lady said she'd kill me if I did.

'I kept talking because that's what I do with animals when they're hurt and scared, and pretty soon they get over being scared. I've got a hang-up with animals, too.

'I could tell she was beginning to calm down a little, at least she let go of the door handle. I even got her to smile once. I forget what I'd been saying. And then I said, "I'm sorry about what happened to you back there," and suddenly she started to cry.

'Man, that got me so shook. Nothing gets me shook like chicks crying.' Mike stopped here, and I gave him another drag on my cigarette.

'That's funny,' I said. ' Chicks crying bore me. Go on, Mike, finish your story.'

'Well, I didn't know what to say to her. I finally said, "Hey, don't cry," which never does any good. She kept on sobbing and now and then I'd catch a word or two. I got the idea that she was fed up with getting walked all over by white people. I could see that. I get fed up with getting walked over by the fuzz, teachers, my old man, and the upper-class kids at school. So I could see that. Bryon, do you know that my old man keeps my mother from coming to see me? Said I was a dumb kid for ever gettin' into this hospital. So anyway, this chick, she tells

me about her problems, and she uses some pretty bad language but nothing I ain't heard before from white chicks. I finally pulled the car over to the curb and reached into my pocket. She sat up straight and got all uptight.

'"What we stoppin' for?" she says, and I said, "I thought I had a handkerchief, but I guess I don't." I pulled back out on the street. She looked at me for a minute — I kept staring straight ahead but I could tell she was watching me — and she said, "Thank you."

'I drove her home. She lived way out on the north side where most of the blacks live; you know where. It is a pretty lousy neighbourhood, about as bad as mine. As I pulled up in front of her house, I could see a bunch of kids hanging around on her porch and in her yard.

'"Well, here you are," I said, a little nervous. For somebody who'd been practising in her mind how to get the door open, she was pretty slow about getting out. That's how it seemed to me, anyway. I think she was tired out from crying so much.

'Then there was all these black kids around my car. Some big guy opened the girl's door and pulled her out and said, "What's the matter, Connie? What happened?" You could tell she'd been crying.

'Then they opened my door and dragged me out. It seemed like there was a hundred black faces staring at me. I guess it was really just about a dozen, but it seemed like a hundred. I just stood there, backed up against the car. Talk about scared — man, was I scared. To top it off, the chick had started crying again so she couldn't talk.'

Mike paused here for a minute. He was staring off in the distance, and when he started talking again, it was slowly, like he was living the whole thing over again.

'The big guy came around to my side of the car. "You hurt her, white boy?"

'"No," I said, and it didn't sound very loud so I cleared my throat and said, "No, I didn't," so loud that it sounded like I was shouting. It was real quiet; you could hear somebody's TV from down the street and a dog barking a block away and Connie's soft sobbing. I could even hear my heart pounding in my ears. Then the big guy said, really quiet-like, "What if we don't believe you?" And I got so scared I was about to cry and said, "Ask her, huh, just ask her!" The guy called across the car, "Connie, what you want me to do with this white cat?"

'And real soft — her voice was so soft, just like her eyes — she said, "Kill the white bastard."

'And sure enough, they almost did.'

from *That Was Then, This Is Now* by S. E. Hinton

Reading for Meaning

1. What does Mike mean when he says 'I was always making like Sir Galahad'?
2. Why did Mike think of himself as 'a sucker'?
3. What hang-up did Mike have?
4. 'I mean, I can see a black guy and a white chick together, and it sure don't bother me.' What does this reveal about Mike's character?
5. Why did the gang get 'all tensed up' when the black girl walked into the drugstore?
6. How did Mike's attitude towards the girl differ from that of the gang?
7. When did Mike begin to feel sorry for the black girl?
8. What stopped the gang from beating up Mike when he protected the black girl?
9. Why did the girl accept Mike's offer of a ride home?
10. What did Mike notice about the girl's appearance as she sat next to him in his Ford?
11. Why did Mike start 'talking to her about just everything'?
12. What idea did Mike get about the reason for the girl's sobbing and feeling fed up?
13. What kind of neighbourhood did the girl live in?
14. 'Talk about scared — man, was I scared.' What was Mike so scared about?
15. After Mike shouted 'No, I didn't', what sounds was he aware of as he waited for the gang's reaction?
16. 'Connie, what you want me to do with this white cat?' What does Connie's reply to this question reveal about her character?
17. What did you learn about Mike's character from this passage?
18. What important ideas about racial prejudice are revealed to us in this passage?

POETRY

POEMS ABOUT PREJUDICE

The Child

I saw him standing on the corner,
A small boy watching the traffic.
But to others he was no ordinary boy,
For his incomplete brain
Punctured his simple exterior.
He was totally happy in his world,
Gazing,
Unaware of cruel eyes
And the mocking voices of other boys
On the opposite kerb.
He ignored them completely,
And the mocking grew more intense.
Suddenly he turned his gaze from the road,
And smiled simply at the onlookers,
Who turned away ashamed.

Valerie Church

Questions

1 What scene is the poet describing at the beginning of the poem?
2 'But to others he was no ordinary boy'. In what ways is the boy 'not ordinary'?
3 What are the boy's feelings as he is standing on the corner?
4 'Unaware of cruel eyes'. Why do you think the boys are being 'cruel'?
5 'And the mocking grew more intense'. How does the boy make the onlookers ashamed?
6 What are your feelings to the boy who 'was no ordinary boy'?

7 What are your feelings towards the boys on the opposite kerb?
8 Why do you think the poet has written this poem?
9 What kind of prejudice has the poet revealed?
10 Do you think this is a good poem? Why or why not?

The Black Drunkard

It only hurts when I'm sober
(my flagon is mostly full)
And I bury my head
In the sweet clean grass
Beside the rivers cool.
I muster all my dignity
To walk, if walk I can
To the pub on the corner of High and Main
To fill up me flagon again.

It's a high, hard road when I sober up
I'm a bull with an outraged pain
I fill me flagon as quick as I can
To cover me eyes again.
It only hurts when I'm sober
That sneer of contempt in the eyes
Of whites in the street as I pass them
Their hypocrisy and their lies
They claim that this land is 'God's country'
If so, then it's 'vacant', 'to let'.
He ain't lived here for two hundred years
Ever since the whites came, I bet!
Their preacher stands down on the corner
He's shouting 'Repent and be saved!'
He turns his head in disgust when
I grin, disbelievin' and wave
It takes more than merely repentin'
To stop our kids starvin' today
To stop them being hung up and crippled
Because of the whites and their way.
It takes more than just bible bashin'
To save all the souls that you hurt
With your greed and your cant
And your land thievin' slant
And those kids that you've stamped into dirt.

It only hurts when I'm sober
The haggard face of my gin
My kids with their bellies all swollen
Trachomaed, legs spindly, starved thin
An' our 'house' a tin shack by the river
No sewerage, no wages, no work
'Cept pickin' peas or red cherries
Where white bosses pay less on wage lurks.

It only hurts when I'm sober
The fact: you've no honour as men.

I blind out that pain through my flagon
I'll try not to get sober again.

Kevin Gilbert

Questions

1 The Aboriginal poet, Kevin Gilbert, adopts the persona of a drunkard to reveal the problems faced by Aborigines in a white society. What words of the drunkard indicate that he spends most of his time drinking?

2 How does the drunkard feel when he becomes sober?

3 What is the attitude of the whites to the drunkard?

4 What is the drunkard suggesting when he says that God 'ain't lived here for two hundred years/Ever since the whites came'?

5 What difficulties do the Aboriginal kids experience living in a white society?

6 'With your greed and your cant/And your land thievin' slant'. What criticism of white society is the poet making here?

7 What is the drunkard's home like?

8 What difficulties does the drunkard have earning a living?

9 Why do you think the drunkard says at the end of the poem 'I'll try not to get sober again'?

10 What examples of racial prejudice can you find in the poem?

11 What are your feelings towards the black drunkard?

12 What is the poet's message in this poem?

13 What steps do you think could be taken to improve the conditions of the Aboriginal people?

14 Do you think this poem could have been written from true life experience? Why?

Ballad of the Landlord

Landlord, landlord,
My roof has sprung a leak
Don't you 'member I told you about it
Way last week?

Landlord, landlord,
These steps is broken down.
When you come up yourself
It's a wonder you don't fall down.

Ten Bucks you say I owe you?
Ten Bucks you say is due?
Well, that's Ten Bucks more'n I'll pay you
Till you fix this house up new.

What? You gonna get eviction orders?
You gonna cut off my heat?
You gonna take my furniture and
Throw it in the street?

Um-huh! You talking high and mighty.
Talk on — till you get through.
You ain't gonna be able to say a word
If I land my fist on you.

Police! Police!
Come and get this man!
He's trying to ruin the government
And overturn the land!

Copper's whistle!
Patrol bell!
Arrest.

Precinct Station.
Iron cell.
Headlines in press:

MAN THREATENS LANDLORD

TENANT HELD NO BAIL

JUDGE GIVES NEGRO 90 DAYS IN COUNTY JAIL

Langston Hughes

Questions

1. What problems does the tenant have with the house he is renting?
2. Why does the tenant refuse to pay the 'Ten Bucks' rent that he owes?
3. Why does the tenant threaten to hit the landlord?
4. How does the landlord deal with the tenant's suggestion of violence?
5. 'Iron cell'. What do these words suggest about the tenant's time in gaol?
6. After reading this poem, what are your feelings about the law?
7. What are your feelings towards the landlord?
8. Do you feel sorry for the tenant? Why?
9. What is the poet's purpose in this poem?
10. Why do you think the poet has recorded the actual words of the newspaper headlines?

Incident

Once riding in old Baltimore
   Heart-filled, head-filled with glee,
I saw a Baltimorean
   Keep looking straight at me.

Now I was eight and very small,
   And he was no whit bigger,
And so I smiled, but he poked out
   His tongue, and called me 'Nigger'.

I saw the whole of Baltimore
   From May until December;
Of all the things that happened there
   That's all that I remember.

Countee Cullen

Refugee

They put a dead dog on my doorstep, with a note.
Illiterate obscenities. Is it
For this I came here in a leaky boat . . .
To be the target of this racist wit?
Our ship of fools! My wife and daughter died
Before they even reached the promised land.
Oh yes, I made it. But I'm dead inside.
I used to teach, back home, but now I stand,
A mindless zombie, on a factory floor.
I should be grateful for the work, they say.
I am. But was I wrong to hope for more?
I can't go back. Yet how am I to stay?
All day I hear the voices, full of hate.
They call me 'slope'. Why won't they call me 'mate'?

Jane Belfield

Questions

1 What horrifying situation confronts the refugee at the beginning of the poem?
2 How does the refugee react to it? What are your feelings about it?
3 By what means did the refugee manage to reach his new country?
4 What suffering has he endured on the way?
5 'I'm dead inside'. What reasons does the refugee have for saying this?
6 What contrast is there between the work now done by the refugee and the work he used to do in his previous land?
7 'Yet how am I to stay?' Why is it difficult for the refugee to remain in his new homeland?
8 What stark contrast is there in the words 'mate' and 'slope'?
9 What emotions does the refugee reveal in this poem?
10 What examples of racial prejudice can you find in the poem?
11 Do you feel sorry for the refugee? Why or why not?
12 Why do you think the poet has written this poem?

Fourteen Men

Fourteen men,
And each hung down,
Straight as a log
From his toes to his crown.

Fourteen men
Chinamen they were,
Hanging on the trees
By their pigtailed hair.

Honest poor men,
But the diggers said, Nay!
So they strung them all up,
On a fine summer's day.

There they were hanging
As we came by,
Grown-ups on the front seat,
On the back seat I.

That was Lambing Flat.
And still I can see
The straight up and down
Of each on his tree.

Mary Gilmore

Questions

1 The incident referred to in the poem was the outcome of an attack by white gold diggers on the Chinese miners at Lambing Flat in 1861. What horrifying picture does the poet present you with in the first verse?

2 What are your feelings towards the white diggers?

3 According to the poet, what kind of men were the Chinese miners?

4 What evidence in the poem can you find to show that the incident has made a lasting impression on the poet?

5 How does the poet make this story seem true to life?

6 Why do you think the poet has written this poem?

7 Do you think the title 'Fourteen Men' is a good one? Why? What title would you have given the poem?

8 What does this poem show you about racial prejudice?

In Australian history the black tracker was an Aboriginal person whose eyesight was so keen and whose bushcraft was so skilled that he could follow even the slightest signs and pick up the track of an animal or a lost human being.

Black trackers were with Eyre, an explorer of the central and western parts of the continent, and with Burke and Wills, the doomed explorers who found a way from the south to the north of Australia.

The Black Tracker

He served mankind for many a year
Before the jeep or the wireless.
He walked, he loped, no thought of fear,
Keen-eyed, lithe and tireless.

He led Eyre to the western plains;
He went with Burke and Wills;
He put Nemarluk* back in chains;
He found the lost in the hills.

He found hair and spittle dry:
He found the child with relief.
He heard a mother's joyful cry
Or a mother's wail of grief.

He found the lost one crawling south,
Miles away from the track.
He siphoned water, mouth to mouth,
And carried him on his back.

He heard the white man call him names,
His own race scoffing, jeering.
'A black man playing white man games,'
They laughed and pointed, sneering.

No monument of stone for him
In your park or civilised garden.
His deeds unsung, fast growing dim —
It's time you begged his pardon.

Jack Davis

* Nemarluk — Aboriginal murderer of the early nineties, captured after a long search by Bul-Bul, who is recognised as the greatest of Australia's black trackers.

Questions

1 What has replaced the black tracker?
2 'He walked, he loped'. How is 'loping' different to 'walking'?
3 How does the poet prove to us that the black tracker used to be an important member of any team going out into the bush?
4 What tiny signs of life could lead the black tracker to a lost child?
5 What words in the poem show that the child was sometimes found too late?
6 How did the black tracker save 'the lost one' who was miles away from the track?
7 What example of racial prejudice can you find in the poem?
8 Why did his own race jeer and scoff at him?
9 What achievements of the black tracker do you admire most?
10 Why do you think the poet Jack Davis wrote this poem?

WRITING

PLANNING AND WRITING A TALK

1 What is the purpose of your talk?

Careful preparation is the key to the success of any talk. Although your talk can be about nearly any subject, it is useful to decide and write down the purpose of your talk. For example, you may have decided to give a talk on bushwalking. Is the purpose of your talk to give information? Is its purpose to entertain? Do you want to convince your audience of the pleasures of bushwalking? Obviously you may feel that your talk should be informative, entertaining *and* convincing. However, try to clarify its most important purpose.

2 Consider your audience

You must next consider the group you are going to speak to, with the aim of immediately gaining their attention and keeping it. Is your audience a specialist group, say, members of a bushwalking club? Is it mostly male, mostly female or mixed? What is its average age? The examples you give, the stories and jokes you tell must be tailored to suit the make-up of your audience. Your audience will respond favourably if you have considered them properly.

"I will now explain the progressive methods by which your children are taught – so keep quiet, sit up straight and don't fidget."

The length of time you have to speak is important. If you intend to speak for a long time you may need slides, a tape, a video or interesting objects to demonstrate (such as a rucksack or hiking boots). This will help to keep your audience interested.

Finally, the place where you are going to give your talk is important. You must make sure your voice will carry to every corner of a big hall. Speaking to a small group in a cosy room is often much less of a strain on the speaker.

3 Make sure your talk has a beginning, a middle and an end
Write out your talk first. Then you can clearly structure it to make sure it has a definite beginning, a middle and an end. Here are some beginnings to consider. Note that each one is interesting and likely to hold an audience's attention.

A talk on cars
Fellow car owners. I'd like to begin my talk by telling you what my mechanic said to me the other day when I put my car in for its annual service. 'Mister,' he said, patting my car on its hood with one hand, 'if I was you I'd keep the oil and change the car.' After that I became an expert on car care . . .

A talk on paragliding
Ladies and gentlemen, the first time I went paragliding I landed in someone's backyard pool. It caused a commotion, especially since the pool was full of people enjoying themselves till I arrived. Since then I've worked hard to understand the sport and . . .

A talk on exercise
Boys and girls, let me tell how jogging once saved my life . . .

A talk on giving a talk
Students and staff. Thank you for inviting me. You know, the human brain is a wonderful organ because it never stops thinking from the time of your birth until the moment you stand up to give a talk. I hope . . .

A TALK ON THE GREAT OUTDOORS

Now let's look at a talk by Fred Dagg, a character created by comedian John Clarke. As you read you will notice that the talk is informal and that its purpose is to entertain rather than to inform or convince. Since it was a radio talk, its audience was mixed and perhaps full of people who remembered unpleasant experiences in the bush that were caused by lack of expertise. The questions that follow the talk will help you to understand how the speaker achieved his purpose.

In the Bush

Gidday. I'd like to have a look at one of the great outdoor activities, and I'm referring here of course to the age-old business of tramping, or hiking, or bushwalking, or bush sitting down and resting, depending on how you feel about it.

The first thing to do is avail yourself of a certain amount of equipment, a pair of good sturdy boots, so that you can wear holes in your pair of good sturdy socks and get a comprehensive range of good sturdy blisters on your pseudopodia. You'll need a pack of some sort so that you can carry essential supplies into the unknown, and drink them when your interest in endemic dicotyledons is flagging.

The main thing to remember before embarking on one of these little adventures, is that you'll get lost, and when you get lost there are several cardinal rules to bear in mind or you'll remain lost more or less interminably.

The first rule to take account of once you've achieved lostness is not to panic. You should ignore this rule. There's nothing wrong with a good panic, in fact it's a cleansing experience and if you can't go through a bit of good blind hysterical panic out in the sticks, where can you go? There are killjoys about though and you can't be too careful. Of course, if you don't panic, don't panic about it, you'll probably panic later.

There's probably someone in your party who knows how to use his watch as a compass, and which berries are edible and how to light a fire with two pieces of dehydrated pizza. This person is called a natural leader and should be tied to a tree and ignored. The best thing to do is wait until night falls and then simply navigate your way home using the stars.

This is a fairly simple business and you don't have to know where the Panhandle is relative to due west. All you do is pick out some celestial landmark. Venus is a good one, and try to remember where it is relative to where you live. Then of course all you've got to do is keep walking until it's in that position and you'll be home.

You might be a street or two out, but the blisters on your feet will have raised you to a height of about thirty feet above the houses and you should be able to make out the roof of your own residence and make your way towards it in your own time.

from *Daggshead Revisited* by John Clarke

Questions

1 How does the opening of the talk reveal that it is to be informal?

2 What makes the first paragraph interesting and likely to keep an audience interested enough to listen to the rest of the talk?

3 What humorous twist does Fred Dagg give to the consideration of footwear?

4 What is important about the pack you carry?

5 Why is it important to panic?

6 What should you do if you don't panic?

7 '... how to light a fire with two pieces of dehydrated pizza'. What bushcraft skill is this expression mocking?

8 What should happen to any natural leader that appears?

9 How does Fred Dagg poke fun at the skill of navigation?
10 How is exaggeration used to bring the talk to a satisfying ending?
11 Did you like this talk? Why or why not?
12 What is the purpose of the talk? Does it achieve its purpose?

SPEECH WRITING

A speech is a special and very formal kind of talk given on ceremonial occasions such as weddings, welcomes and public openings. Men and women, such as politicians, who are expected to give frequent speeches often employ skilled speech writers. Speeches are often read to an audience as the words and phrases in a speech often need to be communicated accurately.

Here is one of the most famous speeches ever written and spoken. It is a wartime speech of Winston Churchill, and its purpose was to rally the British nation to face the threat of an invasion from the German army. As you read this stirring speech note how its formality reflects the gravity of the situation. At the same time, a powerful appeal is made to the patriotic emotions of the British people. What effect do you think was intended by the repetition of 'we shall fight'?

Winston Churchill's Speech

I have, myself, full confidence that if all do their duty, if nothing is neglected, and if the best arrangements are made, as they are being made, we shall prove ourselves once again able to defend our island home, to ride out the storm of war, and to outlive the menace of tyranny, if necessary for years, if necessary alone. At any rate, that is what we are going to try to do. That is the resolve of His Majesty's Government — every man of them. That is the will of Parliament and the nation. The British Empire and the French Republic, linked together in their cause and in their need, will defend to the death their native soil, aiding each other like good comrades to the utmost of their strength. Even though large tracts of Europe and many old and famous States have fallen or may fall into the grip of the Gestapo and all the odious apparatus of Nazi rule, we shall not flag or fail. We shall go on to the end, we shall fight in France, we shall fight on the seas and oceans, we shall fight with growing confidence and growing strength in the air, we shall defend our island, whatever the cost may be, we shall fight on the beaches, we shall fight on the landing grounds, we shall fight in the fields and in the streets, we shall fight in the hills; we shall never surrender, and even if, which I do not for a moment believe, this island or a large part of it were subjugated and starving, then our Empire beyond the seas, armed and guarded by the British Fleet, would carry on the struggle, until, in God's good time, the new world, with all its power and might, steps forth to the rescue and liberation of the old.

The House of Commons, June 4, 1940

YOUR TURN TO WRITE

Imagine you are one of the following people and prepare the kind of talk or speech that could be given.

- a sales person promoting a new product
- a school principal at an assembly
- a guest at a wedding
- a coach to a team
- a national parks ranger to tourists
- a police officer to a school group
- a politician to a crowd
- a TV personality talking about his or her experiences
- an astronaut describing a journey to outer space and back
- a general to his soldiers

LANGUAGE

PROPAGANDA

Propaganda is a way of using language to change viewpoints and alter behaviour. The word 'propagate' means to spread or increase. From this word comes the much more sinister word 'propaganda', meaning a spread of ideas and beliefs across society with the purpose of promoting a particular viewpoint ahead of all others. Propaganda is also usually associated with a highly organised assault on all the senses through posters, broadcasts, repetitive slogans etc. Fortunately, there is usually propaganda for and against any belief system. However, in wartime, or under a dictatorship, propaganda is likely to become the sole means of spreading a system of beliefs aimed at altering the behaviour of people so that they conform with the ideals that rule the state.

Propaganda manipulates emotions such as love, hate, fear, anger, vengeance and guilt to convey its basic messages. The final appeal of propaganda is to emotions rather than to reason or common sense.

Awesome displays of power, trumpet fanfares, speeches and flags are often used to promote a god-like image of a leader. Here is an eyewitness description of the arrival of Hitler at a Nazi rally during the Second World War. Notice that many of the words the writer uses in the description are concerned with emotions.

HITLER'S ARRIVAL

In the 'Lowenbrau' I heard him speak for the first time . . . [I had never met] so hot a breath of hypnotic mass excitement. It was not only the special tension of these weeks, of this day. 'Their own battle songs, their flags, their own symbols, their own salute'. For hours, endless booming military music; for hours, short speeches by subordinate leaders. When was he coming? Nobody can describe the fever that spread in this atmosphere. Suddenly there was a movement at the back entrance. Words of command. The speaker on the platform stopped in mid-sentence. Everybody jumped up, saluting. And right through the shouting crowds and streaming flags the one they were waiting for came with his followers, walking quickly to the platform, high right arm raised stiffly. He passed by me quite close and I saw his thin, pale features contorted as if by inward rage, cold flames darting from his protruding eyes, which seemed to be searching out enemies to be conquered. Did the crowd give him this mysterious power? Did it come from him to them?

by Professor K.A. von Muller, who was present at a Nazi rally in 1923

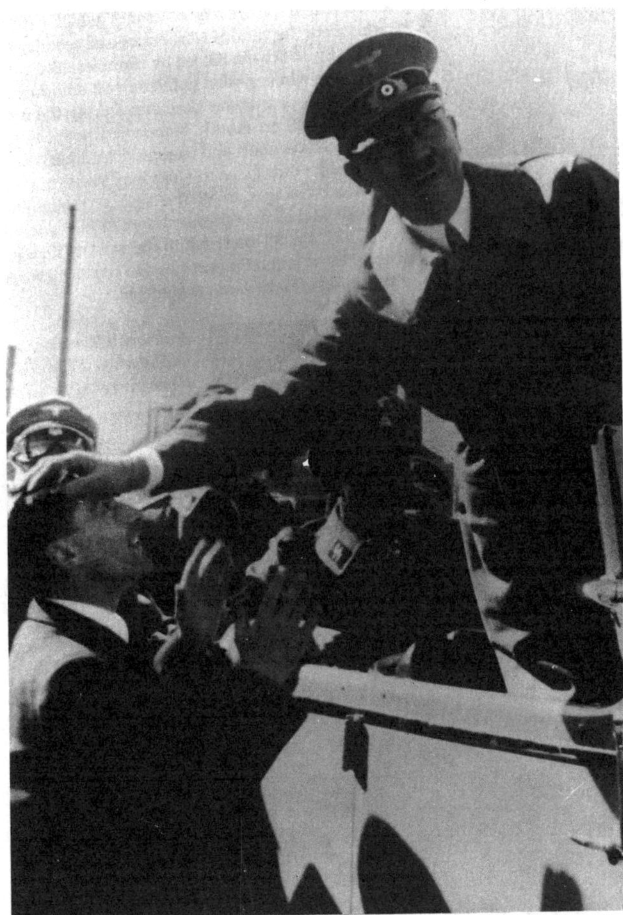

The Führer receiving the adulation of an admirer in 1938

Questions

1 '. . . so hot a breath of hypnotic mass excitement.' What do these words reveal about the crowd?

2 What four typical features of the propaganda-inspired rally were present?

3 What was the question that everyone was asking?

4 How did the speaker on the platform react to the leader's arrival?

5 What did everybody do?

6 What gesture did Hitler make as he walked to the platform?

7 '. . . I saw his thin, pale features . . .' What emotion did the writer believe was contorting Hitler's face?

8 What did the writer think of Hitler's eyes?

9 What was the mystery that surrounded Hitler's presence?

10 How is the power of propaganda revealed in this extract?

PROPAGANDA IN ACTION

Propaganda achieved its most infamous triumph in Nazi Germany. The Nazis used propaganda to spread a belief of the superiority of the German people. All other peoples, in particular the Jews, were considered inferior and so could be legitimately conquered and enslaved in the interests of German aggrandisement. Patriotism became a religion in the Nazi state and German youth became the target of powerful propaganda. In this quotation, taken from a speech by Hitler, German youth is idealised. Notice how they are favourably compared to familiar objects. Why is this quotation a piece of propaganda?

HITLER'S VIEW OF GERMAN YOUTH

What we look for from our German youth is different from what people wanted in the past. In our eyes the German youth of the future must be slim and slender, swift as the greyhound, tough as leather, and hard as Krupp steel.

Adolf Hitler in a speech, December 1938

A poster can be a very powerful and effective propaganda tool. Study the poster opposite and then answer these questions.

Questions

1 How do the German boys in the poster resemble Hitler's ideal German youth?

2 The German words at the top of the poster, 'Hinaus mit allen Storenfrieden!' have been translated into English as 'Out with all Troublemakers!' What do these words show about Nazi Germany's attitude to its opponents?

3 Who do you think are the little people fleeing near the feet of the Hitler youth? What impression of them is the artist trying to create?

4 Why do you think the two youths are depicted as giants?

5 How is the Nazi state symbolised?

6 The words at the bottom of the poster translate into English as 'Unity of Youth in the Hitler Youth!' Why could these words be likely to appeal to young Germans?

7 What comments would you make about the drummer in the poster?

8 Why is this poster a piece of clever propaganda?

A HITLER YOUTH PROPAGANDA POSTER

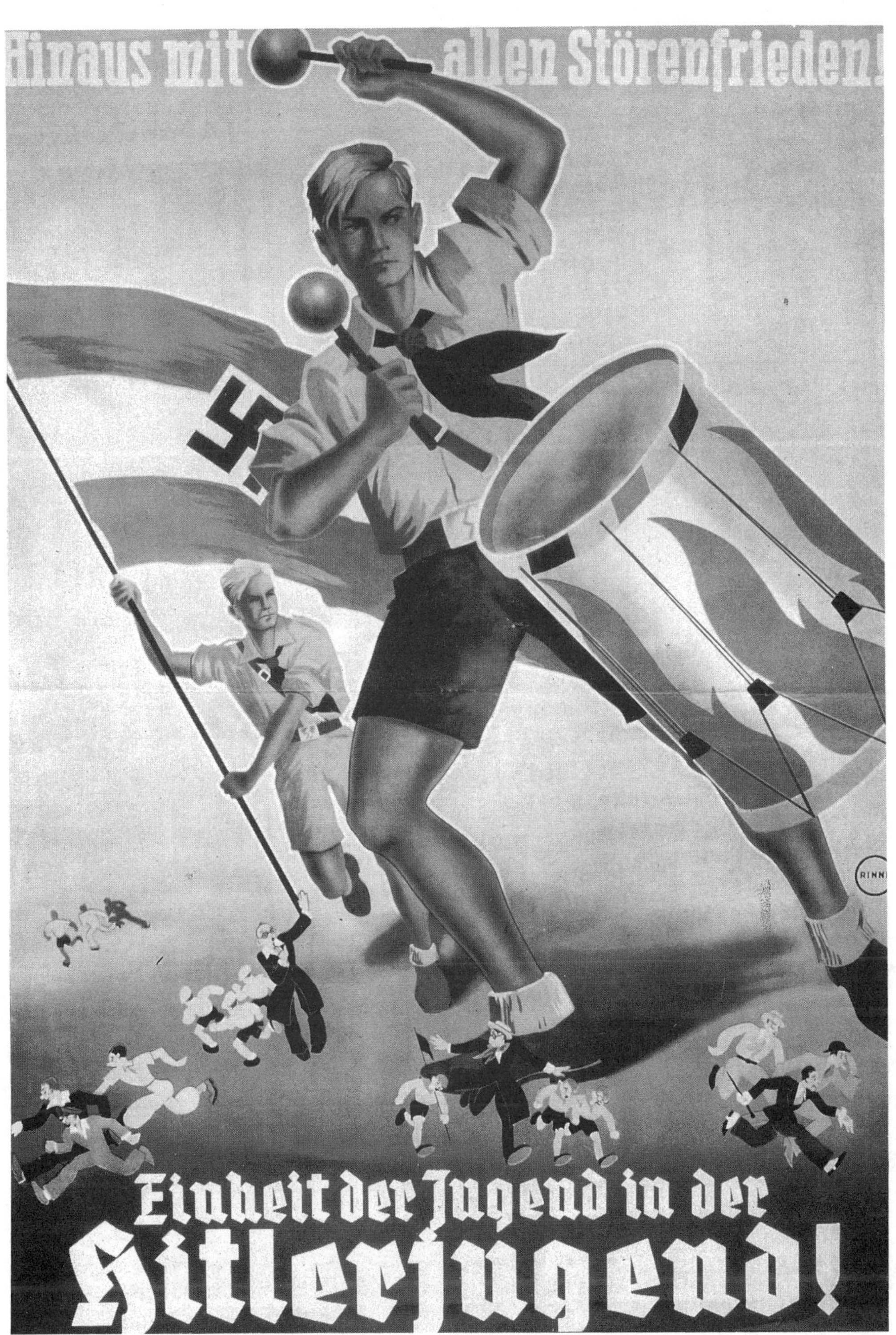

A BRITISH PROPAGANDA POSTER FROM THE FIRST WORLD WAR

Questions

The poster opposite features Lord Kitchener who was the British secretary of war during the First World War.

1 Why do you think Lord Kitchener's finger is pointing directly at the reader?
2 Why do you think Lord Kitchener is in uniform?
3 Why is the word 'YOU' emphasised?
4 Why do you think the words 'God Save The King' have been included?
5 Why do you think this propaganda poster achieved a successful increase in recruitment levels for the army?

Library Research

Collect other examples of the language and art of the propagandist. Select those you consider would have been most effective in their intention and present each of these with your analysis in a short illustrated talk to your class.

GETTING IT RIGHT

CONFUSING WORD PAIRS

Past/passed
Past means 'gone by in time' when it is an adjective or descriptive word. For example:

- In the past month there have been fewer accidents.

Passed is a verb or action word and means 'went by'. For example:

- The bus passed the hotel on its way to the airport.

Accept/except
Accept means 'receive' or 'agree to'. For example:

- I accept the gift on behalf of the school.

Except means 'with the exception of' or 'leaving out'. For example:

- Except for the boy chewing gum, all the class may leave the room.

Lose/loose
Lose means 'to part with by accident or carelessness and be unable to find'. For example:

- You will lose your watch if the strap breaks.

Loose means 'slack, not tight'. For example:

- That knot is too loose and must be tightened.

Choosing the Correct Word

Complete each of the following sentences by selecting the correct word from the pair in the brackets.

1 For the .... three summers the weather has been hot. (past/passed)
2 Several police officers .... the boys as they sat in the park. (passed/past)
3 The .... year has been full of surprises. (passed/past)
4 All the youths .... my friend were allowed to leave the dressing shed. (accept/except)
5 The prison officers .... the court's ruling. (except/accept)
6 The attendant found all the boy's possessions .... his ID card. (except/accept)
7 Try not to .... your money on your way home. (lose/loose)
8 The mechanic found that a .... battery connection caused the car's starting problems. (lose/loose)
9 The dentist found one .... tooth which he had to extract. (loose/lose)
10 You will .... marks if you make spelling mistakes. (lose/loose)

DRAMA

Gregory's Girl

by Bill Forsyth

CHARACTERS

Boy 1 **Boy 2** **Boy 3** **Boy 4** **Boy 5** **Boy 6**	boys trying out for the school football team
Phil	the football coach
Dorothy	the only girl trying out for the team
Andy **Gregory** **Charlie**	keen spectators

Setting: A football field with a football goal

THE FOOTBALL TRIAL

Six boys appear. They are the aspiring strikers. They are keen but lack style. They are not natural footballers.

Boy 1 Give us the ball will you.
Boy 2 These bloody boots are too small.
Boy 3 I must be mad.
Boy 1 I said give us the ball.
Boy 3 Why do I want to play for the worst team in the history of schoolboy football?
Boy 2 I think I've tied them up too tight.
Boy 1 For Godsake give us a touch.
Boy 4 (*He has the ball*) This ball's too heavy.

(Phil comes up to the group. He has a clipboard and a stop watch. He is disappointed at the turn-out.)

Phil Where's the rest then?
Boys Rest, sir?
Phil Is this all there is?
Boy 5 There's rehearsal for the play, sir.
Phil Play rehearsal! Good God, no wonder the school's a sporting disaster. No priorities.
Boy 2 Sir, could I go and change . . .
Phil Right. Let's get going. You all know what I'm looking for . . . a goal scorer . . . and that means two things . . . ball control, shooting accuracy and the ability to *read the game* . . . three things. So this trial will allow me to assess these two . . . three . . . particular aspects of your skills. *(Phil notices one boy's feet.)* What's the idea of sandshoes, boy? No boots?

(The boy shakes his head.)

Boy 6 I'll get some if I get the place.
Phil No, that's a dead loss son . . . there's no point in carrying on . . . go and get changed. We play in real boots in this school, from the word go.

(The boy wanders off to the school building.)

Right. Simple ball control. I want you to trot with the ball at your feet, fifty yards and back . . . two lines . . . go!

The boys do their best. Some disappear off stage. Dorothy walks up to Phil. She is dressed in an immaculate track suit.)

Both sides of the foot! Let me see complete control . . .

(Dorothy approaches the group. Phil presumes that she is on some errand or other and gives her little attention.)

(Shouting to boys off stage) I want it faster now . . . come on . . . What d'you want, lass? Get some pace into it! Anybody can *walk* with a ball . . .

Dorothy *(Waiting patiently)* Sir . . .

Phil What is it, dear?

Dorothy The trial. I'm here for the trial.

Phil This is football here, sweetheart . . . maybe Miss McAlpine is up to something with the hockey team, I don't know, but this here is football . . . boys . . .

Dorothy That's right. Football trials eleven a.m. I saw the notice.

Phil There's been a slight misunderstanding, dear, it was boys I meant . . . for the trials.

Dorothy Didn't say so on the notice . . . just said 'talented players'.

Phil That's a shame you picked it up wrongly . . . but I'm afraid I can't do anything now.

(The boys have given up their dribbling and have gathered round.)

Dorothy You didn't *say* boys only. You're not allowed to anyway. I want a trial.

Phil Not possible, dear . . . not today . . . we don't have a spare ball . . . We can fix something later on though, I'll talk to Miss McAlpine.

(Dorothy deftly flicks up a ball.)

Dorothy Here's one.

Phil *(Tries to ignore her but knows she is still there)* Two basic skills . . . control and . . . the other one. Trotting with the ball again . . . two lines . . . lots of speed . . . On you go.

(Dorothy joins one of the lines. Her ball control is superb. None of the boys can touch her. Gregory, Andy and Charlie are watching from the side.)

Andy He's not going to let her play.

Gregory He's letting her play.

Andy I'm not denying I'd fancy a bit.

Gregory Look at that control.

Andy What about the body contact. It's a physical game.

Gregory Body contact!

Andy He'll not let her play. He can't.

Gregory She can play alright.

Phil Into twos now, out from the goal. I want to see some penetration work and a shot for the goal. One attack and one defend. Let's see who's first in the net . . . go!

(The six hopefuls line themselves up in three pairs. Dorothy is one of the attacking three. She easily escapes from her defender and slams the ball into the net.)

Do it again. Same pairs.

(The same thing happens. Phil gets tougher.)

Three shots each at goal. Now . . . accuracy . . . best of three shots.

(Phil goes into goal. Dorothy has no trouble getting the ball past him, whilst he saves easily the feeble attempts of the boys.)

Dorothy I think I can manage okay from the open angle. Could we try a few tight in? Off the line.
Phil You can't score from there, girl.
Dorothy Not off the line, no, but tighter. I can't find the angle. Look.
Phil *(Walks out of the goal)* Not now! Right, boys, that's it. Just show me some stamina now . . . once round the field and back to the dressing rooms. It's only half a mile and should be tackled as a sprint . . . On your way.

(They go. Dorothy ahead already. Phil walks over to the watching group of boys. He is worried.)

Andy Would you like me to have a go in goal?
Phil No!
Andy She didn't look that tricky from here.
Phil You never did understand angles.
Andy What you reckon Gregory?
Gregory I'd pick her from any angle.
Andy Now you're letting sex cloud your judgement.
Gregory Who me?
Andy She'd never get that close in a real game.
Phil You're right there.
Gregory As close as she liked. *(He is not following the argument.)*
Andy Some of the teams we've had to face. They'd chew her up and spit her out.
Phil It's bottle that counts, these days.
Gregory Bottle?
Andy Gotta have bottle. Like a bloke's got bottle.
Phil Stamina. You can't expect it from a girl. She's got technique, but stamina's a different thing altogether.

(At that moment Dorothy runs in. She is breathing, but not hard. There is no sign of the rest. They will straggle in.)

Gregory God!
Dorothy Well?
Phil I'll let everyone know in the fullness of time . . . I'll pass the word to Miss McAlpine.
Dorothy I was the best. You *know* I was the best!
Phil Okay, dear, you *were* the best. You're good . . . but it's not that simple. It could be out of my hands . . . we'll have to see . . .
Dorothy If I was the best I should be in the team. The notice said so . . .
Phil You might very well get into the team . . . I said we'll see . . . You could get in . . . we'll work it out soon . . .

(Phil moves off for his office. Dorothy follows him.)

Dorothy You've got to put me on the team list . . . I want to sign something. You've got to let me sign something . . .

(The two of them hurry past Gregory and the other two.)

Gregory What a dream . . .

from *Gregory's Girl*, adapted by Andrew Bethell from the novel by Bill Forsyth

Questions

1 As the scene opens on the four grumbling boys, what do we learn about the quality of the team they are thinking of joining?
2 What does Phil think about the school's attitude to sport?
3 What is Phil looking for in a successful footballer?
4 What does Phil claim that school footballers must do 'from the word go'?
5 Why does Phil pay little attention to Dorothy?
6 How does Phil patronise Dorothy?
7 How does Dorothy argue that the trial isn't just for boys?
8 What is Phil's excuse for not giving her a trial?
9 How does Dorothy perform at goal shooting?
10 'It's bottle that counts these days.' What is 'bottle'?
11 Why doesn't Phil expect Dorothy to have it?
12 How does Dorothy prove him wrong?
13 What does Phil agree with Dorothy about?
14 What is Gregory's final comment on Dorothy?
15 What makes Dorothy an interesting character in this scene from *Gregory's Girl*?
16 'All good drama contains conflict.' How is conflict achieved in this play?
17 What does this piece of drama teach us about discrimination?
18 What is this scene's setting?

4

SOCIETY UNDER SIEGE

NOVELS

Boxer

When the animals rebelled and took over Manor Farm, forcing their human owners to leave, everything seemed wonderful. But gradually the pigs took over the leadership and the other animals sometimes seemed no more than slave labour. Boxer, the horse, was one of the most faithful workers. This passage shows how the pigs, led by Comrade Napolean, with Squealer as his 'public relations' representative, use corruption and deceit to protect their leadership privileges.

There lay Boxer, between the shafts of the cart, his neck stretched out, unable even to raise his head. His eyes were glazed, his sides matted with sweat. A thin stream of blood had trickled out of his mouth. Clover dropped to her knees at his side.

'Boxer!' she cried, 'how are you?'

'It is my lung,' said Boxer in a weak voice. 'It does not matter. I think you will be able to finish the windmill without me. There is a pretty good store of stone accumulated. I had only another month to go in any case. To tell you the truth, I had been looking forward to my retirement. And perhaps, as Benjamin is growing old too, they will let him retire at the same time and be a companion to me.'

'We must get help at once,' said Clover. 'Run, somebody, and tell Squealer what has happened.'

All the other animals immediately raced back to the farm-house to give Squealer the news. Only Clover remained, and Benjamin, who lay down at Boxer's side, and, without speaking, kept the flies off him with his long tail. After about a quarter of an hour Squealer appeared, full of sympathy and concern. He said that Comrade Napoleon had learned with the very deepest distress of this misfortune to one of the most loyal workers on the farm, and was already making arrangements to send Boxer to be treated in the hospital at Willingdon. The animals felt a little uneasy at this. Except for Mollie and Snowball, no other animal had ever left the farm, and they did not like to think of their sick comrade in the hands of human beings. However, Squealer easily convinced them that the veterinary surgeon in Willingdon could treat Boxer's case more satisfactorily than could be done on the farm. And about half an hour later, when Boxer had somewhat recovered, he was with difficulty got on to his feet, and managed to limp back to his stall, where Clover and Benjamin had prepared a good bed of straw for him.

For the next two days Boxer remained in his stall. The pigs had sent out a large bottle of pink medicine which they had found in the medicine chest in the bathroom, and Clover administered it to Boxer twice a day after meals. In the evenings she lay in his stall and talked to him, while Benjamin kept the flies off him. Boxer professed not to be sorry for what had happened. If he made a good recovery, he might expect to live another three years, and he looked forward to the peaceful days that he would spend in the corner of the big pasture. It would be the first time that he had had leisure to study and improve his mind. He intended, he said, to devote the rest of his life to learning the remaining twenty-two letters of the alphabet.

However, Benjamin and Clover could only

be with Boxer after working hours, and it was in the middle of the day when the van came to take him away. The animals were all at work weeding turnips under the supervision of a pig, when they were astonished to see Benjamin come galloping from the direction of the farm buildings, braying at the top of his voice. It was the first time that they had ever seen Benjamin excited — indeed, it was the first time that anyone had ever seen him gallop. 'Quick, quick!' he shouted. 'Come at once! They're taking Boxer away!' Without waiting for orders from the pig, the animals broke off work and raced back to the farm buildings. Sure enough, there in the yard was a large closed van, drawn by two horses, with lettering on its side and a sly-looking man in a low-crowned bowler hat sitting on the driver's seat. And Boxer's stall was empty.

The animals crowded round the van. 'Good-bye, Boxer!' they chorused, 'good-bye!'

'Fools! Fools! shouted Benjamin, prancing round them and stamping the earth with his small hoofs. 'Fools! Do you not see what is written on the side of that van?'

That gave the animals pause, and there was a hush. Muriel began to spell out the words. But Benjamin pushed her aside and in the midst of a deadly silence he read:

'"Alfred Simmonds, Horse Slaughterer and Glue Boiler, Willingdon. Dealer in Hides and Bone-Meal. Kennels Supplied." Do you not understand what that means? They are taking Boxer to the knacker's!'

A cry of horror burst from all the animals. At this moment the man on the box whipped up his horses and the van moved out of the yard at a smart trot. All the animals followed, crying out at the tops of their voices. Clover forced her way to the front. The van began to gather speed. Clover tried to stir her stout limbs to a gallop, and achieved a canter. 'Boxer!' she cried. 'Boxer! Boxer! Boxer!' And just at this moment, as though he had heard the uproar outside, Boxer's face, with the white stripe down his nose, appeared at the small window at the back of the van.

'Boxer!' cried Clover in a terrible voice. 'Boxer! Get out! Get out quickly! They are taking you to your death!'

All the animals took up the cry of 'Get out, Boxer, get out!' But the van was already gathering speed and drawing away from them. It was uncertain whether Boxer had understood what Clover had said. But a moment later his face disappeared from the window and there was the sound of a tremendous drumming of hoofs inside the van. He was trying to kick his way out. The time had been when a few kicks from Boxer's hoofs would have smashed the van to matchwood. But alas! his strength had left him; and in a few moments the sound of drumming hoofs grew fainter and died away. In desperation the animals began appealing to the two horses which drew the van to stop. 'Comrades, comrades!' they shouted. 'Don't take your own brother to his death!' But the stupid brutes, too ignorant to realise what was happening, merely set back their ears and quickened their pace. Boxer's face did not reappear at the window. Too late, someone thought of racing ahead and shutting the five-barred gate; but in another moment the van was through it and rapidly disappearing down the road. Boxer was never seen again.

Three days later it was announced that he had died in the hospital at Willingdon, in spite of receiving every attention a horse could have. Squealer came to announce the news to the others. He had, he said, been present during Boxer's last hours.

'It was the most affecting sight I have ever seen!' said Squealer, lifting his trotter and

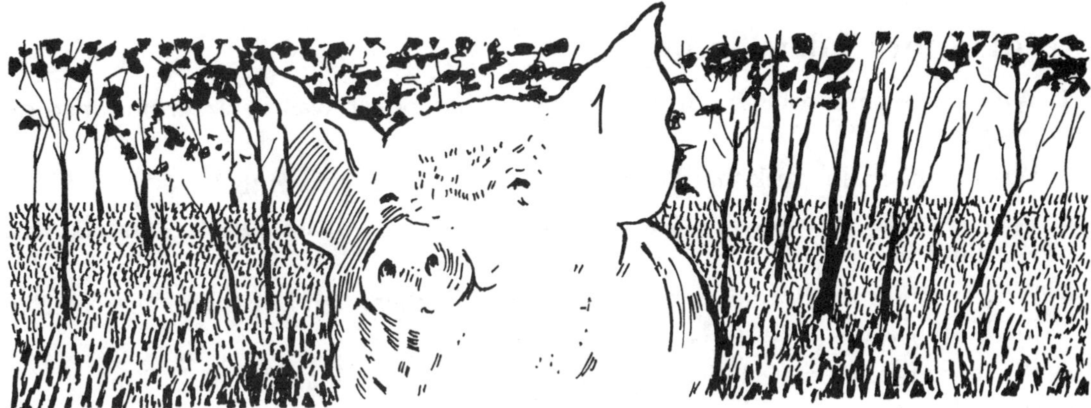

wiping away a tear. 'I was at his bedside at the very last. And at the end, almost too weak to speak, he whispered in my ear that his sole sorrow was to have passed on before the windmill was finished. "Forward, comrades!" he whispered. "Forward in the name of the Rebellion. Long live Animal Farm! Long live Comrade Napoleon! Napoleon is always right." Those were his last words, comrades.'

Here Squealer's demeanour suddenly changed. He fell silent for a moment, and his little eyes darted suspicious glances from side to side before he proceeded.

It had come to his knowledge, he said, that a foolish and wicked rumour had been circulated at the time of Boxer's removal. Some of the animals had noticed that the van which took Boxer away was marked 'Horse Slaughterer', and had actually jumped to the conclusion that Boxer was being sent to the knacker's. It was almost unbelievable, said Squealer, that any animal could be so stupid. Surely, he cried indignantly, whisking his tail and skipping from side to side, surely they knew their beloved Leader, Comrade Napoleon, better than that? But the explanation was really very simple. The van had previously been the property of the knacker, and had been bought by the veterinary surgeon, who had not yet painted the old name out. That was how the mistake had arisen.

The animals were enormously relieved to hear this. And when Squealer went on to give further graphic details of Boxer's death-bed, the admirable care he had received, and the expensive medicines for which Napoleon had paid without a thought as to the cost, their last doubts disappeared and the sorrow that they felt for their comrade's death was tempered by the thought that at least he had died happy.

Napoleon himself appeared at the meeting on the following Sunday morning and pronounced a short oration in Boxer's honour. It had not been possible, he said, to bring back their lamented comrade's remains for interment on the farm, but he had ordered a large wreath to be made from the laurels in the farmhouse garden and sent down to be placed on Boxer's grave. And in a few days' time the pigs intended to hold a memorial banquet in Boxer's honour. Napoleon ended his speech with a reminder of Boxer's two favourite maxims, 'I will work harder' and 'Comrade Napoleon is always right' — maxims, he said, which every animal would do well to adopt as his own.

On the day appointed for the banquet, a grocer's van drove up from Willingdon and delivered a large wooden crate at the farmhouse. That night there was the sound of uproarious singing, which was followed by what sounded like a violent quarrel and ended at about eleven o'clock with a tremendous crash of glass. No one stirred in the farmhouse before noon on the following day, and the word went round that from somewhere or other the pigs had acquired the money to buy themselves another case of whisky.

from *Animal Farm* by George Orwell

Reading for Understanding

1 What were three of the early indications that Boxer was in a serious medical predicament?

2 What is the main work that Boxer has been involved in recently?

3 Why is Boxer hopeful that Clover and the others will be able to complete the windmill without him?

4 Why are the animals uneasy when Squealer tells them that Boxer will be treated in the hospital at Willingdon?

5 What are Boxer's expectations and intentions for the remainder of his life?

6 Why are most of the animals unaware at first that Boxer is being taken away from the farm?

7 Explain why the description of the van driver adds to the reader's sense that something is not right about what is happening to Boxer.

8 How does Benjamin reveal that he has greater intelligence than the other animals?

9 What evidence is there that Boxer *does* understand Clover's message?

10 How might Boxer's departure have been prevented if the animals had thought quickly enough?

11 How does Squealer use his description of Boxer's death to call the animals back into line?

12 What tiny action by Squealer betrays his insincerity?

13 Why does Squealer seem suited to the task of handling 'public relations' for the pigs?

14 What really happened to Boxer?

15 Identify two ways in which the pigs made use of Boxer's death?

16 By what actions, in this passage, do Clover and Benjamin reveal their love for Boxer?

17 What evidence is there in the passage to show that most of the animals are gullible (easily deceived)?

18 What do we learn of Boxer's character from this passage?

The Scorpion

Sometimes it's hard to know which is worse — the bite of a deadly scorpion or the callous behaviour of a fellow human being.

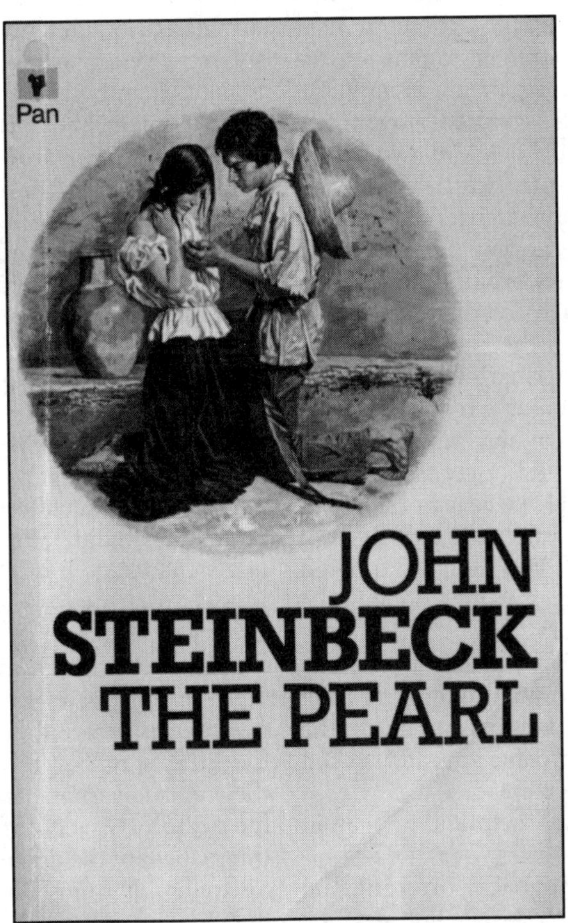

It was a tiny movement that drew their eyes to the hanging box. Kino and Juana froze in their positions. Down the rope that hung the baby's box from the roof support a scorpion moved slowly. His stinging tail was straight out behind him, but he could whip it up in a flash of time.

Kino's breath whistled in his nostrils and he opened his mouth to stop it. And then the startled look was gone from him and the rigidity from his body. In his mind a new song had come, the Song of Evil, the music of the enemy, of any foe of the family, a savage, secret, dangerous melody, and, underneath, the Song of the Family cried plaintively.

The scorpion moved delicately down the rope towards the box. Under her breath Juana repeated an ancient magic to guard against such evil, and on top of that she muttered a Hail Mary, between clenched teeth. But Kino was in motion. His body glided quietly across the room, noiselessly and smoothly. His hands were in front of him, palms down, and his eyes were on the scorpion. Beneath it in the hanging box Coyotito laughed and reached up his hand towards it. It sensed danger when Kino was almost within reach of it. It stopped, and its tail rose up over its back in little jerks and the curved thorn on the tail's end glistened.

Kino stood perfectly still. He could hear Juana whispering the old magic again, and he could hear the evil music of the enemy. He could not move until the scorpion moved, and it felt for the source of the death that was coming to it. Kino's hand went forward very slowly, very smoothly. The thorned tail jerked upright. And at that moment the laughing Coyotito shook the rope and the scorpion fell.

Kino's hand leaped to catch it, but it fell past his fingers, fell on the baby's shoulder, landed and struck. Then, snarling, Kino had it, had it in his fingers, rubbing it to a paste in his hands. He threw it down and beat it into the earth floor with his fist, and Coyotito screamed with pain in his box. But Kino beat and stamped the enemy until it was only a fragment and a moist place in the dirt. His teeth were bared and fury flared in his eyes and the Song of the Enemy roared in his ears.

But Juana had the baby in her arms now. She found the puncture with redness starting from it already. She put her lips down over the puncture and sucked hard and spat and sucked again while Coyotito screamed.

Kino hovered; he was helpless, he was in the way.

The screams of the baby brought the neighbours. Out of their brush houses they poured — Kino's brother Juan Tomás and his fat wife Apolonia and their four children crowded in the door and blocked the entrance, while behind them others tried to look in, and one small boy crawled among legs to have a look. And those in front passed the word back to those behind — 'Scorpion. The baby has been stung.'

Juana stopped sucking the puncture for a moment. The little hole was slightly enlarged and its edges whitened from the sucking, but the red swelling extended farther around it in a hard lymphatic mound. And all of these people knew about the scorpion. An adult might be very ill from the sting, but a baby could easily die from the poison. First, they knew, would come swelling and fever and tightened throat, and then cramps in the stomach, and then Coyotito might die if enough of the poison had gone in. But the stinging pain of the bite was going away. Coyotito's screams turned to moans.

Kino had wondered often at the iron in his patient, fragile wife. She, who was obedient and respectful and cheerful and patient, could arch her back in child pain with hardly a cry. She could stand fatigue and hunger almost better than Kino himself. In the canoe she was like a strong man. And now she did a most surprising thing.

'The doctor,' she said. 'Go to get the doctor.'

The word was passed out among the neighbours where they stood close-packed in the little yard behind the brush fence. And they repeated among themselves. 'Juana wants the doctor.' A wonderful thing, a memorable thing, to want the doctor. To get him would be a remarkable thing. The doctor never came to the cluster of brush houses. Why should he, when he had more than he could do to take care of the rich people who lived in the stone and plaster houses of the town?

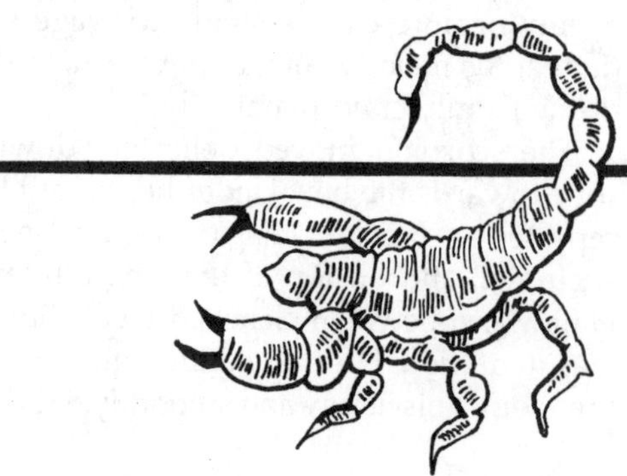

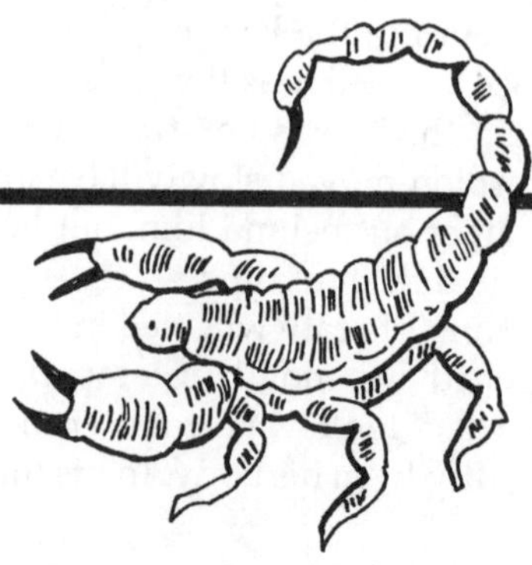

'He would not come,' the people in the yard said.

'He would not come,' the people in the door said, and the thought got into Kino.

'The doctor would not come,' Kino said to Juana.

She looked up at him, her eyes as cold as the eyes of a lioness. This was Juana's first baby — this was nearly everything there was in Juana's world. And Kino saw her determination and the music of the family sounded in his head with a steely tone.

'Then we will go to him,' Juana said, and with one hand she arranged her dark-blue shawl over her head and made of one end of it a sling to hold the moaning baby and made of the other end of it a shade over his eyes to protect him from the light. The people in the door pushed against those behind to let her through. Kino followed her. They went out of the gate to the rutted path and the neighbours followed them.

The thing had become a neighbourhood affair. They made a quick soft-footed procession into the centre of the town, first Juana and Kino, and behind them Juan Tomás and Apolonia, her big stomach jiggling with the strenuous pace, then all the neighbours with the children trotting on the flanks. And the yellow sun threw their black shadows ahead of them so that they walked on their own shadows.

They came to the place where the brush houses stopped and the city of stone and plaster began, the city of harsh outer walls and inner cool gardens where a little water played and the bougainvillaea crusted the walls with purple and brick-red and white. They heard from the secret gardens the singing of caged birds and heard the splash of cooling water on hot flagstones. The procession crossed the blinding plaza and passed in front of the church. It had grown now, and on the outskirts the hurrying newcomers were being softly informed how the baby had been stung by a scorpion, how the father and mother were taking it to the doctor.

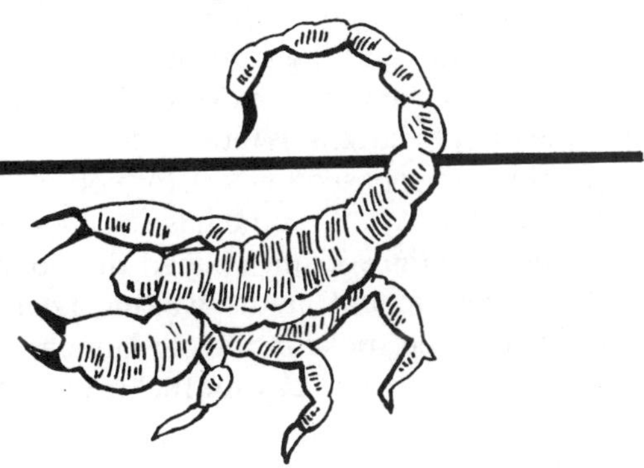

And the newcomers, particularly the beggars from the front of the church, who were great experts in financial analysis, looked quickly at Juana's old blue skirt, saw the tears in her shawl, appraised the green ribbon on her braids, read the age of Kino's blanket and the thousand washings of his clothes, and set them down as poverty people and went along to see what kind of drama might develop. The four beggars in front of the church knew everything in the town. They were students of the expressions of young women as they went in to confession, and they saw them as they came out and read the nature of the sin. They knew every little scandal and some very big crimes. They slept at their posts in the shadow of the church so that no one crept in for consolation without their knowledge. And they knew the doctor. They knew his ignorance, his cruelty, his avarice, his appetites, his sins. They knew his clumsy abortions and the little brown pennies he gave sparingly for alms. They had seen his corpses go into the church. And, since early mass was over and business was slow, they followed the procession, these endless searchers after perfect knowledge of their fellow men, to see what the fat lazy doctor would do about an indigent baby with a scorpion bite.

The scurrying procession came at last to the big gate in the wall of the doctor's house. They could hear the splashing water and the singing of caged birds and the sweep of the long brooms on the flagstones. And they could smell the frying of good bacon from the doctor's house.

Kino hesitated a moment. This doctor was not of his people. This doctor was of a race which for nearly four hundred years had beaten and starved and robbed and despised Kino's race, and frightened it too, so that the indigene came humbly to the door. And, as always when he came near to one of this race, Kino felt weak and afraid and angry at the same time. Rage and terror went together. He could kill the doctor more easily than he could talk to him, for all of the doctor's race spoke to all of Kino's race as though they were simple animals. And as Kino raised his right hand to the iron ring knocker in the gate, rage swelled in him, and the pounding music of the enemy beat in his ears, and his lips drew tight against his teeth — but with his left hand he reached to take off his hat. The iron ring pounded against the gate. Kino took off his hat and stood waiting. Coyotito moaned a little in Juana's arms, and she spoke softly to him. The procession crowded close, the better to see and hear.

After a moment the big gate opened a few inches. Kino could see the green coolness of the garden and little splashing fountain through the opening. The man who looked out at him was one of his own race. Kino spoke to him in the old language. 'The little one — the first-born — has been poisoned by the scorpion,' Kino said. 'He requires the skill of the healer.'

The gate closed a little, and the servant refused to speak in the old language. 'A little moment,' he said. 'I go to inform myself,' and he closed the gate and slid the bolt home. The glaring sun threw the bunched shadows of the people blackly on the white wall.

In his chamber the doctor sat up in his high bed. He had on his dressing-gown of red watered silk that had come from Paris, a little tight over the chest now if it was buttoned. On his lap was a silver tray with a silver chocolate pot and a tiny cup of egg-shell china, so delicate that it looked silly when he lifted it with his big hand, lifted it with the tips of thumb and forefinger and spread the other three fingers wide to get them out of the way. His eyes rested in puffy little hammocks of flesh and his mouth drooped with discontent. He was growing very stout, and his voice was hoarse with the fat that pressed on his throat. Beside him on a table was a small Oriental gong and a bowl of cigarettes. The furnishings of the room were heavy and dark and gloomy. The

pictures were religious, even the large tinted photograph of his dead wife, who, if masses willed and paid for out of her own estate could do it, was in Heaven. The doctor had once for a short time been a part of the great world and his whole subsequent life was memory and longing for France. 'That,' he said, 'was civilised living' — by which he meant that on a small income he had been able to keep a mistress and eat in restaurants. He poured his second cup of chocolate and crumbled a sweet biscuit in his fingers. The servant from the gate came to the open door and stood waiting to be noticed.

'Yes?' the doctor asked.

'It is a little Indian with a baby. He says a scorpion stung it.'

The doctor put his cup down gently before he let his anger rise.

'Have I nothing better to do than cure insect bites for "little Indians"? I am a doctor, not a veterinary.'

'Yes, Patron,' said the servant.

'Has he any money?' the doctor demanded. 'No, they never have any money. I, I alone in the world am supposed to work for nothing — and I am tired of it. See if he has any money!'

At the gate the servant opened the door a trifle and looked out at the waiting people. And this time he spoke in the old language.

'Have you money to pay for the treatment?'

Now Kino reached into a secret place somewhere under his blanket. He brought out a paper folded many times. Crease by crease he unfolded it, until at last there came to view eight small misshapen seed pearls, as ugly and grey as little ulcers, flattened and almost valueless. The servant took the paper and closed the gate again, but this time he was not gone long. He opened the gate just wide enough to pass the paper back.

'The doctor has gone out,' he said. 'He was called to a serious case.' And he shut the gate quickly out of shame.

And now a wave of shame went over the whole procession. They melted away. The beggars went back to the church steps, the stragglers moved off, and the neighbours departed so that the public shaming of Kino would not be in their eyes.

For a long time Kino stood in front of the gate with Juana beside him. Slowly he put his suppliant hat on his head. Then, without warning, he struck the gate a crushing blow with his fist. He looked down in wonder at his split knuckles and at the blood that flowed down between his fingers.

from *The Pearl* by John Steinbeck

Reading for Understanding

1 Though the scorpion's tail was not initially curled ready to sting, it was still dangerous. Why was it so dangerous?

2 What did Juana do to guard against the scorpion?

3 What actions of the scorpion showed that it sensed danger?

4 Why did the scorpion fall?

5 What did Juana do to try to stop the poison spreading in Coyotito?

6 What were the usual symptoms of scorpion bite in a child?

7 Why was it such 'a wonderful thing, a memorable thing', for Juana to want the doctor?

8 Why did the neighbours believe the doctor would never come to see the baby?

9 How did the beggars from the front of the church usually conduct their financial appraisal of people?

10 Why did they follow the procession to the doctor's house?

11 What mixture of emotions did Kino feel before knocking at the doctor's gate?

12 How did this mixture of emotions affect his behaviour as he knocked at the gate?

13 Why do you think the doctor's servant does not speak in 'the old language' on the first occasion?

14 What do we learn about the doctor's character from his response to Kino's request for help?

15 Why does the servant finally shut the gate quickly?

16 What emotions lie behind Kino's action at the end of this passage?

17 From this incident, what do we learn of Kino's character? Support your view with evidence from the passage.

18 From this incident, what do we learn about Juana's character? Give evidence from the passage.

The Nursery

Ivan Pavlov was a famous Russian psychologist who, at the turn of the century, studied ways of training animals to act with specific behaviour under predetermined conditions. In this passage, novelist Aldous Huxley takes a frightening look into the future to see how some of Pavlov's discoveries could be used by society.

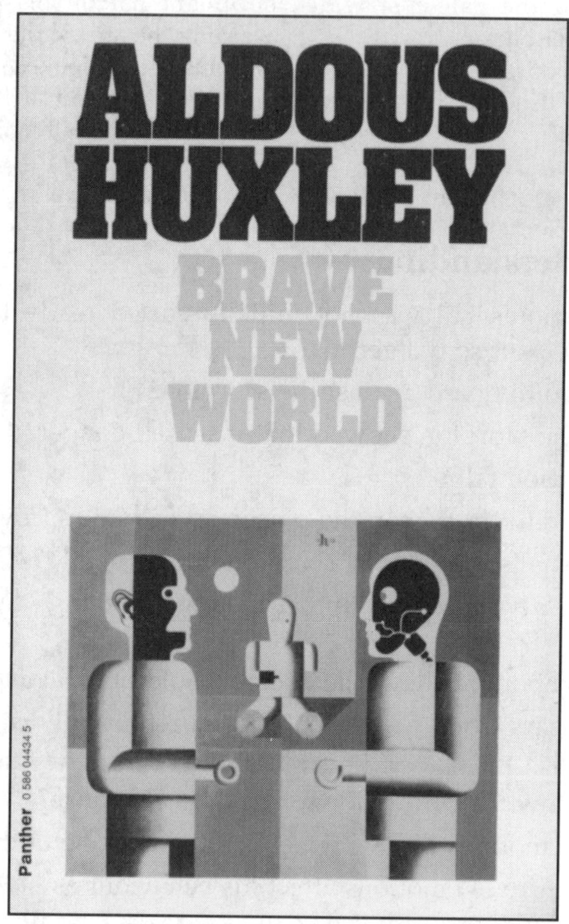

INFANT NURSERIES. NEO-PAVLOVIAN CONDITIONING ROOMS, announced the notice board.

The Director opened a door. They were in a large bare room, very bright and sunny; for the whole of the southern wall was a single window. Half a dozen nurses, trousered and jacketed in the regulation white viscose-linen uniform, their hair aseptically hidden under white caps, were engaged in setting out bowls of roses in a long row across the floor. Big bowls, packed tight with blossom. Thousands of petals, ripe-blown and silkily smooth, like the cheeks of innumerable little cherubs, but of cherubs, in that bright light, not exclusively pink and Aryan, but also luminously Chinese, also Mexican, also apoplectic with too much blowing of celestial trumpets, also pale as death, pale with the posthumous whiteness of marble.

The nurses stiffened to attention as the D.H.C. came in.

'Set out the books,' he said curtly.

In silence the nurses obeyed his command. Between the rose bowls the books were duly set out — a row of nursery quartos opened invitingly each at some gaily coloured image of beast or fish or bird.

'Now bring in the children.'

They hurried out of the room and returned in a minute or two, each pushing a kind of tall dumb-waiter laden, on all its four wire-netted shelves, with eight-month-old babies, all exactly alike (a Bokanovsky Group, it was evident) and all (since their caste was Delta) dressed in khaki.

'Put them down on the floor.'

The infants were unloaded.

'Now turn them so that they can see the flowers and books.'

Turned, the babies at once fell silent, then began to crawl towards those clusters of sleek colours, those shapes so gay and brilliant on the white pages. As they approached, the sun came out of a momentary eclipse behind a cloud. The roses flamed up as though with a sudden passion from within; a new and profound significance seemed to suffuse the shining pages of the books. From the ranks of the crawling babies came little squeals of excitement, gurgles and twitterings of pleasure.

The Director rubbed his hands. 'Excellent!' he said. 'It might almost have been done on purpose.'

The swiftest crawlers were already at their goal. Small hands reached out uncertainly, touched, grasped, unpetalling the transfigured roses, crumpling the illuminated pages of the books. The Director waited until all were happily busy. Then, 'Watch carefully,' he said. And, lifting his hand, he gave the signal.

The Head Nurse, who was standing by a switchboard at the other end of the room, pressed down a little lever.

There was a violent explosion. Shriller and ever shriller, a siren shrieked. Alarm bells maddeningly sounded.

The children started, screamed; their faces were distorted with terror.

'And now,' the Director shouted (for the noise was deafening), 'now we proceed to rub in the lesson with a mild electric shock.'

He waved his hand again, and the Head Nurse pressed a second lever. The screaming of the babies suddenly changed its tone. There was something desperate, almost insane, about the sharp spasmodic yelps to which they now gave utterance. Their little bodies twitched and stiffened; their limbs moved jerkily as if to the tug of unseen wires.

'We can electrify that whole strip of floor,' bawled the Director in explanation. 'But that's enough,' he signalled to the nurse.

The explosions ceased, the bells stopped ringing, the shriek of the siren died down from tone to tone into silence. The stiffly twitching

bodies relaxed, and what had become the sob and yelp of infant maniacs broadened out once more into a normal howl of ordinary terror.

'Offer them the flowers and the books again.'

The nurses obeyed; but at the approach of the roses, at the mere sight of those gaily-coloured images of pussy and cock-a-doodle-doo and baa-baa black sheep, the infants shrank away in horror; the volume of their howling suddenly increased.

'Observe,' said the Director triumphantly, 'observe.'

Books and loud noises, flowers and electric shocks — already in the infant mind these couples were compromisingly linked; and after two hundred repetitions of the same or a similar lesson would be wedded indissolubly. What man has joined, nature is powerless to put asunder.

'They'll grow up with what the psychologists used to call an "instinctive" hatred of books and flowers. Reflexes unalterably conditioned. They'll be safe from books and botany all their lives.' The Director turned to his nurses. 'Take them away again.'

Still yelling, the khaki babies were loaded on to their dumb-waiters and wheeled out, leaving behind them the smell of sour milk and a most welcome silence.

One of the students held up his hand; and though he could see quite well why you couldn't have lower-caste people wasting the Community's time over books, and that there was always the risk of their reading something which might undesirably decondition one of their reflexes, yet . . . well, he couldn't understand about the flowers. Why go to the trouble of making it psychologically impossible for Deltas to like flowers?

Patiently the D.H.C. explained. If the children were made to scream at the sight of a rose, that was on grounds of high economic policy. Not so very long ago (a century or thereabouts), Gammas, Deltas, even Epsilons, had been conditioned to like flowers — flowers in particular and wild nature in general. The idea was to make them want to be going out into the country at every available opportunity, and so compel them to consume transport.

'And didn't they consume transport?' asked the student.

'Quite a lot,' the D.H.C. replied. 'But nothing else.'

Primroses and landscapes, he pointed out, have one grave defect: they are gratuitous. A love of nature keeps no factories busy. It was decided to abolish the love of nature, at any rate among the lower classes; to abolish the love of nature, but *not* the tendency to consume transport. For of course it was essential that they should keep on going to the country, even though they hated it. The problem was to find an economically sounder reason for consuming transport than a mere affection for primroses and landscapes. It was duly found.

'We condition the masses to hate the country,' concluded the Director. 'But simultaneously we condition them to love all country sports. At the same time, we see to it that all country sports shall entail the use of elaborate apparatus. So that they consume manufactured articles as well as transport. Hence those electric shocks.'

'I see,' said the student, and was silent, lost in admiration.

from *Brave New World* by Aldous Huxley

Reading for Understanding

1 What is there about the entrance to the nursery to suggest it is not really a 'friendly' place?
2 How are the nurses attired and what does this suggest about the theory of raising children being followed here?
3 What do we learn about the Director from his first words?
4 What colour were the babies dressed in and what view of them does this reveal?
5 Besides the sameness of the colour they were dressed in, what else was unusual about the group of babies?
6 What was the initial response of the babies when they were turned to see the rose petals and coloured books?
7 How did nature play a part in enhancing the attractiveness of the rose petals and books?
8 What did the Director wait for, prior to giving the signal?
9 'The Head Nurse . . . pressed down a little lever.' What did this cause to happen?
10 What emotion was produced in all the babies by throwing the first lever?
11 What changes in the babies' screams were produced by the electric shock?
12 What specific linkages were being produced in the babies' minds by this kind of terrible experience?
13 What two sense impressions were left behind when the babies were wheeled out?
14 Why was the Director seeking to train the children not to like books?
15 'A love of nature keeps no factories busy.' What priority of the regime does this statement reveal?
16 Explain the solution that was found so that the masses continued to use public transport into the country.
17 Why is the student 'lost in admiration' at the end?
18 What emotional response do you have to this passage?

POETRY

POEMS ABOUT SOCIETY

Enter Without So Much as Knocking

Memento, homo, quia pulvis es, et in pulverem reverteris . . .

Blink, blink. HOSPITAL. SILENCE.
Ten days old, carried in the front door in his
mother's arms, first thing he heard was
Bobby Dazzler on Channel 7:
Hello, hello, hello all you lucky people and he
really was lucky because it didn't mean a thing
to him then . . .

A year or two to settle in and
get acquainted with the set-up; like every other
well-equipped smoothly-run household, his included
one economy-size Mum, one Anthony Squires-
Coolstream-Summerweight Dad, along with two other kids
straight off the Junior Department rack.

When Mum won the
Luck's-A-Fortch Tricky-Tune Quiz she took him shopping
in the good-as-new station-wagon (£495 dep. at Reno's).
Beep, beep. WALK. DON'T WALK. TURN
LEFT. NO PARKING. WAIT HERE. NO
SMOKING. KEEP CLEAR/OUT/OFF GRASS. NO
BREATHING EXCEPT BY ORDER. BEWARE OF
THIS. WATCH OUT FOR THAT. My God (beep)
the congestion here just gets (beep)
worse every day, now what the (beep beep) does
that idiot think he's doing (beep beep and BEEP).

However, what he enjoyed most of all was when they
went to the late show at the local drive-in, on a clear night
and he could see (beyond the fifty-foot screen where
giant faces forever snarled screamed or made
incomprehensible and monstrous love) a pure
unadulterated fringe of sky, littered with stars
no-one had got around to fixing up yet; he'd watch them
circling about in luminous groups like kids at the circus
who never go quite close enough to the elephant to get kicked.

Anyway, pretty soon he was old enough to be
realistic like every other godless
money-hungry back-stabbing miserable
so-and-so, and then it was goodbye stars and the soft
cry in the corner when no-one was looking because
I'm telling you straight, Jim, it's Number One every time
for this chicken, hit wherever you see a head and
kick whoever's down, well thanks for a lovely
evening Clare, it's good to get away from it all
once in a while, I mean it's a real battle all the way
and a man can't help but feel a little soiled, himself,
at times, you know what I mean?

Now take it easy
on those curves, Alice, for God's sake,
I've had enough for one night, with that Clare Jessup,
hey, ease up, will you, watch it —

Probity & Sons, Morticians,
did a really first-class job on his face
(everyone was very pleased) even adding a
healthy tan he'd never had, living, gave him back for keeps
the old automatic smile with nothing behind it,
winding the whole show up with a
nice ride out to the underground metropolis:
permanent residentials, no parking tickets, no taximeters
ticking, no Bobby Dazzlers here, no down payments,
nobody grieving over halitosis
flat feet shrinking gums falling hair.

Six feet down nobody interested.

Blink, blink. CEMETERY. Silence.

Bruce Dawe

Questions

1 '. . . he/really was lucky because it didn't mean a thing/to him then . . .' What does the poet see as one positive aspect of infancy?

2 Judging from the description of the child's family ('one economy-size Mum' etc.), how does the poet want us to view them?

3 On the shopping trip they seem to be confronted with all kinds of signs and instructions. What impression of the modern civilised world is being created by the poet here?

4 What delighted the young child most in his early years?

5 '. . . littered with stars/no-one had got around to fixing up yet'. What view does the poet seem to have about the relationship between people and nature?

6 How does the poet describe people who are 'realistic'?

7 Identify one statement quoted in the poem that is frequently pushed as 'wisdom' for us to live by.

8 What impression of the man's feelings for Clare do we get from the way he speaks to her, and how does he *really* feel about her? What evidence is there for your opinion?

9 How does this man die?

10 How does the poet seem to view the undertaker's work and the whole death and burial sequence?

11 What is the effect of starting and ending the poem with similarly structured sentences?

12 How would you describe the poet's attitude to birth, life and death in the modern world?

13 What emotions does the poet arouse in you? Why?

14 The poet has placed the Latin in words *Memento, homo, quia pulvis es, et in pulverem reverteris* underneath the title of the poem. Their meaning in English is 'Remember, O man, because you are dust, you will return to dust'. How do these words relate to the poet's message in the poem?

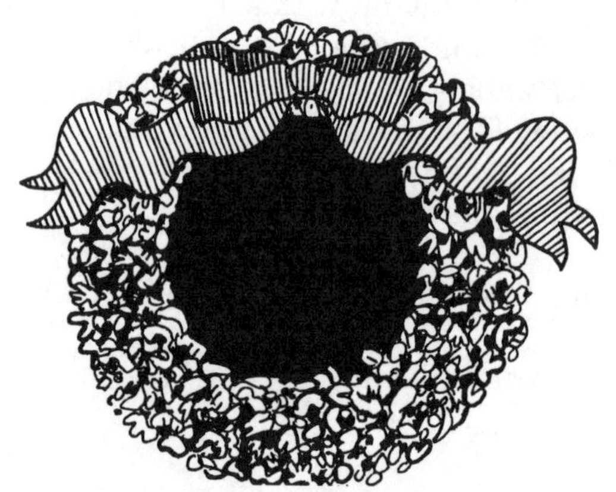

Shantytown

High on the veld upon that plain
And far from streets and lights and cars
And bare of trees, and bare of grass,
Jabavu* sleeps beneath the stars.

Jabavu sleeps.
The children cough.
Cold creeps up, the hard night cold,
The earth is tight within its grasp,
The highveld cold without soft rain,
Dry as the sand, rough as a rasp.

The frost rimmed night invades the shacks.
Through dusty ground
Through rocky ground
Through freezing ground the night cold creeps
In cotton blankets, rags and sacks
Beneath the stars Jabavu sleeps.

One day Jabavu will awake
To greet a new and shining day.
The sound of coughing will become
The children's laughter as they play
In parks with flowers where dust now swirls
In strong-walled homes with warmth and light.
But for tonight Jabavu sleeps
Jabavu sleeps. The stars are bright.

Anonymous

* *Shantytown area near Johannesburg in South Africa*

Questions

1 What aspects of a well-established community are missing from Jabavu according to the first verse?

2 What indication do we have of health problems in Jabavu?

3 'Cold creeps up, the hard night cold'. What does the poet want us to sense about the cold?

4 Identify two similes in the second verse that describe the harshness of the highveld.

5 'The frost rimmed night invades the shacks'. Why is 'invades' an effective word here?

6 What is the effect of the repetition in 'Through dusty ground/Through rocky ground/Through freezing ground . . .'?
7 What do the people of Jabavu use to protect themselves against the cold?
8 What emotion does the poet express in the final verse?
9 What changes does the poet anticipate for the Jabavu of future years?
10 What is the effect of the final sentence 'The stars are bright'?
11 How successfully do you think the poet has described Jabavu and his feelings about it?
12 What emotions are stirred in you by this poem? Why?

Song of the City

My brain is stiff with concrete
My limbs are rods of steel
My belly's stuffed with money
My soul was bought in a deal.

They poured metal through my arteries
They choked my lungs with lead
They churned my blood to plastic
They put murder into my head.

I'd a face like a map of the weather
Flesh that grew to the bone
But they tore my story out of my eyes
And turned my heart to stone.

Let me wind from my source like a river
Let me grow like wheat from the grain
Let me hold out my arms like a natural tree
Let my children love me again.

Gareth Owen

Questions

1 What features of a modern city are being described in the first two lines of this poem?

2 A person's belly usually holds the food that energises him or her. What energises the city?

3 'They choked my lungs with lead'. What are the 'lungs' of the city and where has the lead come from?

4 'They churned my blood to plastic'. What is the impact of the word 'plastic'?

5 What do you think the poet means by 'They put murder into my head'?

6 'But they tore my story out of my eyes'. How does this depict the way the city-dwellers have acted?

7 What effect on the city's heart have its inhabitants had?

8 The last verse depicts the city's desires. What does the poet believe the city would like to happen?

9 What response is the city looking for from its inhabitants in the final line?

10 Do you think the poet's personification of the city is an effective technique? What does he achieve by it?

Geography Lesson

When the jet sprang into the sky,
it was clear why the city
had developed the way it had,
seeing it scaled six inches to the mile.
There seemed an inevitability
about what on ground had looked haphaz-
ard,
unplanned and without style
when the jet sprang into the sky.

When the jet reached ten thousand feet,
it was clear why the country
had cities where rivers ran
and why the valleys were populated.
The logic of geography —
that land and water attracted man —
was clearly delineated
when the jet reached ten thousand feet.

When the jet rose six miles high,
it was clear that the earth was round
and that it had more sea than land.
But it was difficult to understand
that the men on the earth found
causes to hate each other, to build
walls across cities and to kill.
From that height, it was not clear why.

Zulfikar Ghose

Questions

1 What causes the city to appear 'scaled six inches to the mile'?

2 What is made clear by the early aerial view of the city?

3 What becomes clear at ten thousand feet that was not clear at a lower height?

4 What facts are revealed about the earth from a height of six miles?

5 Aerial geography can give some important understanding. What is it *not* able to explain?

6 What is the effect of starting each verse with 'When the jet . . .'?

7 How would you describe the view of humankind presented in this poem? Are people seen as basically good or evil? Explain your answer.

8 How would you rate the achievement of this poem? What do you see as the poet's purpose and how successful has he been?

In the past, wild animals were sometimes forced to perform for the entertainment of human beings.

The poet Charles Causley has made this comment about his inspiration for the following poem:

> The 'Dancing Bear' story is a true one and was told to me by my mother when she was in her eighties as though it had happened that very morning.

The word 'bruin' used in the poem is an old word for 'bear'.

My Mother Saw a Dancing Bear

My mother saw a dancing bear
By the schoolyard, a day in June.
The keeper stood with chain and bar
And whistle pipe, and played a tune.

And bruin lifted up its head
And lifted up its dusty feet,
And all the children laughed to see
It caper in the summer heat.

They watched as for the Queen it died.
They watched it march. They watched it halt.
They heard the keeper as he cried,
'Now, roly-poly!' 'Somersault!'

And then my mother said, there came
The keeper with a begging-cup,
The bear with a burning coat of fur,
Shaming the laughter to a stop.

They paid a penny for the dance,
But what they saw was not the show;
Only in bruin's aching eyes,
Far-distant forests, and the snow.

Charles Causley

WRITING

DIFFERENT FORMS OF WRITING

The word **form**, when used to describe writing, means 'kinds', 'formats' or 'styles'. The following, then, could all be described as writing forms:

- poems
- plays
- novels
- letters
- reports

Naturally enough, because each is different, there will be differences from one to another on such things as vocabulary, style and layout. Read the following information about a kidnapping case and respond by doing the writing tasks, each of which requires you to use a different form of writing.

Rock band kidnapped!

Rock mega-star Captain Blood, and his band, Positive Antibodies, were kidnapped *en masse* last night after their big Melbourne concert. The group, travelling in a late model Tarago, disappeared on the way back to their hotel. Their manager reports that he received a phone call from the kidnappers during the night, and that he expects a ransom note to be sent soon. Police are awaiting further developments.

WRITING TASKS

1 Ransom Note

The ransom note has arrived. It asks for five million dollars ransom money and promises further contact by phone. Use your writing skills to complete the ransom note below.

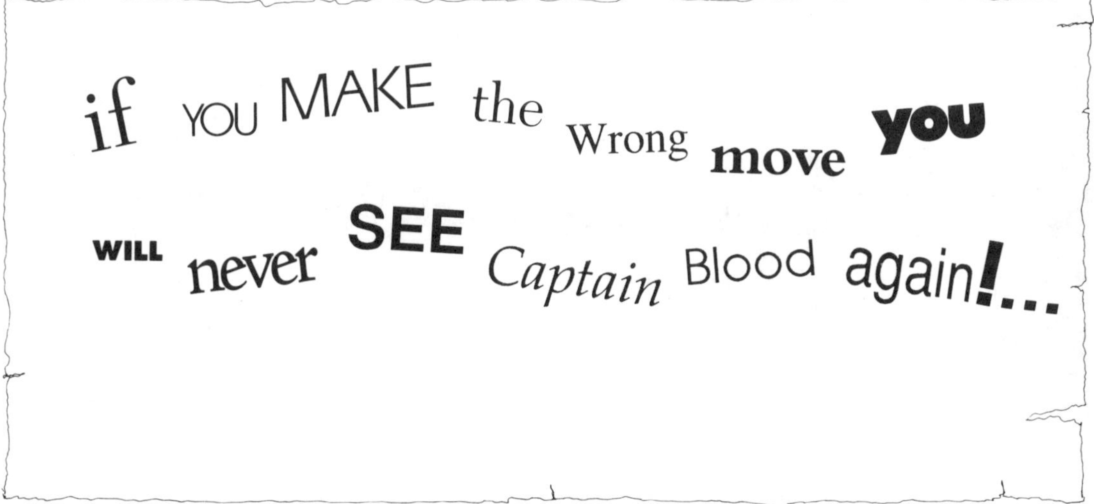

2 Radio News Item

The story is big news! Write the incident of the kidnapping and the ransom note in the form of a news item for a radio station. Begin your news item in the following way:

> **News broadcaster**: And now a newsflash from our news room. Police report that last night the rock mega-star Captain Blood and his group Positive Antibodies were kidnapped after their Melbourne concert . . .

3 Telephone Conversation

The rock group's manager, Augustus Bollocks, has been anticipating a phone call from the kidnappers to give further details of how the payment is to be made. He is concerned to try and establish that the members of the rock group are safe and that the person on the other end of the line is not a hoax caller. Since he is also taping the call he wants to prolong it, in case it can be traced. Create the phone conversation, building on the start below.

> **Bollocks**: Augustus Bollocks
> **Voice**: Mr Bollocks, listen *very* carefully.
> **Bollocks**: . . .

4 Diary Entry

A young student, 'Moose' Hawkins, on his way home from the concert actually witnessed the kidnapping. Moose and two mates were walking on the footpath when the Positive Antibodies' Tarago drove by. Moose has kept a record of what he saw in the form of a diary entry. Complete the entry, building on the introduction below.

Friday 5

Dear Diary

I'm so scared I'm still shaking!

At exactly 1·17 this morning I was walking home along Collins Street, after the Captain Blood concert, when . . .

5 Interview

Moose contacts the police and before long they send two detectives to interview him. They are interested in everything he has to to say, particularly in the details which suggest that the kidnapper may be 'Scarface' Smith and his gang.

Write out a record of the interview between Detective Sam Stevens, Detective Rhoda Bainbridge and Moose.

Sam: Hi! You must be Moose. Thanks for your call to the police station. My name is Sam Stevens and this is Rhoda Bainbridge. We'd like to talk with you about what you witnessed.

Moose: . . .

6 Plan of Police Operation

The police, drawing on information from Moose and other members of the public, have been able to locate the hideout of Scarface and his gang. The gang is holed up in a mansion on the outskirts of Melbourne, where they are believed to be holding Captain Blood and the Positive Antibodies. A plan is devised by the police to surround the house and try to negotiate the release of the rock group in exchange for lesser charges being laid against the kidnappers. If the negotiations fail, an assault on the mansion is planned.

Write out the plan below, including at least eight more steps of your own. Include a diagram of the area showing important locations, such as Police Headquarters, sniper posts and so on.

OPERATION ROCK RELEASE

Step 1: Surround 40 Embargo St with 200 police, fully armed, under the control of Superintendent Ormsby of Tactical Response.
Step 2: Snipers to be stationed on four sides of the kidnapper's house. Locations as marked on the diagram.
Step 3: . . .

7 Negotiations

The police assemble around the mansion and, using the phone, Superintendent Ormsby tries to negotiate the release of the rock group with Scarface. Record the conversation between the police chief and the kidnapper which will terminate with a refusal to negotiate any further by Scarface.

(Sound of phone ringing)
Scarface: Yes. *(harshly)*
Ormsby: Scarface, this is Superintendent Ormsby of Tactical Response. You are completely surrounded . . .

8 Letter to a Friend

Suzie Hallowell lives on Embargo St, not far from the scene of the siege. Her parents own a three-storey house and, with the aid of binoculars, she is able to piece together what happens when the police finally make their assault on the kidnappers' mansion and successfully rescue the rock band. She later writes to her closest friend, Amanda, telling her everything that happened. Complete the letter.

16 Sunny [illegible]
South Spotswood

Dear Amanda
You'll never believe what's happened! I'm still totally spun-out by it myself! On Sunday afternoon our street was invaded by what seemed like half the police in Melbourne....

9 Formal Police Report

After the successful rescue of Captain Blood and the Positive Antibodies, and the capture of Scarface Smith and his gang, a formal police report has to be written. Complete the report including special commendation of any officers who performed in an outstanding manner. Use today's date and write under the following sub-headings:

OPERATION ROCK RELEASE
POLICE REPORT

Date: ____________

Location: 40 Embargo St

Officer in charge: ____________

Sequence of events: ____________

____

____

____

Outcome: ____________

____

Special Commendations: ____________

____

10 Song Lyrics

In the aftermath of the kidnap drama, Positive Antibodies member, 'Pug-fingers' Gormley, writes the lyrics for a rock ballad to be performed by the band. Complete the lyrics.

Saturday evening in Melbourne
Everything's looking good
The band is hot and the kids have got
Their eyes on Captain Blood
. . .

LANGUAGE

LANGUAGE IN EVERYDAY LIFE

COLLOQUIAL LANGUAGE

Colloquial language is relaxed, friendly, informal language. It is the language that friends use when they talk or when they write to each other. Notice that it makes use of common, widely used words and phrases.

G'day Steve. How'd the weekend go?

Ah, not so good. The weather was lousy for the beach on Saturday and the surf was flat as a pancake. Then to top it all off, I busted my sunglasses.

While this language is perfectly good communication between friends, it would be considered inappropriate in a more formal situation. Colloquial language is fine, as long as it is appropriate to the situation.

Colloquial Language in Action

Rewrite each of the following sentences, changing them from colloquial to more formal language. For example:

Colloquial: I've been slogging away for hours and I'm really bushed.
Formal: I have been working hard for hours and I am exhausted.

1 The Principal watched us like a hawk so he could bust anyone who was mucking up.
2 The band was hot and soon the audience were all grooving along.

3 She didn't turn a hair when the ghost first appeared.
4 The driver got crook so we had to change buses.
5 We decided to shoot through before the speeches started.
6 Even if you can't do a good job on the exam question you've got to give it your best shot.
7 'Check out the latest fashions. They're really off!'
8 The economy's on the nose. That's why so many businesses are going to the wall.
9 Don't be conned. He's pulling a swifty on you.
10 She was over the moon about the new hunk who'd moved in next door.

SLANG

Slang is an extreme form of colloquial language. While there is considerable overlap with colloquial language, slang tends to be less widely understood and to pass in and out of use more quickly.

Slang in Action

In relaxed and informal situations, we sometimes resort to slang. Here are ten sentences involving Australian slang. Write the sentences in normal English.

1 The check-out chick was once a dole bludger.
2 I put the bite on my old man for ten bucks.
3 He took me for a demo in his old bomb.
4 What do you do for a crust?
5 He did his block and it was on for young and old.
6 He took a sickie, but he didn't go to the quack.
7 Don't stand there like a stunned mullet, throw some meat on the barbie.
8 The two bikies got busted and were taken to the cop shop.

JARGON

Jargon is a specialised kind of language developed and used by people who share work or interest in a specific area. Areas as diverse as card-playing, cricket, carpentry and computers all have their specialised vocabulary — understood only by those with a knowledge of the particular field.

Cartoon Jargon

'Smash', 'crush' and 'grab' for us are everyday English words. Why do you think they are classed as jargon words in the Hagar cartoon above?

Examining the Jargon of Lifesavers

In this passage from *They're A Weird Mob* by Nino Culotta (John O'Grady), we can see that lifesavers have developed their own specialised language. Nino, a new Australian, who is describing the situation, believes that if he wishes to become a lifesaver he will have to learn their language. See if you can work out the everyday meanings of the jargon words shown in heavy type.

HOW TO BECOME A LIFESAVER

I realised then that they also were lifesavers, who were probably not on duty. And I thought, 'It is all right for lifesavers to swim in rips, but not for anybody else. Therefore, if I wish to swim away from the crowds, I must become a lifesaver.' So I went up to where they were all sitting in and around a canvas enclosure, and I said, 'Excuse me, please, what is the procedure if one wishes to become the lifesaver?'

They laughed. One said, 'Wot's yer time for the four forty?'

Another said, 'Can yer **crack a wave**?'

A third said, 'Saw a **tiddler crack him** a while ago.'

'You can't talk, you went **down the mine** yesterday.'

'Yeah? Wot about Maroubra last Sundy? All on 'e says, an' falls for it himself. Comes up blue in the face, spittin' sand an' seaweed.'

'I **caught a boomer** just after, but.'

'Who didn't.'

'You didn't. Out there like a shag on a rock, yellin Mummy, I'm lonely.'

'I was waitin' for a big one. There was **one out the back.**'

'Did yer crack ut?'

'**Didn't break.** Didn't have me **propeller** with me.'

'There'd be a brown stain if y'ever did **crack a howler,** Bluey.'

'I'd be on my own anyway. None o' yous'd be game.'

'Listen what's talkin'? Be on 'im will yer?'

Not understanding any of this, I decided that they must be speaking the technical language of lifesavers. If I wished to become a lifesaver, I would first have to learn these terms.

from *They're a Weird Mob* by John O'Grady

CLICHE

A cliche is an outworn expression. It has been so over-used that it has lost any originality or vitality. As soon as a cliche is started we know how to finish it. Good speakers and writers tend to avoid cliches because they feel that they are boring for the reader or audience. Here are some examples:

- as silly as a goose
- at a loose end
- give up the ghost

Completing the Cliches

Complete the cliches below by filling in the missing word in each case. The first letter is sometimes given to help you.

1 as brown as a b.................

2 curiosity killed the ....

3 have a frog in one's t.................

4 one big happy f.................

5 something out of the o.................

6 a tale of w.................

7 wave a magic ....

8 an officer and a g.................

9 a miss is as good as a ....

10 a lot of water has flowed under the ....

11 love at first ....

12 good riddance to bad ....

13 bid a fond f.................

14 do yourself a f.................

15 between the devil and the deep blue ....

16 better late than ....

17 as blind as a ....

18 beyond a certain p.................

19 given the benefit of the ....

20 have a whale of a ....

EUPHEMISM

A euphemism is a word or phrase that attempts to cover up the ugliness or unpleasantness of something by presenting it in a more socially acceptable way. For example, a commonly used euphemism for the word 'died' is 'passed away'.

Cartoon Euphemisms

1 What euphemism does the real estate agent use to describe the dilapidated house?

2 What word of Hagar's extends the euphemism?

Euphemisms and Their Meanings

Match each euphemism with its equivalent plain English word or phrase.

Euphemism	Plain English
1 mature	kill
2 a necktie party	dead
3 comfort station	punishment
4 a fib	prostitute
5 neutralise	public toilet
6 surveillance	bookmaker
7 casket	old
8 bring up	guts
9 deceased	poor
10 intestinal fortitude	a hanging
11 negative reinforcement	vomit
12 turf accountant	a lie
13 fallen woman	official spying
14 low-income	coffin

GETTING IT RIGHT

AMBIGUOUS SENTENCES

At times in speech and writing, the meaning of a sentence is ambiguous. That is, the sentence has a double meaning. This is often because a word or word-group occurs in the wrong place in the sentence or is missing.

Example 1

- The golfer won the tournament on his home course wearing red-checked trousers. (incorrect)
- The golfer, wearing red-checked trousers, won the tournament on his home course. (correct)

In this example, the word-group 'wearing red-checked trousers' should be placed alongside 'golfer' so that we don't finish with a confusing humorous picture of a golf course wearing red-checked trousers.

Example 2

- Looking over the fence, a sailing boat unfurled its spinnaker. (incorrect)
- Looking over the fence, we saw a sailing boat unfurl its spinnaker. (correct)

In this example, the missing words 'we saw' have been added so that it does not sound as if the boat is looking over the fence.

Removing the Ambiguity

Rewrite each of the following sentences, removing the ambiguity caused by misplaced or missing words and word-groups.

1 Walking along the road, a car almost hit Frazer.
2 The coach instructed the team to tighten their defence in an angry tone of voice.
3 The old lady went to the spot where her husband died every day.
4 Coming over the crest of the hill, a lake surrounded by trees appeared.
5 A wallet was lost by a man with keys inside.
6 The whole class visited their schoolmate who was sick after school.
7 Looking through the keyhole, a funny sight met our eyes.
8 While the boat was sinking the passengers sought safety in the clothes they wore.
9 The priest called in at the hospital where the old man was recovering sometimes.
10 The passenger finally took her seat on the plane with a red face.

DRAMA

The Broadcast

by Maureen Stewart

A dramatic radio announcement suddenly changes everything for a group of school students.

CHARACTERS

Janet | **Andrew**
Lin | **Vicky**
Phil | **Joe**
Kathy | **Voice of announcer**

Students will need to prepare a cassette before performing this play or, if this is difficult, have taped music or a record available, and have someone read the announcer's part off-stage, as though it comes from radio.

The seven students are sitting in a common room. Some are reading, some are doing assignments. Lin and Janet are playing noughts and crosses. There is music playing on a radio (off-stage).

Lin Beat you again, Janet!
Janet This is not my lucky day. Here, try again. I've got a plan this time.
Joe A plan for winning noughts and crosses! Pull the other one!
Janet Just you wait and see. *(They play again)* See! I won! Come on Lin, have another go.
Phil You two seem to spend all your free periods playing that stupid game.
Lin Well, unlike some people I could name, we've finished our assignment, Phil.
Janet That's right. Plan ahead, I always say.
Phil Anyone ever told you that you're a boring goody-goody, Janet Price?

Janet Yes, you. Lots of times. Jealousy is a curse.
Vicky Oh come on, Janet. Phil doesn't have a jealous bone in his body.
Andrew That's a dumb thing to say. Bones don't have feelings. Ever seen a happy bone?
Vicky It's a saying, Andrew. Don't take it literally.
Andrew And don't use big words.
Kathy I wish you'd all shut up! I have to finish this by last period, and I can't concentrate with you jabbering away.
Phil I'm with you, Kathy. If everyone shuts up we can listen to the music for a change.
Vicky Talk about the pot calling the kettle black . . .
Phil Who's talking about that? No-one mentioned a pot or a kettle . . .
Vicky I give up!

(There is silence for about twenty seconds. The only sound is the music from the radio. Then the music stops abruptly, and an announcer's voice is heard from the off-stage radio. As the announcer speaks, the students gradually stop what they are doing and listen intently.)

Voice We interrupt this program to bring you an urgent message. This is a high priority message. Repeat. This is a high priority message. Do not attempt to leave the place where you are now. Repeat. Stay where you are. We are in a state of total emergency, Priority One. Repeat. Total emergency, Priority One. We are in a state of nuclear war. Do not panic. Repeat, do not panic. Stay where you are. We will bring you updates of the situation as soon as possible. You are listening to ACV, the Voice of the People. Repeat. We are in a Priority One emergency situation. Stay exactly where you are until further notice. Do not panic.

(The students look at one another in stunned silence.)

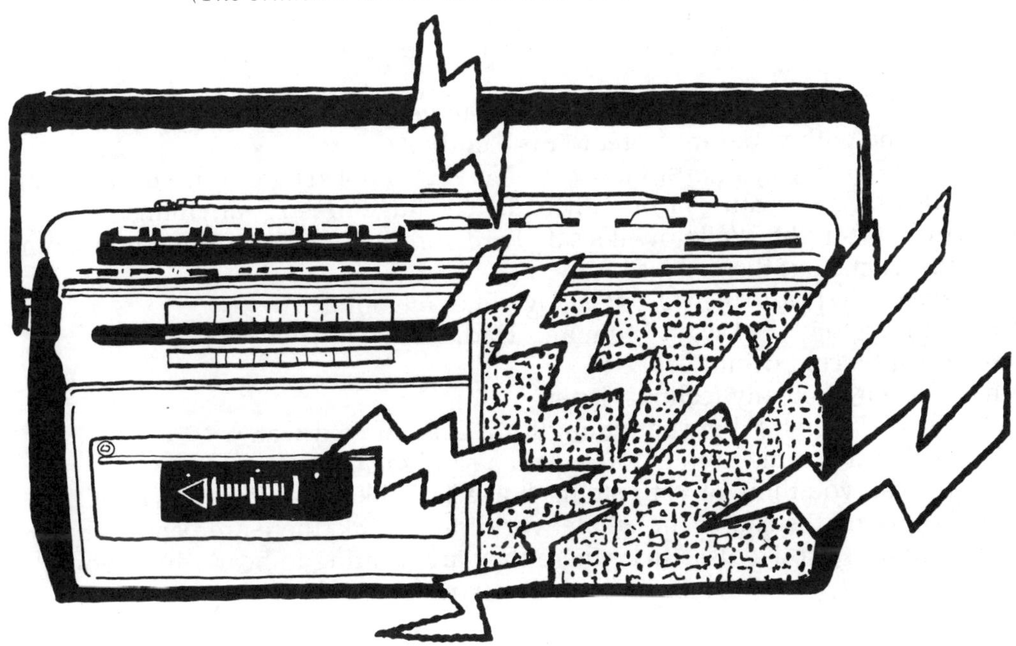

Joe It's a joke.

Phil I'm not so sure, Joe.

Vicky I think it's for real. They've never used Priority One before. Wonder if the street loudspeakers are telling everyone? Mum's doing the garden today.

Kathy Of course they'll tell everyone, Vicky. Oh I wish Mum and Dad were here. Or a teacher. Or someone.

Lin *(Rushing to the door)* I'm getting out of here!

Andrew *(Helping Janet stop Lin running away)* Sit down, Lin! You heard what he said! Stay where you are!

Janet Who knows what's out there, Lin. Stay here!

Lin But my family! I've got to warn them!

Vicky They'll know, Lin. They let everyone know when it's a high priority.

Joe It's a joke. It's got to be. We can't just stay here!

Janet We have to! You heard what he said, Joe. Just relax.

Joe *Relax* she says! What's happening at home? What's going to happen to us? To me?

Phil We don't know Joe. All we know is we have to stay here and wait.

Joe *(Loudly)* Wait? For what?

Janet Look, Joe, it will probably be all over in a few minutes.

Joe All over, you say, calmly, just like that. We'll probably be dead in a few minutes, is that what you're saying?

Janet No, I'm saying the emergency will probably be over in a few minutes, Joe, that's what I'm saying! Don't panic, for heaven's sake!

Joe Panic? Who's panicking?

Lin Me. I'm frightened. The bell should have gone by now for history . . .

Vicky Oh Lin, don't be silly. As if there are going to be normal lessons at this time!

Lin Well where is everyone? What's happening out there?

Janet That's what everyone will be asking, I bet. Come on, Lin, let's play some more noughts and crosses, hey?

Lin Oh, don't be stupid.

Vicky Janet's only trying to get your mind off things, Lin. No need to be nasty.

Andrew Vicky's right. We might as well enjoy the wait. No use thinking of the worst.

Joe Look, I don't know about you lot, but I'm getting out.

Lin I'll come with you. I must get to my family . . .

Andrew *(Standing up against the door)* No you're not. There could be anything out there. Gas, creatures from other planets, huge fires . . . anything.

Phil Andrew's right. We know it's safe here, for the time being. We know nothing about what's out there.

Joe *(Trying to get past Andrew, but failing)* Let me out!

Kathy *(Crying softly)* I want Mum and Dad.

Janet I want a cold drink.

Kathy Haven't you any feelings, Janet?

Janet I'll say. Thirst. I'd give anything for a glass of cold water.

Phil So would I, come to think of it. And a sandwich.

Lin How can you think of your stomach at a time like this? Phil, this could be the end of us all, the end of the whole world! Just think, there are people all over the country just like us, stuck where they are, waiting to hear what's going to happen next, and all you can think of is your stomach!

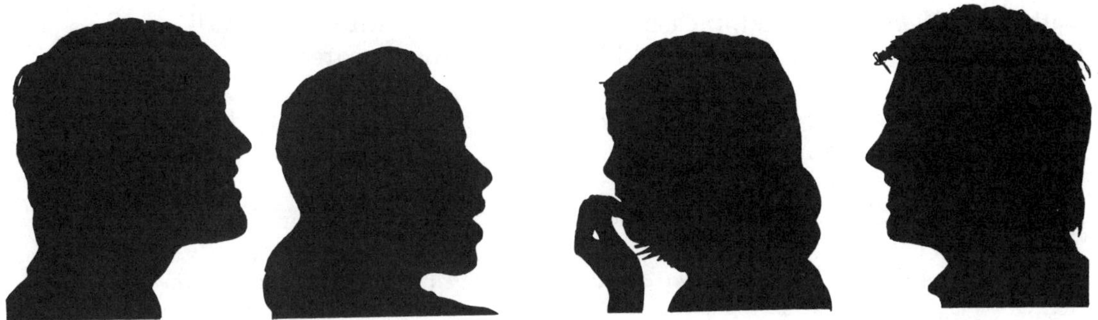

Phil Well no one else is going to think of it, that's for sure.

Joe I suppose you think you're being funny. You're not called Phil the Dill for nothing!

Phil Seeing that it's the end of the world and all that, and you're scared stiff, Joe the Crow, I'll let that one pass.

Lin 'Course he's scared! He's not stupid! We're all scared, only some of us are too scared to show it.

Kathy *(Still crying)* I'm not too scared to show it. I just want Mum and Dad. And my dog.

Janet Oh, come on, Kathy. Grow up.

Andrew She's probably not going to, that's why she's crying.

(At this Kathy starts sobbing.)

Janet That's not funny, Andrew. Come on, Kathy. We're all in the same boat you know.

Vicky At least we get to miss history.

Janet Just when I'd done my assignment, too!

(There is silence for a while, except for whimpers from Kathy. Joe and Lin look towards the door occasionally, but Andrew is standing at it.)

Phil Well, we might as well make the best of things.

Vicky You're right. Let's tell jokes.

Joe Very funny. At a time like this?

Vicky Well, I need a bit of cheering up, don't you?

Joe No. I just can't stand this waiting.

Lin *(Loudly)* Listen.

(There is a noise like static, then the announcer's voice is heard.)

Voice This is ACV, the Voice of the People. This is a high priority message. Repeat. This is a high priority message. It is known that some of you have moved. You were ordered *not* to move. It is known that some of you have panicked. You were ordered *not* to panic. Those who moved from the place where they heard that we are in a state of total emergency have been vaporised. Repeat. Those who moved have been vaporised. Do not move. We will bring you updates of the situation as soon as possible. Stay calm.

Kathy *(Sobbing)* Oh God, please save me! And save Mum and Dad!
Joe Vaporised! All my family could be dead . . . disappeared . . .
Janet Joe, you don't know that . . .
Vicky Janet, I'm scared now. Mum was doing the garden today. I bet she's moved inside or something . . .
Phil What are we going to do?
Lin I feel terrible. Andrew, what will we do?

(They all look at Andrew, who has moved away from the door.)

Andrew Don't know. Look, it might sound silly, but . . .
Lin But *what*?
Andrew How about we pray?
Vicky It can't do any harm.
Janet Or any good. If there is a God he wouldn't have let this happen.
Kathy Well I'm going to pray. *(She closes her eyes and looks at the ceiling.)* Dear God, if you can hear me, please please save Mum and Dad and me and my dog. Please. I'll be just so good if you do. I'll clean my room every week and be kind to everyone and . . .
Janet What a selfish prayer! What about us?
Kathy *(Sniffling)* Pray for yourself!
Andrew *(Bowing his head)* Dear God. Help all of us, and our families to come through this.
Janet That's more like it.
Joe Vaporised. That means sort of disappearing into thin air, doesn't it?
Andrew Yes.
Lin Oh, how can that happen? This is crazy.
Phil Wonder how they know people have been vaporised? I mean if the people at the radio station aren't moving either, how would they know?
Janet They probably can see through windows. Wish we had windows in here.
Vicky So do I. It's stuffy.
Janet Wonder how long our air will last?
Andrew I hadn't thought of that!
Kathy I wish *she* hadn't. You're just trying to make things worse, Janet.
Janet Why don't you just shut up and pray to God for some extra air just for yourself?
Kathy *(Sobbing again)* Oh you're awful! When we get out of here I'm never going to speak to you again.
Joe I feel like yelling. Maybe someone will come if I do.
Andrew How could they? They'd be vaporised.

Lin Mmmm . . . I don't know how to say this . . . *(She whispers something to Janet.)*
Janet I was thinking the same thing myself. There's just no way.
Phil What are you two whispering about?
Lin Don't tell, Janet.
Janet Well, we're all going to have the same problem sooner or later. Maybe we should talk about it so we can work out a plan . . .
Phil Not one of your plans again!
Janet Well, just wait till *you* want to . . .
Lin Janet! Please!
Vicky This is terrible. I'm thirsty. What if . . . what if we just opened the door? Just a bit?
Joe Yeah. Just a bit. We wouldn't have to move outside or anything like that.
Lin We could see what's going on . . .
Phil I wouldn't . . . what do you reckon, Andrew?
Andrew No. Let's stick to what the broadcast said. Don't you agree, Janet?
Kathy Why ask her? What about me?
Janet That's typical, Kathy. What about me. You, that's all you can think of. Maybe we should let you go out that door and check things out.
Kathy You just want me to be vaporised!
Janet You said it, not me.
Andrew Come on, this is getting us nowhere. Let's vote on it. Hands up if you want the door opened.

(Vicky, Joe and Lin raise their hands. Phil half raises his, then puts it down again.)

Andrew Well, that's settled. Three for it and four against.

(They all sit in silence for a while, except Kathy, who is mumbling prayers and crying.)

Vicky This must be a dream. *(Pinches herself)* Ow! No, it isn't.
Janet We have to get our mind off this somehow . . .
Phil You're kidding! What if this goes on all night . . . and all tomorrow . . .
Lin Oh we just *have* to do something! I've got to get out of here!
Janet I know. Let's all think of the first thing we're going to do when we get out!
Kathy That's dumb.
Andrew It passes the time.
Kathy Well the first thing I'll do is never speak to Janet Price again!
Janet *(Sarcastically)* I'm so upset.
Lin The first thing I'm doing is running home.
Vicky Same here.
Joe I think I'll go to the phone on the corner and ring Mum.
Phil I'll get a drink and a sandwich.
Janet What about you, Andrew?
Andrew I'll thank God, that's what I'll do.
Lin Janet hasn't said what she's going to do.
Janet *(Laughing)* Go to the toilet.

(They all smile except Kathy.)

Kathy That's not a nice thing to say!
Janet Well, it's something we'll have to consider if we're cooped up here much longer!
Phil Has anyone got anything to eat?
Joe Yeah. Here, a chocolate bar. *(He gets it out of his pocket.)*
Vicky I've got some chewing gum somewhere . . . *(She gets some from her pocket.)*
Kathy Can I have some chocolate bar please?
Andrew I think we ought to pool these and divide them later when we're really hungry.
Vicky You're right. *(She and Joe give their offerings to Andrew.)*
Kathy Why can't we have some now?
Janet Just wait for a few hours, Kathy, then you'll really appreciate them.
Lin Listen. *Listen!*

(There is a static-like noise, then the voice of the announcer.)

Voice Attention. This is ACV, the Voice of the People. Attention. This is the end of the state of total emergency. Repeat. There is no longer a state of total emergency. This was a test run only. Repeat. This was a test run only.

(The students sit in silence for a minute.)

Kathy I knew it all the time!
Joe What will they think of next?
Lin Shh! Listen! He hasn't finished!
Voice The test run was carried out for a number of reasons. You will hear about those in due course. But, for now, we want you to consider two things: One, if you were with others, what did you learn about those you were with at the time of the emergency? Two, and more importantly, what did you learn about yourself?

(The students look silently at each other.)

Questions

1 In this play, which student shows personality qualities that cause you to see him/her as:

- **(a)** the most practical?
- **(b)** the strongest?
- **(c)** the most selfish?
- **(d)** the most fragile?
- **(e)** the most concerned about others?

2 Which student do you most identify with? Why?

3 What is there about the radio message that convinces the students not to treat it as a joke?

4 Which of the students do you see emerging as the leader? What qualities about this person make him/her the leader in this situation?

5 Consider how differently the students handle their fear and anxiety. Identify two different approaches and give examples by quoting from the play.

6 Identify three issues that begin to emerge as major problems as the seven students contemplate being cooped up in the room for a long period of time.

7 Which student do you react most strongly against? Why?

8 Why do you think people react differently to high levels of stress such as these?

9 What do you see as the single most important issue to address in a situation such as this?

10 How do you think *you* would react in this situation?

11 How difficult would it be to stage this play? What would you do to maximise its impact?

12 What do you see as the writer's purpose for this play? How successful do you rate the play in achieving this purpose and why?

5

FILM APPRECIATION

WHY PEOPLE WATCH FILMS

Every year millions of people all over the world watch films at the cinema or on television screens in their own homes. Most popular films are produced to entertain and allow audiences to relax and escape from the pressures of everyday life. However, films can also be important sources of education and information. Teaching and training films are used in schools, universities and businesses.

Film-making is also a form of artistic expression, like writing or painting. But instead of words or paint, the camera is the means used to express the film-maker's outlook on life. Camera angles catch and emphasise important dramatic scenes. Action is often a more important means of revealing character on the screen than words.

The first films were made in the late nineteenth century. Since then, there have been rapid developments in the scope and sophistication of their settings, plots and characterisation. Today, film production is a multi-million dollar industry. Most films need special-effects equipment, many cameras, elaborate sets and hundreds of technical employees to back up the actors. The huge cost of making a film means that nearly all films must attempt to appeal to a wide public, cutting across the boundaries of education and social standing and giving a democratic flavour to this mass entertainment industry.

HOW FILMS ARE CLASSIFIED

Films that possess similarities in style and content are said to belong to the same **genre**. For example, an audience expects at least a gunfight and probably a stage-coach chase to occur whenever a Western movie is shown, and so most films that possess such features belong to the Western genre or category. Films that show battle scenes and tell stories of military heroism belong to the War genre.

Matching Genres and Films

On the left are some of the main genres used to classify films. See if you can match up famous films from the list on the right with each of the genres.

Genres	**Films**
Crime/police	*Gallipoli*
Comedy	*High Noon*
Historical epic	*Lethal Weapon*
Horror	*Lonely Hearts*
Musical	*Crocodile Dundee*
Romance	*Puberty Blues*
Science fiction	*The Exorcist*
Sport	*The Sound of Music*
War	*Gone with the Wind*
Western	*Star Wars*
Youth	*Phar Lap*

HOW FILMS ARE CONSTRUCTED

A film is a story in pictures and, like any story, a film must have characters, scenes, settings and a storyline or plot. As film actors portray a character they use gestures, facial expressions, body language and voice to persuade the audience that the scenes unfolding on the screen are convincingly real. Camera angles such as distant shots, close-ups of faces and wide views of scenery have become meaningful to cinema-going audiences who expect each change of camera angle to reveal new aspects of drama and emotion. For example, zooming in on an actor's face brings an emotion such as fear into sharp focus and causes it to dominate the screen. Because close-ups reveal the details of the gestures and expressions accompanying every piece of dialogue, film actors need to concentrate on every movement they make to ensure it is true to the personality of the character they are portraying.

CHARACTER

Here are two actors portraying a tough stockman and an old timer in a scene from the film *The Man from Snowy River*. Look carefully at their facial expressions. What emotion or feeling does each man's face portray?

SETTING

The setting or scenery dominates this picture taken during the filming of *The Man from Snowy River*. How would you describe this film's setting?

ACTION AND PLOT

Action is the essential ingredient that keeps the plot unfolding in a film. What action is going on in this scene from *The Man from Snowy River*?

SCENE STRUCTURE

The screenplay or story of a film is made up of numerous scenes, with each scene moving the story forward one more step. Each scene is responsible for presenting a single action filmed with the cameras holding one angle. Every time the camera angles change a new scene begins. A single piece of dramatic action forms a scene.

Each scene must have a setting or a place where the action takes place. If the scene is to be filmed indoors, the letters INT (meaning 'interior') are placed in the script. If the scene is to be shot outdoors, the letters EXT (meaning 'exterior') are used. As well as place, the time when the action happens in a scene must be known. Is it day or night, morning or afternoon? For example:

EXT. SCHOOL STEPS. DAY, *or*
INT. KITCHEN. NIGHT

Scenes can be made up of characters speaking (dialogue). However, most scenes contain a mixture of action and dialogue. The following scene from a film script will clarify a number of the points we have been discussing.

The film *Breaker Morant* deals with the experiences of Harry Morant, soldier, horseman and poet, in the Boer War. He was arrested and accused, together with Peter Handcock, a fellow soldier, of murdering Boer civilians. As the scene begins, Major Thomas, who commands the escort party, walks into the condemned cell to take Harry and Peter outside to be executed.

Breaker Morant

MORANT'S CELL. INT. DAWN

MORANT *looks up as the door opens. The* ESCORT PARTY OF HIGHLANDERS *is waiting.* THOMAS *walks into the cell.* MORANT *picks up his last letters.*

MORANT: Cheer up. You look like you're going to a funeral.

THOMAS: Harry . . .

MORANT: Don't worry about it, Major. It's been a good run. There's nothing for me in England any more and . . . back in Australia . . . well they say you've had it when you need a couple of brandies before you can get up on a wild horse.

(MORANT *gives* THOMAS *the letters.*)

MORANT: See these get sent for me, will you? One to my mother in Hampshire, one to my girl in Devon.

(THOMAS *waits.* MORANT *hands him the sheet of verse.*)

And see this little effort gets published, eh? We poets do crave immortality.

(Their eyes meet. They shake hands.)

MORANT *steps outside, with the* ESCORT PARTY. THOMAS *remains in the cell.*

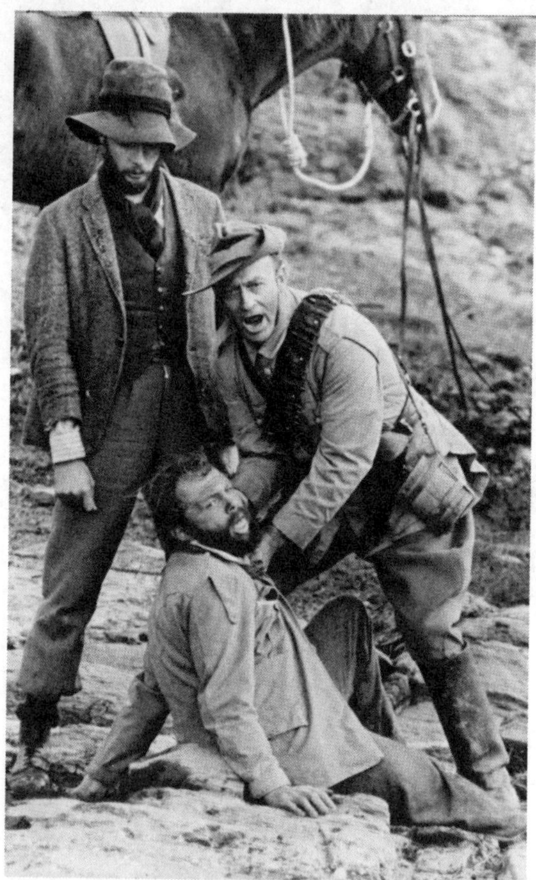

A scene from the film *Breaker Morant*

Questions

1 What is the scene's setting?

2 How are place and time indicated in the script?

3 What movements begin the scene?

4 What does Morant reveal about his character in this scene?

5 How are action and dialogue mixed in this scene?

6 What does this scene reveal about the relationship between Thomas and Morant?

AN ACADEMY AWARD WINNING FILM

Now let's look at another example of screenplay. This time it is a long sequence from the film *My Left Foot*. This film portrays the life of Christy Brown, who was born with brain damage. After much suffering he overcame the great disability of not being able to communicate by learning to use his left foot as a means of writing and painting. He managed this with such success that later in his life he became a famous writer and painter.

In this sequence, Christy uses his left foot to communicate with members of his family for the first time. It is a wonderful moment for Christy and for his family.

My Left Foot

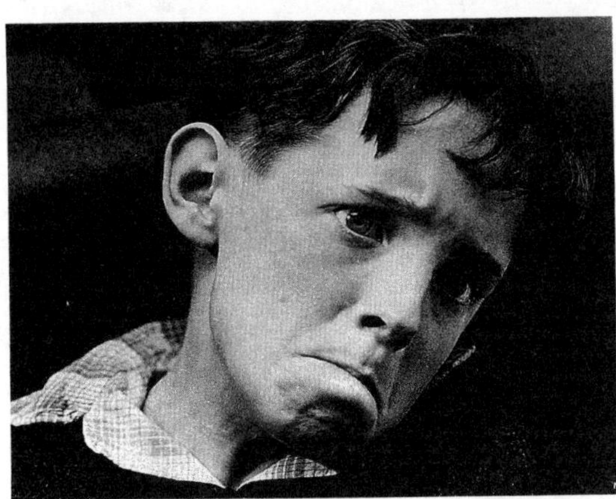

INT. CHRISTY'S HOUSE. NIGHT

Everybody is sitting around. MR BROWN *is sitting reading the paper in bad humour. The children are doing their homework.* CHRISTY *is sitting there with the chalk between his toes. He has drawn a straight line. Hold on:* CHRISTY'*s foot as he makes another line at a 45-degree angle to the first.*

SHEILA: Look at Christy, Mammy. He's making a triangle.

(CHRISTY *finishes the line, looks at everybody looking at him and then raises his foot to finish the figure. He starts halfway up one of the lines.)*

MR BROWN: He's starting in the wrong place.

(CHRISTY *tries to join the two lines together, but his foot gives up and it ends in a squiggle. Then* MR BROWN *takes the chalk in his hand. He draws a triangle.)*

Look, Christy, that's a triangle.

(CHRISTY *looks at him furiously. Rubs out his father's line.)*

MRS BROWN: It's not a triangle, it's an A.

(CHRISTY *grunts a deep strong grunt of acknowledgement. There is something primitive and territorial about it. It is his first articulation in the film. The father eyes him warily, sits back and looks at* MRS BROWN. *All the kids are watching* CHRISTY. *Tom comes through the door.)*

TOM: What's up?

MR BROWN: Keep quiet.

TOM *(Slight threat)* All I said was 'What's up?'

MR BROWN: And all I said was 'Keep quiet.'

(He starts to take off his belt.)

TOM: *(Standing)* All I said was . . .

(The father lets out a primal roar.)

MR BROWN: Sit down.

(TOM *sits, mesmerised and slightly embarrassed. Close on:* CHRISTY *as he watches the tribal war.* MRS BROWN *rushes from the room and comes back with some money in her hand.)*

MRS BROWN: Here.

MR BROWN: What's that?

MRS BROWN: Money. Go and have a drink.

MR BROWN: Where did you get it?

MRS BROWN: From the fairies. Go and get a drink for yourself.

MR BROWN: I don't need a drink. I just need to be obeyed in my own home.

(CHRISTY *has picked up the chalk again and is drawing on the floor again. They all watch him. He again draws the beginning of a triangle or an A. He stops when he completes two sides.)*

MRS BROWN: Go on, Christy.

(CHRISTY *starts at the outside of the second line and draws another line back up at an angle of 45 degrees.*)

SHARON: He's drawing another triangle.

(CHRISTY *finishes the line. They all watch him.*)

MRS BROWN: That's an M.

(*Another deep primitive grunt from* CHRISTY. *He immediately starts on another letter. Close on: his face, and you would think he was having a baby as the sweat stands out on his brow. He draws a curious half-moon and then goes on to make a primitive O.*)

O.

(*Nobody is able to talk. All have been dumbstruck by* CHRISTY. *He continues drawing on the floor and there is a magical effect to the lettering, almost as if he were discovering the letters, as if they were his own shapes newly thought up, a strange alphabet springing from a deep urge to communicate. He makes the T.* MR BROWN *is transfixed and mouths the word* MOT. CHRISTY *continues on and does the letter H. All the children during the time* CHRISTY *is drawing have edged towards the mother. Involuntarily the younger ones have put their arms around her legs.* MR BROWN *stands alone, unaware in the drama that he has become isolated. When* CHRISTY *draws the E, one of the kids says 'Mother', but* MRS BROWN *stops her with a raised finger, afraid that any break in the silence will destroy the magic. The perspiration on* CHRISTY'S *brow is translucent. He continues drawing the R with a maniacal energy. When he finishes he looks at the father, defiance, anger and ten years' frustration released in a minute.* MR BROWN *is stunned;* MRS BROWN *and all the children wait on his reaction.* MRS BROWN *appears calm and assured, an interior knowledge made flesh.*)

MR BROWN: Good Jesus, holy Jesus, suffering Jesus. (*Picks* CHRISTY *up.*) You're a Brown all right.

Christy's a Brown. (*Holds him aloft like a chalice.*)

Christy Brown. Give me that money, woman.

(MRS BROWN *gives him the money.*)

EXT. STREET. NIGHT

MR BROWN *carries* CHRISTY *out on to the street, followed by* TOM *and* BENNY, *his two eldest sons. Doors start to open and windows are pulled back to see what's going on.* MR BROWN *stands silhouetted in the glow of a lamp.*

MR BROWN: This is Christy Brown. My son. Genius.

(*He walks on.*)

INT. PUB. NIGHT

MR BROWN *walks into the pub and plonks* CHRISTY *down on the bar.*

MR BROWN: Give this man a drink.

(*The barman pulls a pint for the father and gives* CHRISTY *a 7-Up.*)

Straw.

(*The barman produces a straw and the crowd gathers round to watch* CHRISTY. *He watches them and then bangs his foot on the table. The father doesn't know what he wants.*)

MAN: He wants the pint.

(MR BROWN *puts the straw in the pint and* CHRISTY *drinks. It tastes awful. The crowd laugh.* CHRISTY *watches, furious, and then he gets his head down to the straw and takes a sizeable sup. The crowd all applaud him.* CHRISTY *beams and bangs the table with his foot. He is part of the man's world at last.*)

MR BROWN: There's nothing wrong with this fellow.

from *My Left Foot*, by Shane Connaughton and Jim Sheridan

Questions on the Screenplay

1 As the sequence opens, what is the setting indicated for the camera?

2 What camera direction emphasises the way in which Christy is trying to communicate?

3 How do we learn of Christy's deeply felt need to communicate without assistance?

4 How does Christy's mother react to her son's attempts to write the word 'mother' with his left foot?

5 How does the camera focus on the emotional effort Christy is making to communicate?

6 How does Mr Brown react to his son's success in writing the word 'mother'?

7 How are two settings outside the Brown's house indicated to the camera?

8 How does Christy show that he is 'part of the man's world at last'?

9 What kind of conflict occurs in this sequence?

10 What is the climax of this sequence?

11 Why is the ending satisfying?

12 Think of your own title for this sequence.

NOVEL AND SCREENPLAY

A novel often provides the inspiration for a film script. Film producers are always on the look out for novels that can be made into films. Often enormous fees are paid for the film rights of a novel. Of course, sometimes successful film scripts are turned into novels.

On the following pages you will find a passage from the novel *Gallipoli* and the corresponding film script. Note that the setting is the battleground at Gallipoli where the Australians are fighting the Turks in the First World War. The scene takes place at just the moment when Australian soldiers are about to climb from their trenches and make a futile attack on entrenched Turkish forces.

In the book and the film, Major Barton is the commanding officer. Archy and Frank are two soldiers who are firm friends. In civilian life Archy and Frank were superb sprinters who competed against each other. In fact, Archy won the famous Kimberley Gift Race. In the scenes that follow, Archy is about to participate in an attack on the Turks, just as Frank races to bring the news that the attack has been cancelled. Once again, Archy wins his race but it is his last.

Read and compare the novel passage with the screenplay. The questions that follow the extracts will guide you in making your comparison.

Gallipoli — The Novel

'We're going, lads,' he said. 'I know every one of you will do your utmost. Good luck to you all, and God bless you.' He turned away and grasped the climbing peg.

Archy slowly took off his Kimberley Gift medal and hung it from one of the climbing pegs. As though in a dream he seemed to hear Uncle Jack's voice again, to see the pepper trees behind the house, the cockatoos in white clouds at sunset, to hear the thunder of rain on the corrugated iron roof. Pictures ran across his mind's eye, fast as summer lightning: Billy Snakeskin. Zac. Stumpy and the camel. Mary Stanton. Frank learning to ride. The images flickered and ran together and he heard himself saying softly: 'What are your legs, boy? *Springs. Steel springs.* And what are they going to do, boy? *Hurl me down the track.* How fast can you run, boy?' Tears rained from his eyes and pattered on the bloody dust of the trench floor. 'How fast can you run, boy? *Fast as a leopard!* Then let's see you do it!'

The silver whistle shrilled.

Archy was over the parapet and among the dead. For a second it was breathlessly still: cordite smoke from the Turkish guns eddied among the bodies.

Then the gunfire crashed around him. He ran as he had never run before, head high, rifle forgotten. He was alone, at the head of the field. 'How fast can you run, boy? *Like a leopard!*'

He was still running with head high, his eyes half-closed, when the nearest Maxim gun team clipped a fresh belt into their weapon, and Archy fell with a roaring in his ears. Lieutenant Gray, on the firestep, turned irritably as someone seized him by the arm.

'Dunne!'

Frank sank to the floor of the trench, 'It's cancelled! General Gardner's Orders!' Then he screamed a long cry of anger and rage and was violently sick. Lieutenant Gray slowly holstered his revolver. He looked at the dead and the dying in the trench and the bloody debris in no-man's-land.

'My God,' he said. 'My God.'

Something winked in the early sunlight. Frank looked at it dully, uncomprehending. Then he recognised it, as it twirled on its watered silk ribbon, catching the sun. Archy's Kimberley Gift medal.

from *Gallipoli* by Jack Bennett

Gallipoli — The Screenplay

BARTON:

All right, men, we're going.

(pause)

I want you all to remember who you are . . .

Two soldiers embrace.

BARTON:

. . . You're the Tenth Light Horse. Men from Western Australia. Don't forget it. Good luck.

SOLDIER *(to Barton):*

Good luck, sir.

BARTON:

You too.

One soldier removes the wedding ring from his finger and places it on the handle of his bayonet. Another writes a letter in haste. Another plunges his bayonet into the sandbags of the trench and places his watch around it. One bayonet, stuck into the sandbags, holds a letter addressed to Mr Wallace Hamilton, and the Kimberley Gift medal hangs by its ribbon on the bayonet. Archy takes deep breaths in preparation for the attack in the same way as he prepared for his races.

Frank is still racing. He is driving his body to its limits. Time is running out.

The rifles are in position. Men are quietly mumbling last prayers.

VOICE:

Though I walk through the valley of the shadow of death, I shall fear nothing . . .

Frank fights his way past a couple of donkeys on the hillside of Anzac Cove.

Archy's last race, from the film *Gallipoli*

Archy, in the trench, begins psyching himself for the attack.

ARCHY:

What are your legs?
Springs. Steel springs.
What are they going to do?
They're going to hurl me down the track.
How fast can you run?
As fast as a leopard.
How fast are you going to run?
(loudly)
As fast as a leopard.
Then let's see you do it.

The men prepare to move out.

In the support trench, Frank furiously pushes his way through.

FRANK

Gangway! Gangway! Gangway!
Urgent message.

Major Barton cocks his revolver and raises the gun over his head to give the signal. Lt Gray places his whistle in his mouth. Frank desperately makes his way through the trench. He is so close.

FRANK:

Gangway!

The whistle blows. Frank is too late.

Archy heads up and over. The men yell as they go over the top. They advance across no-man's-land and are cut down.

Frank screams in anguish. He is too late.

FRANK:

Aghhh.

Archy, running across no-man's-land, drives his muscles to the utmost of their capacity. He has dropped his rifle and is sprinting his last race. Inevitably he is hit by a machine gun blast but it appears as though he has just breasted an invisible tape.

from *Gallipoli: The Screenplay* by David Williamson

Gallipoli Questions — Novel and Screenplay

1 Why do you think the screenplay leaves out the sounds from his past that Archy hears as he takes off his Kimberley medal?

2 As Archy prepares to fight, Frank races to bring the news that the attack has been cancelled. How does the screenplay differ from the novel in its treatment of Frank's race?

3 In the trench, Archy psyches himself up for the attack. Why do you think the screenplay is like the novel in its treatment of Archy's moment of personal crisis?

4 'Action is the life blood of a film.' How does the screenplay stress the action as Frank arrives at the trench too late to save Archy?

5 The novel and the screenplay end very differently. Why do you think the screenplay chose the ending of Archy running across no-man's-land rather than ending with the Kimberley Gift medal catching the sun?

WRITING A SCREENPLAY FROM A NOVEL

Below is a passage from the novel *All The Green Year* by Don Charlwood. Read the passage carefully with the aim of turning it into a piece of screenplay. The three characters in the passage are teenage boys. One of them, Johnno, has spent the haircut money his father gave him on going to the pictures. However, his mate Squid swears that he knows how to cut hair and goes to work enthusiastically with a pair of clippers. Begin your screenplay in this way:

> INT. A SPACE UNDER SQUID'S HOUSE. DUSK
> SQUID *flourishes clippers and a towel.* JOHNNO *is seated on a decrepit chair under a light. He looks apprehensive.*
>
> SQUID: What style d' y' want it done?

If you are in doubt about how to proceed as you write your screenplay from the novel, look back at the scripts from *My Left Foot* or *Gallipoli.*

The Haircut

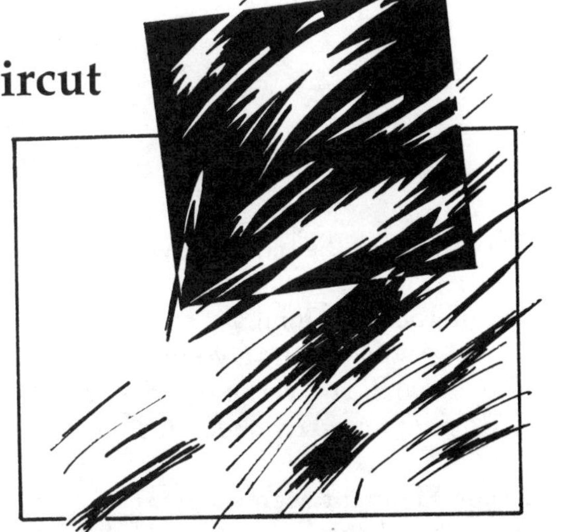

Squid came back with the clippers and a towel. 'What style d' y' want it done?'

'Oh hell!' Johnno burst out. 'Do it the same way it's always done.'

Squid pulled one of the decrepit chairs under the light and waved Johnno into it. Johnno glanced at us as if he were a victim for electrocution. He sank into it and Squid tucked in the towel.

'Been wet, don't you reckon, sir?'

'For gawd's sake just hurry!' begged Johnno.

He had his head bowed and Squid was ploughing an experimental furrow. Certainly he seemed to have the art, even to the flourishes of the clippers. 'Nothink to it,' he murmured.

It was when he went over the furrow a second time that my heart faltered. It was so deep now that I knew there would by no way of fixing it. It was no use saying anything. I sank into a chair and looked at the ground between my feet, hardly able to bear what was happening.

I don't think Squid realised what he had done till three or four furrows lay side by side and a heap of ginger hair was scattered on the ground.

'Trouble is,' he said, standing back, 'trouble is you've had it the wrong style before.'

'Just leave it the way it was,' said Johnno distractedly.

It was too late for this. Squid began examining Johnno's head more frequently. After each examination he gave a clip here and and a clip there. Johnno was beginning to look like a parrot with a large crest.

'Well,' said Squid a little uneasily. 'I reckon a bit off the front will about fix it.'

He took out the scissors and clicked them a few times in the air and held the comb with one finger nicely raised. I turned away again and looked at the bag walls and began wishing we had never met Johnno at all. Next time I looked I could hardly believe it was Johnno's head. Squid had fixed it, all right. In fact he himself was standing back with his mouth open.

'Is it finished?'

'Well,' said Squid, recovering himself, 'it needs a sort of — smoothing over, that's about it.'

Johnno ran his hand over it. 'Oh gawd,' he cried, 'it's all up and down!' He turned to me desperately. 'Charlie, it's hacked about, isn't it?'

I felt half sick for him. 'A bit,' I admitted, 'but not too bad —'

'Will my old man notice it?'

'No,' said Squid hurriedly.

'But Charlie, do *you* reckon he'll notice it?'

I was casting about for an answer when we heard Mrs Peters coming into the house. Squid said urgently, 'We better go up and you better go, Johnno.'

'I'm clearing out, all right,' said Johnno, feeling his head again. 'I — I don't know what the hell to do.'

From upstairs Mrs Peters cried, 'Bird-ie.'

'Just getting the wood,' yelled Squid.

Outside it was dusk and fog was rising over the sea. Through the trees I could see the lights at 'Thermopylae', yellow-looking in the damp air.

'I'll be late home, too,' said Johnno hoarsely.

'It's only a quarter to six,' I told him.

'Ah, well,' he said resignedly. 'So long.'

'So long,' I said.

But Squid said nothing.

from *All the Green Year* by Don Charlwood

WRITING YOUR OWN FILM SCRIPT

Choose one of the plots below and, using your imagination, write your own screenplay.

1 Hobgoblins (Comedy/thriller)
At a big movie studio a young guard opens a locked vault and out pour the hobgoblins. They have the power of being able to tap into the human mind and force their victims to do anything the hobgoblins wish.

2 The Elephant Man (Drama)
A terribly deformed but highly intelligent man is displayed as a freak at side shows. His life is one of ridicule and fear as some of his viewers attempt to exploit his deformity even further by removing the mask he must wear. He is at last rescued by a kindly doctor.

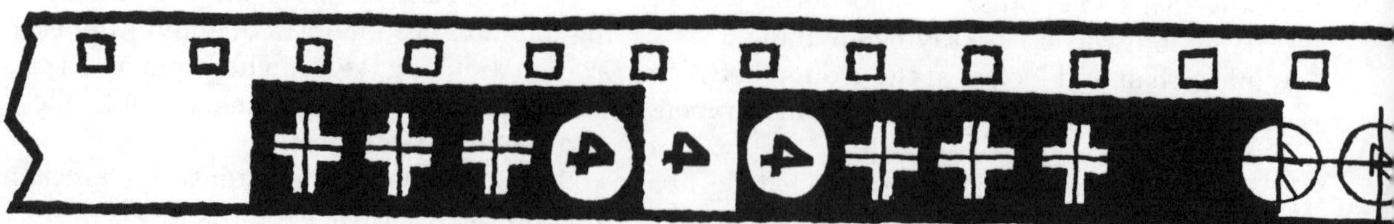

3 Lord of the Flies (Thriller)
After a plane crash a group of school boys are left alone on a deserted tropical island. Most of the boys become savages in a society where only might is right.

4 The Girl I Want (Comedy)
An intelligent schoolgirl called Amy sets out to attract her dream boy, who is the school's most popular football player, by changing her intellectual image. However, while she implements her plan the football star decides to change his image to attract an intellectual type of girl, namely Amy.

5 Predator (Thriller)
A commando team is hired by the US government for a rescue mission in the South American jungle. Their leader is the muscular Schwarzenegger. The rescue team is stalked by an other-world predator!

6 Tunnels (Thriller)
In the ancient underground sewers of the city, a subterranean creature controls a group of slaves. Pam and Sharon descend and the trouble begins.

7 The Wonder Years (Comedy)
A teenager gets his first pimple a few days before family friends visit with their beautiful daughter. The teenage boy tries every pimple cure he can find.

8 Goddess of Love (Comedy)
A statue of the goddess Venus comes alive after a young man slips a ring on her finger as a joke. The problem is that he was just about to get married to a real young woman. Now he has to juggle the two.

9 Big (Comedy)
A 12-year-old boy who makes a wish to be BIG finds that he is suddenly changed into a 35-year-old man. Problems arise when he becomes a businessman and falls in love with his female boss.

10 Ghost (Comedy/thriller)
A ghost desperately tries to communicate with his live girlfriend without frightening her to death. The ghost conceives the idea of employing a reluctant messenger as a go-between.

DESIGNING YOUR OWN FILM POSTER

A popular way of advertising a film is the poster. A poster is always designed to attract the film-goer so its impact must be immediate and unforgettable. As well as the dramatic visual image it presents, a poster must suggest the film's story in a few well-chosen words. It must also name the stars and the producers.

All these features of a successful film poster are present in the *Young Einstein* poster opposite. Study it carefully, then design your own poster for a real or imagined film.

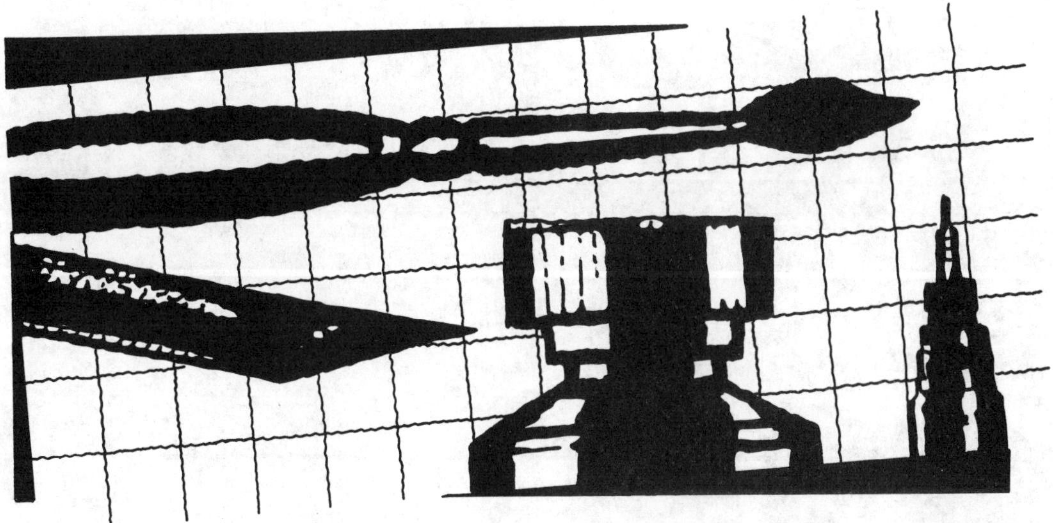

6

PLANET EARTH

NOVELS

The Killing

In a powerful description Jeremy Lucas takes us into the world of a family of killer whales as they experience tragedy.

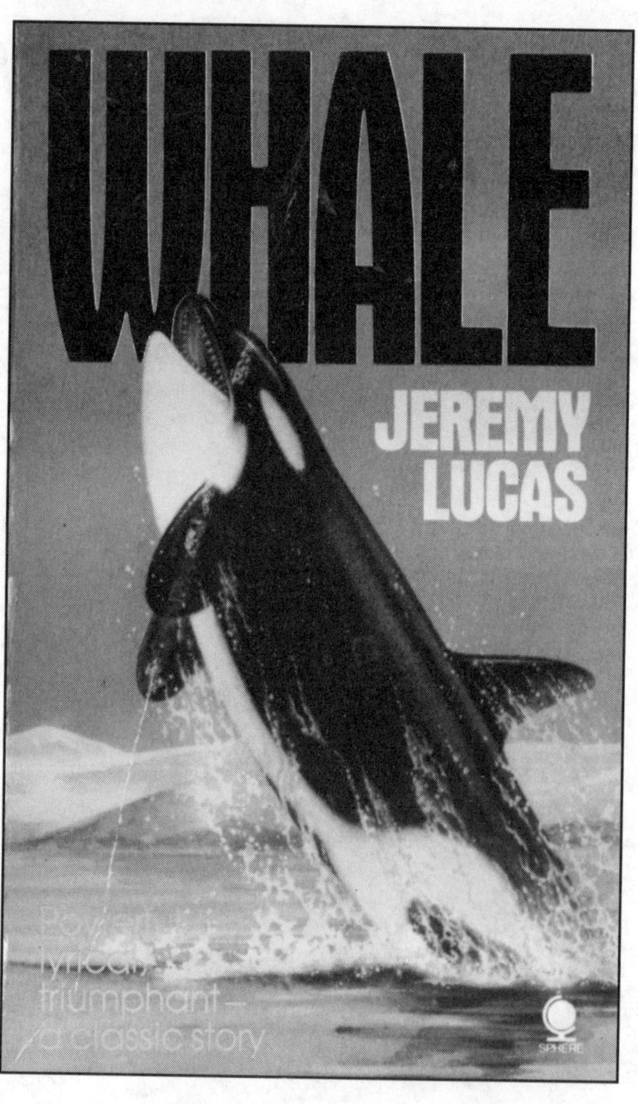

The moment he had planned, the moment he had hoped for. Now it was here it was somehow unreal, impossible. He lifted the gun very slowly. It was a heavy, old gun, a 0.44 calibre that had been used for stags back in his mainland days. He stared along the sights as another wave washed gently over Orion's back. Like a stationary submarine the whale just wallowed in the swell. And then he started forward, and in that movement his back nudged above the surface. Orion, in a carefree glow of triumph after the intense joy of his kill, began to turn. The man's finger closed over the trigger as he watched the dark shape inch over the sand. He could see every detail in the now clear water, even the white splash behind the whale's eye.

The huge rounded flippers wafted gently to and fro. Quietly the immense dorsal lifted high above the waves, followed by the back and the smooth round head; and then even the white splash poked above the surface.

The brief, trigger-squeezing moment changed everything. The rifle's crash was stunning in its intensity: an alien, evil sound in a peaceful Hebridean isle.

The seals on the beach kicked up sand in their panic. Many rushed for the sea, ignoring the threat of the killer whale. Others repeatedly circled their calves, barking insistently and continuously, not knowing what to do, not understanding this new threat. The gulls again rose screaming into the air. A falcon, making a plummeting dive on a rock-dove over the moor, suddenly met the shock wave, broke off his attack, and fled for the sanctuary of his eyrie in the cliffs not far away.

A surge of water had been passing over Orion's back as the bullet struck. A column of white shot into the air, but the water was a flimsy shield. It was not enough. The bullet slammed and exploded in the the whale's neck, boring through the blubber as if it did not exist. Then two vertebrae splintered. The fragments of bone and lead tore through the upper part of his body, causing agony in their travel. Some pierced a lung, and the pain flooded uncontrollably over his entire body.

He jerked convulsively, tail flukes lashing for the very last time above the waves. Releasing the air he had taken in on his last blow in one long, drawn-out submarine scream, blood and air rushed from his blow hole, and foamed obscenely on the surface. He kicked twice, and then again, as he moved weakly away from the beach towards the open sea, leaving behind him a plume of blood like dark smoke hanging in the air; Orion's life-blood welling out into the ocean, leaving a streak like a scar on the face of the deep.

He managed to reach the surface, and made an agonised rasping noise that was a pitiful gasp for air, while the nausea swept through him. Air bubbled and foamed from both his blow hole and the wound. He kicked and bucked. Helpless in the confusion, the shock and the pain, he rolled in the disgustingly crimson sea all around him. He sank, spinning and twisting, choking and drowning in his own blood.

Sabre and his mother were half a mile off the beach when the bullet struck. They heard the thud of the impact followed by the terrifying scream. They both burst into a pulsing swim towards Orion, totally oblivious to any danger that must lie with him. They knew only that he was in terrible pain, that he needed them. By the time they reached Orion he was bumping on the sea-bed, enveloped in a large cloud of blood still billowing from the wound.

The big bull was twice their size, but between them they lifted him towards the surface, turned him, and forced his back above the waves. He drew a hoarse weak breath and wallowed uselessly in the water, his great dorsal slapping the waves as it rolled drunkenly from side to side.

In his own state of shock the crofter stared at the scene unfolding before him. It was all outside his previous experience: some nightmare that just could not be real. He dropped the gun and it fell unnoticed on to the rocks. How could it happen? Deer and rabbits would bolt from their stricken comrades. Why should Grampus behave like this? How could a beast that killed like the whale act like this? Even as the first blood rose to the surface, and Orion screamed, the man saw the two shadows streaking towards the beach. Why didn't they go? Why must it be like this? The killer whale rolling helplessly out there, with his family struggling to keep him on the surface and push him to safety.

While the white-hot agony burnt along Orion's spine, Sabre and Nightshadow fought for his life, and the crofter willed him to die. But the big whale would not die yet. It would be several hours of energy-sapping agony before the wound took him: several hours while Orion swam his last pain-filled miles, fighting a battle that he could only lose. Hours, while Sabre and his frantic mother exhausted themselves for the dying whale.

Orion rolled over revealing a belly that was no longer white, but rose-tinted with his own blood. As he was rolled upright his bent dorsal swept above the surface, carrying water which sprayed in a vermilion fan into the waves.

The crofter swung around and stumbled off; unseeing; horrified; utterly shocked. The blanket fell from his shoulders. He never returned for his possessions, and they were carried away by the tide, the gun smashed by the waves against the weed-flecked stones.

Slowly the beach returned to normal. The seals settled, and the gulls began their scavenging day. Once again the falcon's shadow flicked, fork-winged, across the moor. Soon the animals of the island's shore had forgotten the shocking dawn, and to remind them there was only an ugly red stain running out to sea.

For the whales, however, the horror was far from over. Sabre and his mother pushed the bull slowly away from the beach towards the sanctuary and peace of deep water. Orion was helpless, and they knew that he would die. His once powerful flukes hung limp and useless. He had barely enough energy to breathe, and occasionally he sobbed a long weak moan from somewhere deep inside. And sometimes, when they nudged him a little too hard in their struggles to support him, the pain would shake his entire body, and he would scream, and the she-whale would cry to him.

Throughout the day his family kept Orion on the surface, pushing him gently to the west. He grew weaker by the hour, while his wound bled less freely. As the sun set in their path, the stricken whale took a last compulsive breath, gave a short cry of good-bye, and all agony drifted away with his life. They released him then, and watched the great whale, pink belly upwards, fall on his last journey to the sea floor. And when the darkness had swallowed him up they swam off into the dusk.

The red stain off Seal Island was gone by morning. With it had disappeared the fear the animals had known for the previous few days. For the seals there was no longer terror at the sight of the huge black fin cutting towards one of their comrades.

from *Whale* by Jeremy Lucas

Reading for Understanding

1 What was the killer whale doing at the start of the passage?
2 What emotions is Orion experiencing at the beginning of this passage and why is he experiencing this?
3 What damage did the bullet cause in Orion's body?
4 Where does Orion head after being shot?
5 What evidence is there that the bullet is already having its effect as the killer whale moves out to sea?
6 What is the immediate reaction of the other killer whales when they hear Orion's scream?
7 What did Sabre and Nightshadow do for Orion when they reached him? Why was this difficult?
8 Why is the crofter shocked by the actions of Orion's family?
9 Why doesn't the crofter return for his possessions? What is it that has so overwhelmed him?
10 As the animals on the island return to normal, what is the only reminder of the dawn tragedy?
11 What causes Orion to scream occasionally as he is pushed out to deep water?
12 Why is Orion's death, in some respects, a relief to him?
13 What qualities of character are shown by the whale family in their care for Orion?
14 What techniques has the writer used to make this passage more personal and effective?
15 What emotions did you experience as you read this extract?
16 How successful would you rate this passage in terms of the author's purpose? Why?

Firestorm

In forest country, a man flees for his life in front of a raging forest fire.

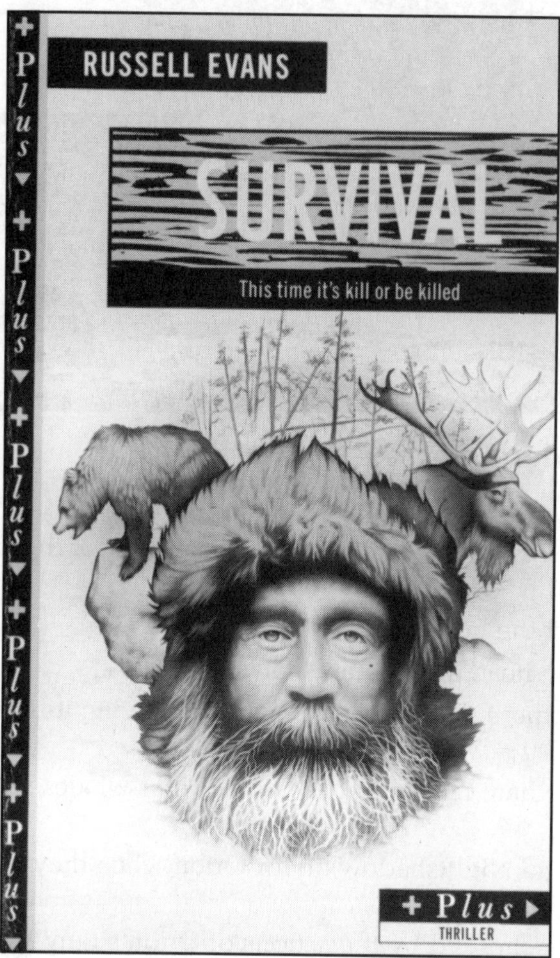

The smoke was coming from the west, driven on a brisk breeze, and he turned sideways to it to listen. 'It'll be like thunder,' Rogojin had told him. 'Like no noise you've ever heard.'

It was more like a continuous roll of explosions, more like those massive artillery barrages Ivanov had read about.

He scrambled up a spruce and gasped at what he saw. The western skyline, in a wide arc from north to south, was hidden under a thick bank of smoke which glowed a fiery red, fanned by the wind into a pulsating furnace which was sweeping towards him at an alarming pace.

With frantic speed he packed his haversack and set off east at a steady lope, his one thought to reach the river, some twelve miles away. Narrow as it was, the river provided the only break in the forest which might serve as a barrier to the flames.

Ivanov maintained a breath-rasping pace,

stopping only to listen for the thunder of the fire behind him. He had no time now to climb a tree to look back: the wind had risen and streamers of smoke eddying past convinced him he was losing ground.

He was now conscious, for the first time since being in the taiga, of animal life around him. He saw nothing at first, only heard the creak and rustle of creatures making their way, like him, at speed through the woods. But as the smoke increased and the roaring of the fire cut out all the other sounds, he caught a glimpse of a bear ahead of him.

He thought to change direction slightly, but at that moment a lynx bounded across his path, its teeth bared in a fixed snarl of fear. It didn't give him so much as a passing glance, and he realised he need not worry about the bear. No animal had a mind for anything but escape from the awesome fury of the fire.

He was running now, weaving in and out of the trees, taking direction from the moving canopy of smoke which blotted out the sky above him. He tried to avoid thickets and overgrown clearings, but again and again he stumbled into them and found himself scrambling over toppled tree trunks and through tangled copses of young birch.

His breath was coming in shuddering gasps and he had little control over his legs, which felt heavy as lead, calf and thigh muscles twitching spasmodically. The fire could now be felt in the wind, like a hot blanket on his back, and he was bathed in sweat, which filled his eyes and blurred his vision.

He tried to leap over a fallen tree, but his legs buckled under him, and as he fell to the ground he took in a lungful of smoke which doubled him up in a paroxysm of coughing. He struggled to his feet to avoid the smoke swirling at knee level and fought to control his coughing, gulping for air with the strident rasping of a drowning man.

As soon as he could breathe again he wiped the sweat from his face with his sleeve and looked round him. The woods had been darkened by the pall of smoke overhead, but he could see clearly enough to observe how the smoke at knee level moved in scattered spurts, spreading upwards to meet the smoke overhead. In between were pockets clear of smoke.

Telling himself to stop charging through the woods like a panicking bear, Ivanov walked swiftly from one clear patch to another, muffling his face with his sleeve where the smoke rose above his head. At first he made steady progress due east, but then he found that in following the smokeless pockets he was travelling almost parallel with the fire.

Fighting an impulse to run, he stopped and faced east — towards the river. A warm current of air swirled past him, and for a joyous moment he thought the wind had swung round, was now blowing against the fire. But then the horrifying truth made him stagger forward in a lurching trot. He was in the fire draught, on the edge of the dread hurricane which sucked all before it into the maw of the furnace.

The thunder of the blaze seemed all round

him now, and the forest was bathed in an eerie red light, yet he saw no flames. The hot breeze blowing against him became a wind, bending the trees, searing his lungs. He knew he had only moments now before his agony was ended, and he determined to keep moving, to die on his feet.

Suddenly he was falling, tumbling head over heels down a steep bank to find himself sitting in water. 'The river!' he shouted, but the sound emerged as a croak from his scorched lips. On his hands and knees he shuffled through the water, searching for a deep pool.

At that point the river had made one of its loop-like curves, splitting into two channels with a strip of sand and pebbles in between. In the channel running against the east bank Ivanov found a pool which was shoulder deep. He gasped as the icy water closed about him. A moment ago he was being scorched and now he was being frozen.

But the wild scene unfolding before him took all thoughts from his own condition. The blanket of smoke flying high on the westerly wind had deepened to blot out all light from the sun, and the ghostly red twilight he'd noticed in the woods was spreading over the river.

The roaring of the still unseen flames mingled with the howling winds of the firestorm to become a high pitched screech, a mad keening which made Ivanov cringe in his pool, horrified by its sheer savagery.

The trees on the west bank bent to the blast of the firestorm and then exploded into flames from top to bottom. They didn't burn as Ivanov imagined they would. With resin oozing out of them, and already dried to tinder by the firewind, the trees just disintegrated — reduced to carbon in one explosive puff.

Some instinct made him snatch a deep breath and duck his head. As he did so he felt the water rise, as though sucked up by the vacuum created by the fire, and warm currents welled up from the river bed. For an awful moment he thought the water was beginning to boil.

Lungs bursting, Ivanov cautiously raised his head to find the air still hot and thick with smoke which swirled over the river from the blackened wilderness on the west bank.

He turned to the east and staggered back, awestruck. The fire had leapt the river and now he was seeing it from behind, a wall of flame towering a hundred feet above the taiga, twisting and dipping, swaying and curling in a ballet of destruction.

Ivanov dragged himself wearily from the water onto the strip of sand between the channels. The air was still warm, but breathable now, and the smoke was thinning fast. The sun broke through and glistened on something wet and brown lying half out of the water. He leant forward, peering uncertainly, his eyes smarting from the smoke. It was an elk, a full grown bull, its lungs burnt out in the hot blast when the firestorm leapt the river.

The elk moved feebly and Ivanov despatched it with one slash of Petrisky's hunting knife across the jugular. As he watched it bleed, holding the antlered head to keep the gash in its throat open, he shook his head in bemused wonderment. That forest fire, which had so nearly cost him his life, had given him what he came so far for: a deer.

from *Survival* by Russell Evans

Reading for Understanding

1 Why did the oncoming fire sound 'like a continuous roll of explosives'?
2 How did Ivanov manage to see the full extent of the raging fire?
3 What one thought dominated as he set off running?
4 What were the earliest indications of animal life that he noticed?
5 Why was there no need to fear the bear or any other animal?
6 What were some of the obstacles Ivanov encountered as he ran?
7 What caused the air to rush back towards the fire?
8 What irony struck Ivanov as he plunged into the deep pool?
9 What preoccupied him as he waited in the pool?
10 What indication was there of just how thick the smoke was?
11 Why did Ivanov 'cringe' in horror in the pool?
12 Why was Ivanov surprised by the way the trees just exploded?
13 Why did the water level rise as the fire passed overhead?
14 What fear briefly struck him as he stayed under the water?
15 Why had the elk died?
16 What caused Ivanov 'bemused wonderment'?
17 What qualities of character are revealed by Ivanov in this passage? Explain by referring to the passage.
18 Write a comment on your personal response to this piece of writing.

Shark!

When the old man finally catches his huge fish, he hopes that the struggle is over. But he still has to bring it back to land.

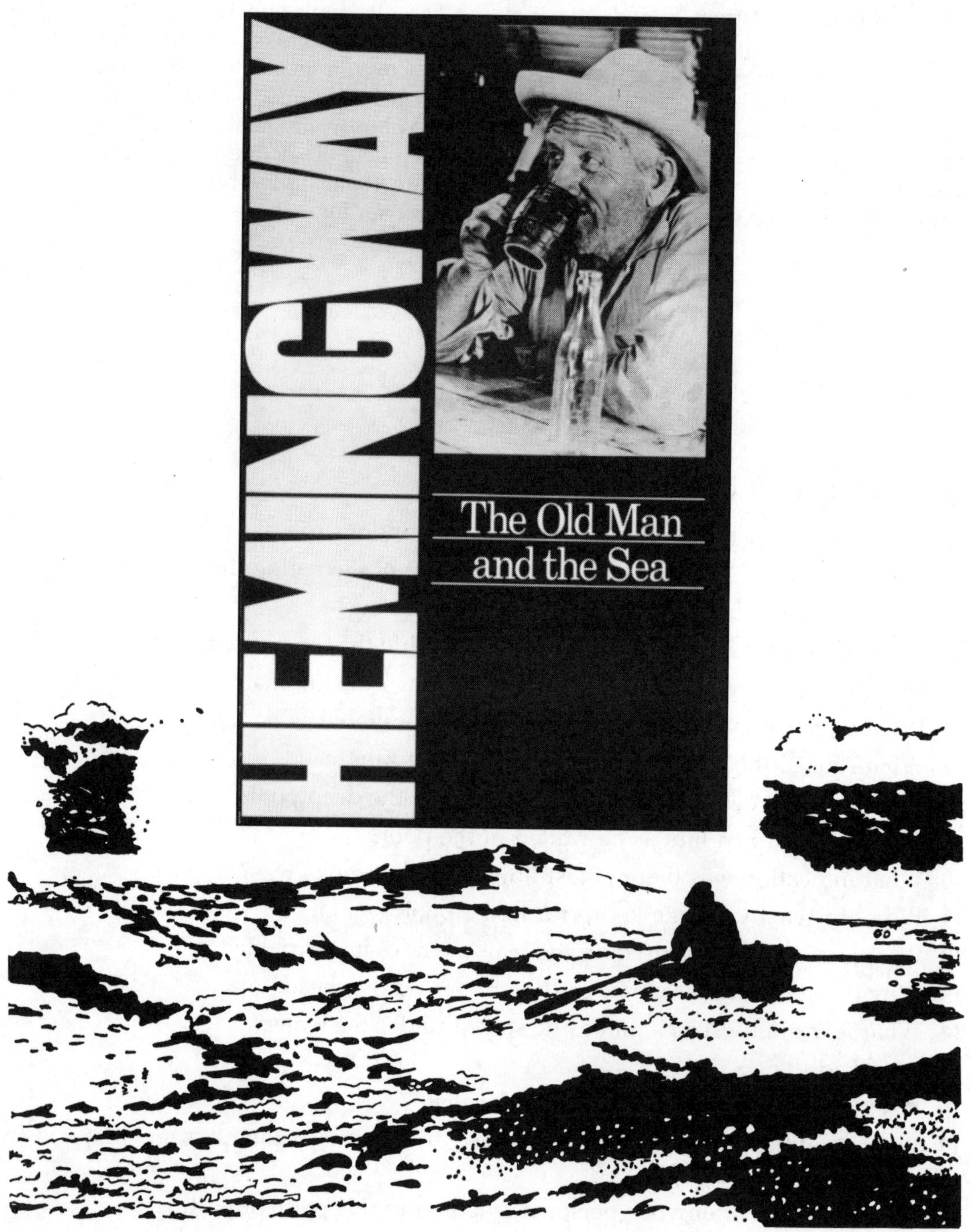

He made the fish fast to bow and stern and to the middle thwart. He was so big it was like lashing a much bigger skiff alongside. He cut a piece of line and tied the fish's lower jaw against his bill so his mouth would not open and they would sail as cleanly as possible. Then he stepped the mast and, with the stick that was his gaff and with his boom rigged, the patched sail drew, the boat began to move, and half lying in the stern he sailed south-west.

They sailed well and the old man soaked his hands in the salt water and tried to keep his head clear. There were high cumulus clouds and enough cirrus above them so that the old man knew the breeze would last all night. The old man looked at the fish constantly to make sure it was true. It was an hour before the first shark hit him.

The shark was not an accident. He had come up from deep down in the water as the dark cloud of blood had settled and dispersed in the mile-deep sea. He had come up so fast and absolutely without caution that he broke the surface of the blue water and was in the sun. Then he fell back into the sea and picked up the scent and started swimming on the course the skiff and the fish had taken.

Sometimes he lost the scent. But he would pick it up again, or have just a trace of it, and he swam fast and hard on the course. He was a very big Mako shark built to swim as fast as the fastest fish in the sea and everything about him was beautiful except his jaws. His back was as blue as a swordfish's and his belly was silver and his hide was smooth and handsome. He was built as a swordfish except for his huge jaws which were tight shut now as he swam fast, just under the surface with his high dorsal fin knifing through the water without wavering. Inside the closed double lip of his jaws all of his eight rows of teeth were slanted inwards. They were not the ordinary pyramid-shaped teeth of most sharks. They were shaped like a man's fingers when they are crisped like claws. They were nearly as long as the fingers of the old man and they had razor-sharp cutting edges on both sides. This was a fish built to feed on all the fishes in the sea, that were so fast and strong and well armed that they had no other enemy. Now he speeded up as he smelled the fresher scent and his blue dorsal fin cut the water.

When the old man saw him coming he knew that this was a shark that had no fear at all and would do exactly what he wished. He prepared the harpoon and made the rope fast while he watched the shark come in. The rope was short as it lacked what he had cut away to lash the fish.

The old man's head was clear and good now and he was full of resolution but he had little hope. It was too good to last, he thought. He took one look at the great fish as he watched the shark close in. It might as well have been a dream, he thought. I cannot keep him from hitting me but maybe I can get him. *Dentuso,* he thought. Bad luck to your mother.

The shark closed fast astern and when he hit the fish the old man saw his mouth open and his strange eyes and the clicking chop of the teeth as he drove forward in the meat just above the tail. The shark's head was out of water and his back was coming out and the old man could hear the noise of skin and flesh ripping on the big fish when he rammed the harpoon down onto the shark's head at a spot

where the line between his eyes intersected with the line that ran straight back from his nose. There were no such lines. There was only the heavy sharp blue head and the big eyes and the clicking, thrusting, all-swallowing jaws. But that was the location of the brain and the old man hit it. He hit it with his blood-mushed hands driving a good harpoon with all his strength. He hit it without hope but with resolution and complete malignancy.

The shark swung over and the old man saw his eye was not alive and then he swung over once again, wrapping himself in two loops of the rope. The old man knew that he was dead but the shark would not accept it. Then, on his back, with his tail lashing and his jaws clicking, the shark ploughed over the water as a speed-boat does. The water was white where his tail beat it and three-quarters of his body was clear above the water when the rope came taut, shivered, and then snapped. The shark lay quietly for a little while on the surface and the old man watched him. Then he went down very slowly.

'He took about forty pounds,' the old man said aloud. He took my harpoon too and all the rope, he thought, and now my fish bleeds again and there will be others.

He did not like to look at the fish any more since he had been mutilated. When the fish had been hit it was as though he himself were hit.

But I killed the shark that hit my fish, he thought. And he was the biggest *dentuso* that I have ever seen. And God knows that I have seen big ones.

It was too good to last, he thought. I wish it had been a dream now and that I had never hooked the fish.

from *The Old Man and the Sea* by Ernest Hemingway

Reading for Understanding

1 Why did the old man tie the fish's lower jaw against its bill?

2 What evidence is there in the condition of the boat to suggest that the old man is not rich?

3 How was the old man able to judge whether the breeze would last?

4 Why did the old man look at the fish constantly?

5 What was suggested by the way the shark first broke the surface of the ocean?

6 What was there about this Mako shark that was 'beautiful'?

7 What was distinctive about the Mako's teeth?

8 What emotions did the old man experience as he prepared for the shark's attack?

9 What sounds did the old man hear as the shark attacked the fish?

10 Why did the old man aim the harpoon between the shark's eyes?

11 What is the first indication that the harpoon strike has been successful?

12 What does the shark take with him in death?

13 The attack by the shark is like a personal attack for the old man. What action shows that he has taken it personally?

14 Why does the old man wish he had never caught the fish?

15 What qualities of the old man's character are revealed in this passage? Refer to the passage for evidence.

16 What techniques has the writer used to make this a powerful piece of writing?

POETRY

GLIMPSES OF THE ENVIRONMENT

Sanctuary

The road beneath the giant original trees
sweeps on and cannot wait. Varnished by dew,
its darkness mimics mirrors and is bright
behind the panic eyes the driver sees
caught in headlights. Behind his wheels the night
takes over: only the road ahead is true.
It knows where it is going; we go too.

Sanctuary, the sign said. Sanctuary —
trees, not houses; flat skins pinned to the road
of possum and native-cat; and here the old tree stoo
for how many thousand years? that old gnome-tree
some axe-new boy cut down. Sanctuary, it said:
but only the road has meaning here. It leads
into the world's cities like a long fuse laid.

Fuse, nerve, strand of a net, tense
bearer of messages, snap-tight violin-string,
dangerous knife-edge laid across the dark,
what has that sign to do with you? The immense
tower of antique forest and cliff, the rock
where years accumulate like leaves, the tree
where transient bird and mindless insect sing?
The word the board holds up is Sanctuary,
and the road knows that notice-boards make sense,

but has no time to pray. Only, up there,
morning sets doves upon the power-line.
Swung on that fatal voltage like a sign
and meaning love, perhaps they are a prayer.

Judith Wright

Questions

1 What are the 'panic eyes the driver sees/caught in the headlights'?

2 In the second verse the poet outlines several things that the word 'sanctuary' seems to indicate. Identify two of these.

3 What does the poet mean when she writes that the 'old gnome-tree' was cut down by some 'axe-new' boy?

4 The road is like 'a long fuse laid'. What is the poet implying here?

5 Who does the poet address in the third verse?

6 How does the poet see the road, judging from her descriptive labels in the third verse?

7 The doves are seen as 'perhaps . . . a prayer'. What would be the content of the prayer that they represent.

8 The road and the sign 'Sanctuary' are presented as being in opposition. What does the road represent in this poem?

9 How does the poet appear to feel about the Sanctuary?

10 What qualities do you find most impressive in this poem? Give examples.

The Heron

The heron stands in water where the swamp
Has deepened to the blackness of a pool,
Or balances with one leg on a hump
Of marsh grass heaped above a muskrat hole.

He walks the shallow with an antic grace.
The great feet break the ridges of the sand,
The long eye notes the minnow's hiding place.
His beak is quicker than a human hand.

He jerks a frog across his bony lip,
Then points his heavy bill above the wood.
The wide wings flap but once to lift him up.
A single ripple starts from where he stood.

Theodore Roethke

I Am a Fire

I want to dance, to leap, to twist,
To jump and creep, to fall back at every gust of wind,
To flare up every second of my life.
I'm red — I want to be yellow.
I'm orange — I want to be green.
I'm blue — I want to be red.
I'm dark — and I want to be light.

I take another form every second.
Horses are riding through my forests
And disappear as suddenly as they came.
Deep caverns form and disform.
Forests rise up and fall back.
The trees are my flame.
I am a happy fire,
Happy because I can do whatever I want.

Dancing, leaping, twisting, swirling,
Flaring, creeping and jumping,
Crackling and roaring as I do.
The smell of burning reaches the people around me,
The smoke drifts up and up till it reaches the heavens,
And then just fades away,
And sadly I die, slowly, slowly, slowly.

Alison Smith

Questions

1. 'I want to dance, to leap, to twist'. What quality of the fire is being emphasised here?
2. How does the poet depict the sudden changes of colour in a fire in the first verse?
3. What emotion does the poet see the fire as having and why does it feel this way?
4. What sound-words does the poet use to depict the fire in the last verse?
5. What three physical senses in humans does the fire affect? Find support for your view in the last verse.
6. What emotion does the poet attribute to the fire as it dies? Quote a line to support your claim.
7. This poem is an extended personification of fire. How does the poet achieve this?
8. What impact did the poem have on you and how would you rate its quality as a poem?

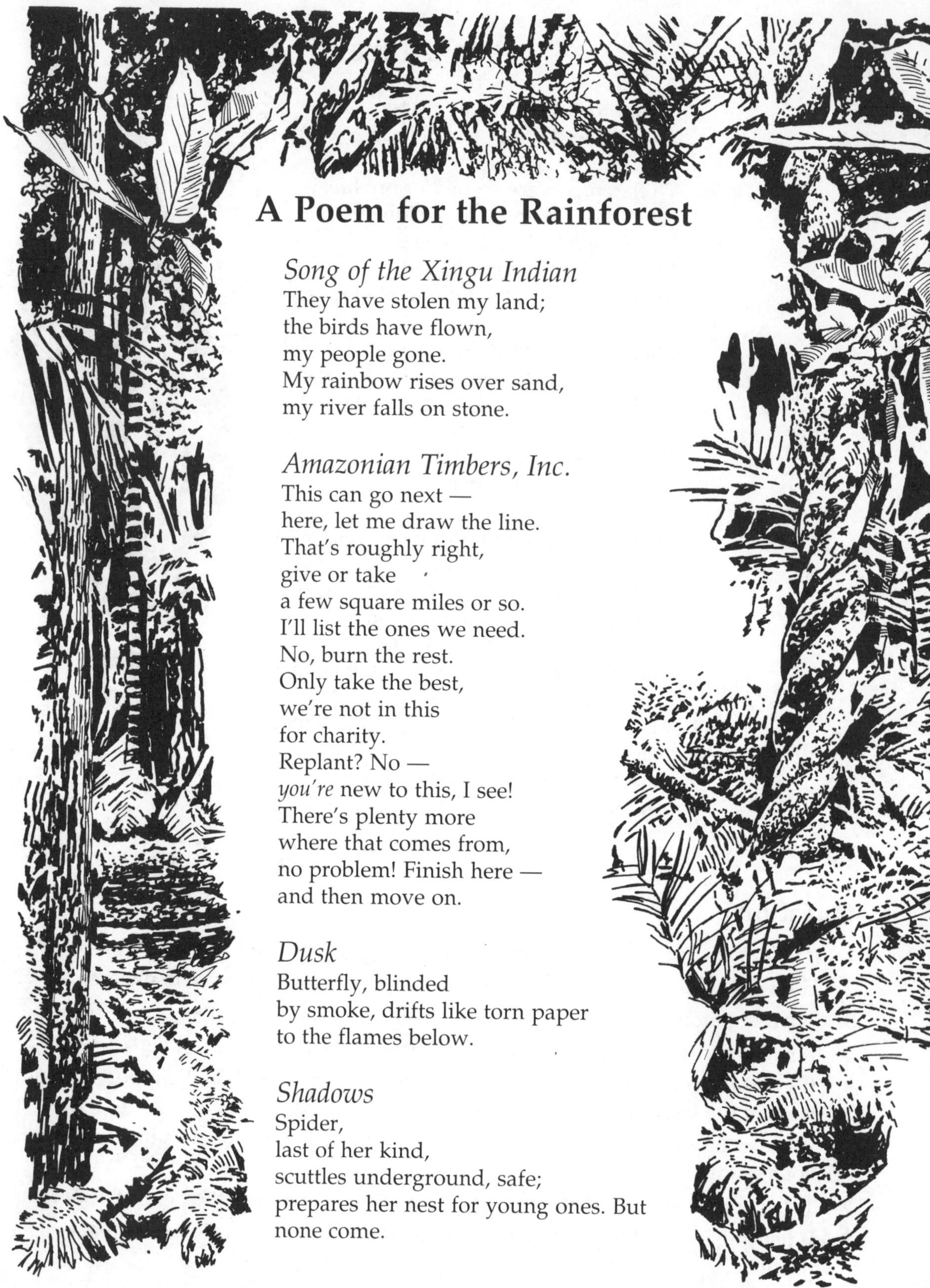

A Poem for the Rainforest

Song of the Xingu Indian
They have stolen my land;
the birds have flown,
my people gone.
My rainbow rises over sand,
my river falls on stone.

Amazonian Timbers, Inc.
This can go next —
here, let me draw the line.
That's roughly right,
give or take
a few square miles or so.
I'll list the ones we need.
No, burn the rest.
Only take the best,
we're not in this
for charity.
Replant? No —
you're new to this, I see!
There's plenty more
where that comes from,
no problem! Finish here —
and then move on.

Dusk
Butterfly, blinded
by smoke, drifts like torn paper
to the flames below.

Shadows
Spider,
last of her kind,
scuttles underground, safe;
prepares her nest for young ones. But
none come.

The Coming of Night
Sun sinks
behind the high canopy;
the iron men are silenced.

The moon rises,
the firefly wakes.
Death pauses for a night.

Song of the Forest
Our land has gone,
our people flown.
Sun scorches our earth,
our river weeps.

Judith Nicholls

Questions

1 What emotions does the Xingu Indian seem to show in the first section of the poem?

2 'My rainbow rises over sand'. What does this image suggest about the changes that have come to the rainforest?

3 What decisions are being made by the timber company in the second section of the poem?

4 How would you describe the attitude of the timber company to the rainforest?

5 'Butterfly, blinded/by smoke, drifts like torn paper'. What would a butterfly normally be an image of? How is it depicted here?

6 What is the sadness in the world of the spider? What do you think causes this?

7 'Death pauses for a night'. What does the poem mean here?

8 'Our river weeps'. Why is 'weeps' such an appropriate word here?

9 This poem is formed by giving glimpses of the life of the rainforest. How successful do you think this technique is?

10 What feelings are aroused in you by this poem? Why?

Death of a Tree

The power saw screamed,
then turned to a muttering.
She leaned forward,
fell.
A sad abruptness
in the limpness of foliage,
in the final folding of limbs.
I placed my hand on what was left:
one hundred years of graceful beauty ended,
and the underside of leaves pale
blended with the morning rain.
Better for her to have been overpowered
by wind or storm.
That would have been a battle,
a fitter end for such a forest giant
than this ignoble inevitability
because man was involved.
Man is pain.
I walked away and left her,
saddened,
aware of my loss.
Yet — still,
part of the gain.

Jack Davis

Questions

1 'The power saw screamed'. Why is 'screamed' an effective descriptive word here?

2 'She leaned forward'. What effect does the poet achieve by calling the tree 'she'?

3 'Fell'. Just one word on its own describes what happens to the tree. Why is this an effective line?

4 '. . . the limpness of foliage'. Why is the foliage described as limp?

5 What two words does the poet use to describe the living tree?

6 As the writer touches the stump what strikes him about the tree's leaves?

7 Why does he think that it would have been better if the tree had been brought down by a storm or wind?

8 How does the poet view man's intrusion into Nature?

9 What emotion does the poet feel about the death of the tree?

10 'Yet — still,/part of the gain'. What does the poet mean?

11 How would you state the theme or message of this poem?

12 What effect did this poem have on you? Why?

The Elephant

The atrocity
Of the great elephant
In the Milano Zoo: He is
Chained by his leg to the
Floor. His cage is as large
As he is — just a little larger.
He stands there, looking
At adults and children
Pelting him with peanuts and
Garbage, he looks out of his
Tear-shaped eye circled by pink.

I will save you.

His name is Pepsi. He was a gift
From the American Pepsi-Cola Company
To the city of Milano. I wrote
A letter to the company and asked 'Do you
Know what agony this elephant suffers? This
Beast which was named after your beverage?'

I received a reply
On heavy stationery from
The head of the company saying
Zoo conditions in Italy can
Not be helped. He said he was
Taking my letter under advisement.
But there was nothing he could do. He
Ended with a paragraph on zoo
Conditions in general.

Sandra Hochman

WRITING

THE WRITER'S TECHNIQUE

In assessing the quality of a piece of writing we are always interested in how effectively it achieves the writer's purpose. How humorous is it if the writer intended to make us laugh? How much does it stir our emotions if that is the writer's purpose? How vividly does it describe something if that is what the writer wants to do? Effective writing achieves its purpose by clever use of writing techniques such as:

- choice of words
- length of sentences
- rhythmic flow of the sentences
- distinctive features of style

Read through the following passage from Henry Lawson's story 'The Drover's Wife'. While the father is away droving, a snake has entered the hut and the wife is awake guarding her sleeping children. The author's description of this slice of outback life seems to communicate with readers of all ages.

The Snake

It must be near daylight now. The room is very close and hot because of the fire. Alligator still watches the wall from time to time. Suddenly he becomes greatly interested; he draws himself a few inches nearer the partition, and a thrill runs through his body. The hair on the back of his neck begins to bristle, and the battle-light is in his yellow eyes. She knows what this means, and lays her hand on the stick. The lower end of one of the partition slabs has a large crack on both sides. An evil pair of small bright bead-like eyes glisten at one of these holes. The snake — a black one — comes slowly out, about a foot, and moves its head up and down. The dog lies still, and the woman sits as one fascinated. The snake comes out a foot further. She lifts her stick, and the reptile, as though suddenly aware of danger, sticks his head in through the crack on the other side of the slab, and hurries to get his tail round after him. Alligator springs, and his jaws come together with a snap. He misses, for his nose is large, and the snake's body close down in the angle formed by the slabs and the floor. He snaps again as the tail comes round. He has the snake now, and tugs it out eighteen inches. Thud, thud, comes the woman's club on the ground. Alligator pulls again. Thud, thud. Alligator gives another pull and he has the snake out — a black brute, five feet long. The head rises to dart about, but the dog has the enemy close to the neck. He is a big, heavy dog, but quick as a terrier. He shakes the snake as though he felt the original curse in common with mankind. The eldest boy wakes up, seizes his stick, and tries to get out of bed, but his mother forces him back with a grip of iron. Thud, thud — the snake's back is broken in several places. Thud, thud — its head is crushed, and Alligator's nose skinned again.

She lifts the mangled reptile on the point of her stick, carries it to the fire, and throws it in; then piles on the wood and watches the snake burn. The boy and dog watch too. She lays her hand on the dog's head, and all the fierce, angry light dies out of his yellow eyes. The younger children are quieted, and presently go to sleep. The dirty-legged boy stands for a moment in his shirt, watching the fire. Presently he looks up at her, sees the tears in her eyes, and, throwing his arms round her neck, exclaims:

'Mother, I won't never go drovin'; blast me if I do!'

And she hugs him to her worn-out breast and kisses him; and they sit thus together while the sickly daylight breaks over the bush.

from 'The Drover's Wife' by Henry Lawson

Words

Notice the appropriateness of the words chosen. A 'thrill' runs through Alligator's body as he senses the snake moving. The snake's eyes are 'evil'; it is a black 'brute'. She lifts the 'mangled' reptile onto the fire and hugs her child to her 'worn-out' breast as 'sickly' daylight breaks. The words paint the picture vividly in our mind's eye.

Sentence length

What do you notice about the length of the sentences before the snake's death? For example, 'He snaps again as the tail comes round' and 'Thud, thud'. Can you see how this changes when the snake is dead? Suddenly the urgency is gone and the sentences, generally, are longer.

Rhythmic flow

The writing has a balance, a rhythm to it that does not 'jar' or distract us. The rhythm eases us into the scene allowing us to become engrossed without unnecessary disruption.

Notice the balance in: 'The hair on the back of his neck begins to bristle, and the battle-light is in his yellow eyes.' Notice the balance of three pieces of information, each one becoming shorter, in sentences like: 'She lifts the mangled reptile on the point of her stick, carries it to the fire, and throws it in . . .'

Distinctive features of style

This passage is made distinctive by the use of the present tense: 'The room <u>is</u> very close and hot . . .' instead of the more usual 'The room <u>was</u> very close and hot . . .' There is a suggestion of humour in the skinning of Alligator's nose, a feature of Lawson's style. And there is the realism of the young boy's words: 'Mother, I won't never go drovin'; blast me if I do!' This touch, too, adds to the authenticity of the picture created by the writer.

Other ways that writers might achieve a distinctive style include being conversational, formal, flowery or sparse in their writing.

DEVELOPING YOUR OWN WRITING TECHNIQUE

Choose several of the following topics and write two or three paragraphs on each. Pay attention to the selection of words, the variation of sentence length, and the use of rhythm in your writing, and experiment with distinctive features of style.

- Midnight feast
- Seen from the air
- A dream come true
- The longest hour
- Outback scene
- I saw it in a tree!
- A tragic accident
- Poverty!
- Practical jokers
- Environmental disaster
- Freaky fishing trip
- Danger! Keep Out!
- The ocean, my friend
- Dating is for dags
- Heart-broken

LANGUAGE

SATIRE

Satire has been defined as a form of speech, or writing, or artwork that identifies an area of human foolishness or weakness and exposes it to ridicule. The satirist usually seeks to portray an aspect of life in a scornfully amused way. He or she will attempt to provoke the readers, listeners or viewers to see the situation with new eyes, to see the foolishness of it and, hopefully, to alter their attitudes to that which is satirised. Typical tools that the satirist uses are scorn, ridicule, irony, sarcasm, exaggeration and 'sending up' or lampooning.

Golf

Gidday. I'd like to have a few words with you about one of the most paradoxical leisure activities in the recorded annals. If it hadn't made the grade as a leisure activity it could easily have hit the headlines as a form of mentally debilitating torture. I refer of course to the royal and ancient business of golf and if you're not up to a full-frontal lobotomy, then a round or two of golf is probably just what you're after.

It's not a very complicated game and if you can count up to about two or three you should find you'll be looked upon as something of a colossus out there on the sward.

You'll need a pair of two-tone dancing pumps with spikes in the soles. The spikes are put there especially by the designer to help you tell your golf shoes from your other shoes. You'll need a club, which is a stick with a knob on one end of it, and you'll need balls. There are eighteen holes so of course you'll need at least eighteen balls, although for the inexperienced golfer a bag of about a thousand balls would appear to be the minimum requirement.

You step up to something called a tee, you place a ball on a little hatstand, and you give it a good lusty whack with your club. This should whip the little hatstand out from underneath and give you a good clear shot at the ball. You drive the ball as hard as you can down the fairway and you then follow it and hit it around in amongst the trees and across little ponds and through a lot of rather boring sandpits, until eventually of course you lose the ball altogether.

By now you should be anything up to about ten or fifteen yards away from the actual tee where you started, and it's time for phase two. You walk down the fairway towards the green. It's the walking you do in golf that makes it so good for you. As you wander along the fairway you'll hear someone shout 'fore'. This means you've got a golf ball imbedded in the back of your skull. Keep moving now because if you stop you'll seize up altogether.

When you reach the green you take the flag out of the hole and say 'here's looking at you, blue eyes'. This is called a bogie and is considered pretty hot stuff by the bulk of the golfing fraternity. Then you proceed to the next tee and you whack another ball off down the fairway and the whole business is repeated. By the end of the round the eighteen golf balls lodged in the back of your brain should have anaesthetised you to the point where you are no longer bothered by the unbridled tedium of the activity, your head is now worth about $45 on the open market, and it's time to go home.

If you like walking, a bit of physical exercise and the joy of competition I recommend you have a very serious look at stamp collecting.

from *Daggshead Revisited* by John Clarke

Analysis

1 What overall message about golf and golfers is being conveyed in this passage?

2 What main technique is being used in the passage to satirise golf and golfers?

3 How does the introduction 'Gidday' set up an expectation for us about this piece of writing? What expectation is set up?

4 '. . . if you can count up to about two or three you should find you'll be looked upon as something of a colossus out there on the sward.' Comment on the effect of the language here.

5 '. . . for the inexperienced golfer a bag of about a thousand balls would appear to be the minimum requirement.' What technique of satire is being used here?

6 The writer describes a golf tee as 'a little hatstand'. Comment on this description and its effect on the reader.

7 After describing extensive hitting of the golf ball, the satirist writes: 'By now you should be anything up to about ten or fifteen yards away from the actual tee where you started . . .' How would you describe this technique of humour?

8 What is unexpected in the concluding sentence? What effect does it have?

9 How would you describe the satire in this passage? What do you see as its purpose?

10 What response did you have to this piece of satire? Why?

Writing Satire

Choose a sport and write a humorous satirical description of what it involves. Be sure to include a description of the activity, special clothing or equipment and the people who play. Try to make use of techniques such as exaggeration or understatement.

CARTOON SATIRE

SCRIPT TEASE DEPT.

Not even your parents are old enough to remember this, but once upon a time, Hollywood made movies that were original—not sequels or re-makes or outright rip-offs of other films. Nowadays, it's a different story...no, actually, it's the *same* story over and over! That's the problem! Well, we still yearn for those days when a "new movie" really was new! And since none of those overpaid "geniuses" out in Tinseltown can do it, it's up to us *under*paid geniuses over here at MAD to come up with...

TOTALLY ORIGINAL NEVER-BEEN-DONE BEFORE MOVIE PLOTS

ARTIST: GEORGE WOODBRIDGE WRITER: MIKE SNIDER

Teenage hacker Morrie Byte is dumbfounded when, after punching a few simple numbers into his Apple II, *he fails to break into a U.S. Missile Launch Computer!*

A ten-year-old boy who can't wait to grow up meets a 40-year-old man who wants to be a kid again—and—despite the intervention of a benevolent angel—*they resolve their problems without switching bodies!*

A respected Karate Master takes an awkward but eager young American under his wing and is shocked when—despite 6 months of intensive training—*his student is savagely beaten and humiliated by some street punk!*

from *Mad* magazine

Analysis

1 Identify any movies you can that are being satirised in these three cartoons.
2 How do you expect the plot to conclude in each of the three movies? Rewrite the scripts so that they conclude the way you would expect them to.
3 What techniques are being used here to create the satiric effect?
4 What aspect of movies is being satirised in these cartoons?
5 What effect is the satire intended to have in these cartoons? How effective would you rate them?
6 What is your response to these examples of visual satire?

Writing Satire

1 Choose a movie with a well-known plot and, using the models provided, satirise the plot. Draw a satiric cartoon to go with your plot.

or

2 Choose several well-known movies and draft satiric versions of the plots.

POETIC SATIRE

Bankers Are Just Like Anybody Else, Except Richer

This is a song to celebrate banks,
Because they are full of money and you go into them and all
    you hear is clinks and clanks,
Or maybe a sound like the wind in the trees on the hills,
Which is the rustling of the thousand-dollar bills.
Most bankers dwell in marble halls,
Which they get to dwell in because they encourage deposits
    and discourage withdralls,
And particularly because they all observe one rule which woe
    betides the banker who fails to heed it,
Which is you must never lend any money to anybody unless
    they don't need it.
I know you, you cautious conservative banks!
If people are worried about their rent it is your duty to deny
    them the loan of one nickel, yes, even one copper
    engraving of the martyred son of the late Nancy
    Hanks;

Yes, if they request fifty dollars to pay for a baby you must
look at them like Tarzan looking at an uppity ape in the
jungle,
And tell them what do they think a bank is, anyhow, they had
better go get the money from their wife's aunt or ungle.
But suppose people come in and they have a million and they
want another million to pile on top of it,
Why, you brim with the milk of human kindness and you urge
them to accept every drop of it,
And you lend them the million so then they have two million
and this gives them the idea that they would be better
off with four,
So they already have two million as security so you have no
hesitation in lending them two more,
And all the vice-presidents nod their heads in rhythm,
And the only question asked is do the borrowers want the
money sent or do they want to take it withm.
But please do not think that I am not fond of banks,
Because I think they deserve our appreciation and thanks,
Because they perform a valuable public service in eliminating
the jackasses who go around saying that health and
happiness are everything and money isn't essential,
Because as soon as they have to borrow some unimportant
money to maintain their health and happiness they
starve to death so they can't go around anymore
sneering at good old money, which is nothing short of
providential.

Ogden Nash

Analysis

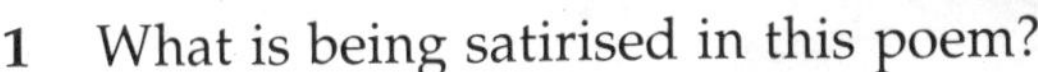

1 What is being satirised in this poem?
2 What aspects of the subject are the focus of the satire?
3 What techniques are being used by Ogden Nash to satirise banks and bankers?
4 Is the satire here savage and biting or gentle and humorous? Support your viewpoint by referring to the poem.
5 Find an example of absurdity as a satiric technique in the poem.
6 How would you describe the purpose of the satirist here?
7 What is your response to this poem?
8 How effective would you rate this poem in terms of its achievement? Why?

Writing Satire

Choose an institution in our society (not banks) and try your hand at satirising in a poem some aspects of that institution.

MORE CARTOON SATIRE

The following cartoon, published in *The Sydney Morning Herald*, sets out to satirise some aspects of the examination system.

Analysis

1 What has the cartoonist done to reduce all exam candidates to uniformity?
2 What is the cartoonist attempting to 'say' by emphasising brains and glasses in the exam candidates?
3 What is the cartoonist 'saying' by his visual portrayal of the exam supervisor?
4 What is the overall message of this satiric cartoon?
5 How effective would you rate this cartoon? Why?

GETTING IT RIGHT

SINGULAR VERBS

The words 'each', 'every', 'either' and 'neither' are always followed by the singular form of the verb. For example:

- Each of us **are** going to the Graduation Ball. (incorrect)
- Each of us **is** going to the Graduation Ball. (correct)

Selecting the Singular Verb

Complete the following sentences by supplying the correct form of the verb.

1 Every student .... encouraged to continue on at school. (was/were)

2 Neither the captain nor the vice-captain .... available to play this week. (is/are)

3 Each large tree in the sanctuary .... accounted for. (is/are)

4 Either this April or next .... been set for the trip overseas. (has /have)

5 Each member of the party .... the decision is wrong. (believe/believes)

6 Every small business owner .... been finding it hard to make ends meet. (has/have)

7 Each of the birds .... infected with disease. (was/were)

8 Neither of the candidates .... a very convincing representative. (make/makes)

DRAMA

ENVIRONMENTAL CONFLICT

Much of the intensity of action in a play or piece of drama occurs because characters have different points of view, different perspectives. Many of the current struggles in our society that we see dramatically portrayed on news broadcasts each day involve differing perspectives on environmental issues.

Look carefully at the advertisement opposite.

The values and viewpoint demonstrated by the Greenpeace movement in this ad would include:

- a concern for the environment
- a desire to stir the public from apathy to action
- a commitment to non-violent action for change

Presumably, the values and viewpoints of the fishermen using driftnetting would include:

- a concern to earn a living and provide for their families
- a desire not to be involved in conflict in doing this

In the clash of people with these different viewpoints and value systems there is great potential for good drama. The drama could highlight any aspect of the situation that you believe would have dramatic interest.

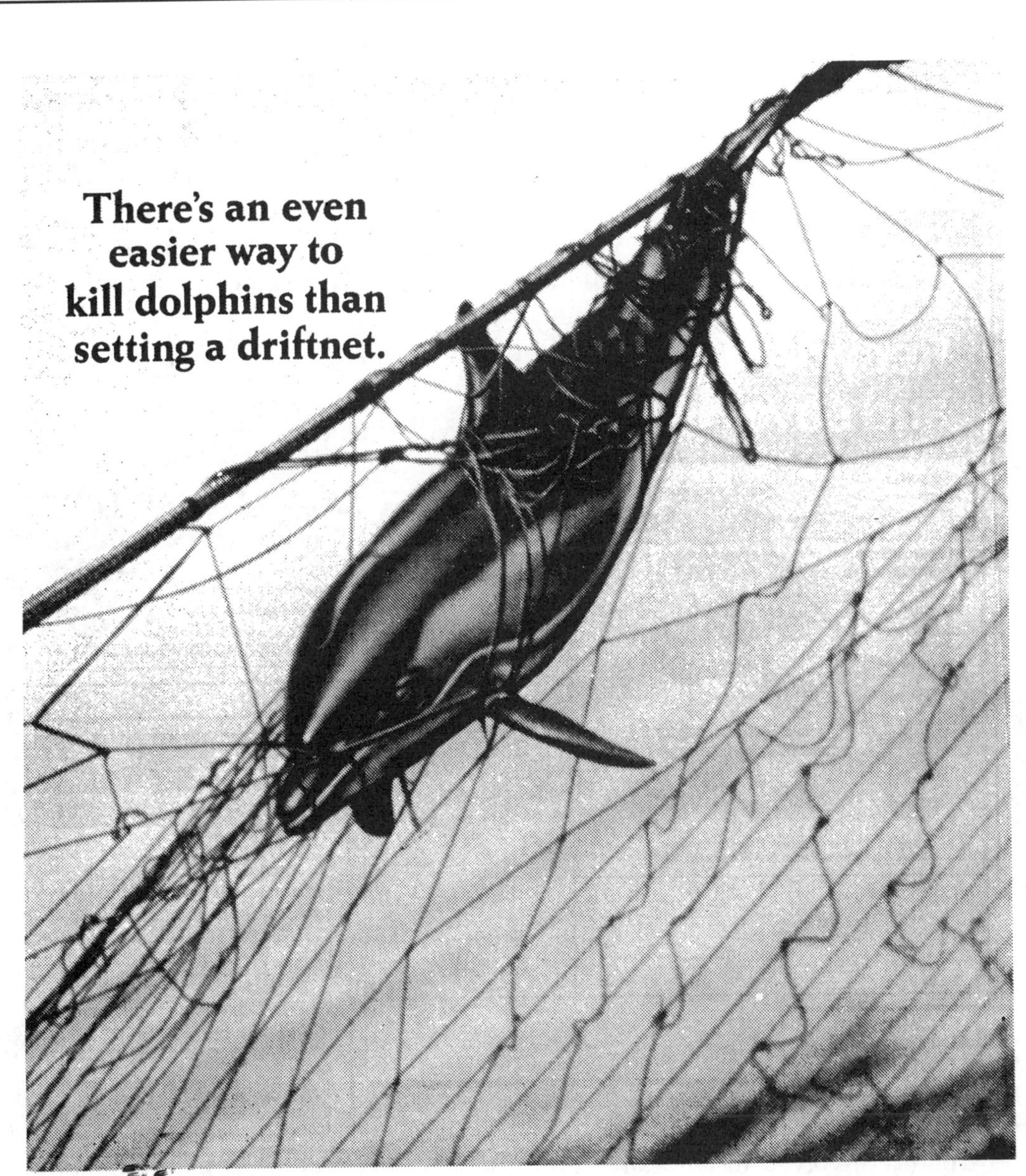

There's an even easier way to kill dolphins than setting a driftnet.

It's turning the page.

A 45-kilometre long "wall of death" is a very efficient way to kill thousands of dolphins.

But apathy works just as well.

We know you care, otherwise you'd have already turned the page.

But please, show you care.

Join Greenpeace.

As a member of Greenpeace you'll get a free subscription to the Greenpeace magazine.

But, more importantly, you'll be there in spirit aboard the new Rainbow Warrior as she continues her non-violent actions against the Taiwanese and Japanese driftnetters.

Together, we can end driftnetting.

GREENPEACE

CLASS ACT-OUTS

1 Divide the class into groups of four to six members.
2 Have each group choose *one* of the following situations and discuss what 'mini-plot' they could develop as an aspect of that situation. The first situation includes a number of possible mini-plots to give you the idea.
3 Decide on characters and the way that you will have your mini-plot develop as a drama. Don't worry about scripting the action. Simply decide on where you want the action to go and improvise your way along.
4 Act out your mini-plot within your group and make any modifications you think are necessary.
5 Present it to the class as one aspect of an environmental conflict.

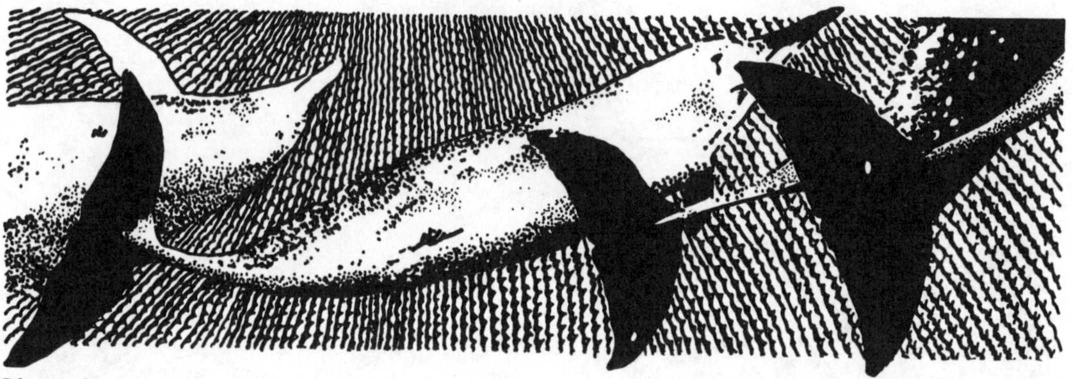

Situations

1 You have been chosen as a team member on the *Rainbow Warrior*. Your purpose as a team is to harass the fishing boats using driftnetting, to try to interfere with their operations without resorting to violence, to capture on film the destructive aspects of driftnetting in order to awaken public concern and so on.

Consider these aspects of the situation and how you could portray them dramatically.

Mini-plots

(a) You are involved in harassment of a fishing boat when suddenly its members produce guns and begin firing on you. What happens? How do you handle the situation? What actions do you take?
(b) The stress of the work begins to produce major conflicts among the members of your crew. What happens? How does everyone cope? How do you cope?
(c) The ship you are on breaks down, and engine repairs are needed but parts have to be air-lifted. In the meantime a huge tropical storm is approaching. What happens? How does the ship come through? How do crew members react?
(d) In a freak accident you are lost overboard at night, only to be picked up by one of the fishing trawlers. How are you received? How do you respond? How do you get back to your ship?

2 Some of you are actively concerned about logging in rainforest areas and the environmental destruction caused, particularly to plant and animal life. You set out to confront timber-workers non-violently. What aspect of this situation would you like to develop into a drama? What action do you take? What response do you get from the timber-workers and their company?

or

You are a worker with a large wood-chip company. Your livelihood depends on your being able to work unimpeded in the forests, helping to cut timber. What are your circumstances? What family responsibilities do you have? How do you handle the clash with environmentalists who threaten your livelihood? What happens?

3 You live in a large city and are concerned about the way the sewage problem is being handled. Most of it is being treated and piped out to sea but there is considerable evidence to suggest that beach pollution is getting worse. You plan a protest march to finish at the office of the Minister for the Environment. However, things don't go quite the way you expect. What happens? How will you present it dramatically?

4 Concerned about the danger represented to the environment by uranium mining and its use in nuclear armaments, you join with others to confront a mining company. You are surprised at the way things turn out. What do you do? What is the outcome?

5 Your pleasant little seaside town is about to be turned into a booming holiday resort with luxury facilities. The impact on the town is likely to be enormous, changing the whole atmosphere of the place you have come to love. Choose a dramatic aspect of this situation and work at portraying it.

6 Upset over the continuing sponsorship by tobacco companies in the world of sport, you and friends set out to stir for changes. You are surprised not only at the vigorous opposition you encounter, but also at *who* opposes you. What do you do and how does it turn out?

7
STRUGGLE

NOVELS

The Death of Piggy

A group of English schoolboys are stranded on a tropical island. Under Ralph's leadership they try, at first, to remain civilised. However, under the cruel leadership of Jack, many of the boys make spears, paint their faces, hunt pigs and become bloodthirsty savages. They reject the civilisation they came from.

A symbol of civilisation in the novel is a conch shell. Whoever holds the conch is allowed a hearing. At the beginning of this scene, Ralph tries to reason with the savages. Later, Piggy, one of the boys who believes in civilised behaviour, holds the conch but it is too late for speech to be effective against the blood lust of the savages.

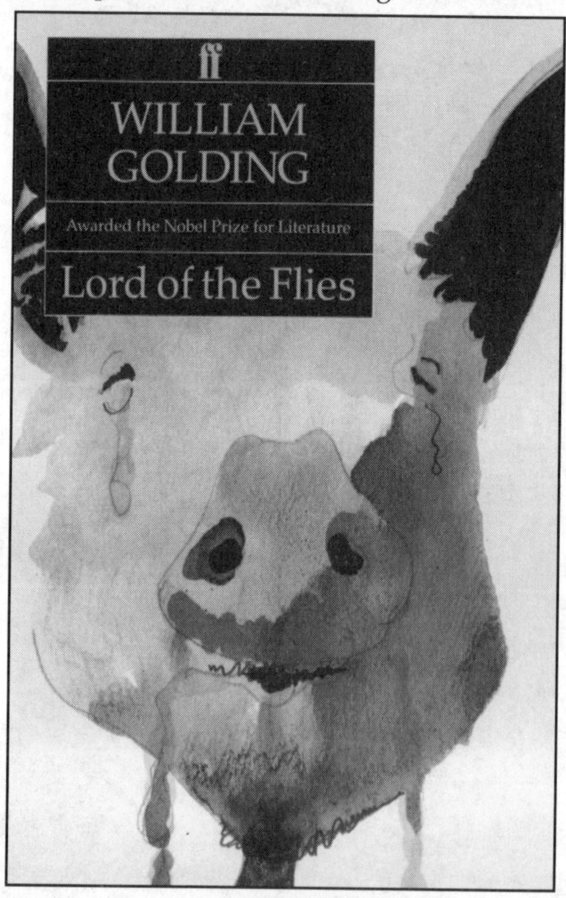

He held out his spear and pointed at the savages.

'Your only hope is keeping a signal fire going as long as there's light to see . Then maybe a ship'll notice the smoke and come and rescue us and take us home. But without that smoke we've got to wait till some ship comes by accident. We might wait years; till we were old —'

The shivering, silvery, unreal laughter of the savages sprayed out and echoed away. A gust of rage shook Ralph. His voice cracked.

'Don't you understand, you painted fools? Sam, Eric, Piggy and me — we aren't enough. We tried to keep the fire going, but we couldn't. And then you, playing at hunting. . . .'

He pointed past them to where the trickle of smoke dispersed in the pearly air.

'Look at that! Call that a signal fire? That's a cooking fire. Now you'll eat and there'll be no smoke. Don't you understand? There may be a ship out there —'

He paused, defeated by the silence and the painted anonymity of the group guarding the entry. The chief opened a pink mouth and addressed Samneric who were between him and his tribe.

'You two. Get back.'

No one answered him. The twins, puzzled, looked at each other; while Piggy, reassured by the cessation of violence, stood up carefully. Jack glanced back at Ralph and then at the twins.

'Grab them!'

No one moved. Jack shouted angrily.

'I said "grab them"!'

The painted group moved round Samneric nervously and unhandily. Once more the silvery laughter scattered.

Samneric protested out of the heart of civilisation.

'Oh, I say!'

'— honestly!'

Their spears were taken from them.

'Tie them up!'

Ralph cried out hopelessly against the black and green mask.

'Jack!'

'Go on. Tie them.'

Now the painted group felt the otherness of Samneric, felt the power in their own hands. They felled the twins clumsily and excitedly. Jack was inspired. He knew that Ralph would attempt a rescue. He struck in a humming circle behind him and Ralph only just parried the blow. Beyond them the tribe and the twins were a loud and writhing heap. Piggy crouched again. Then the twins lay, astonished, and the tribe stood round them. Jack turned to Ralph and spoke between his teeth.

'See? They do what I want.'

There was silence again. The twins lay, inexpertly tied up, and the tribe watched Ralph to see what he would do. He numbered them through his fringe, glimpsed the ineffectual smoke.

His temper broke. He screamed at Jack.

'You're a beast and a swine and a bloody, bloody thief!'

He charged.

Jack, knowing this was the crisis, charged too. They met with a jolt and bounced apart. Jack swung with his fist at Ralph and caught him on the ear. Ralph hit Jack in the stomach

Piggy holding the conch in the 1988 film of *Lord of the Flies*

and made him grunt. Then they were facing each other again, panting and furious, but unnerved by each other's ferocity. They became aware of the noise that was the background to this fight, the steady shrill cheering of the tribe behind them.

Piggy's voice penetrated to Ralph.

'Let me speak.'

He was standing in the dust of the fight, and as the tribe saw his intention the shrill cheer changed to a steady booing.

Piggy held up the conch and the booing sagged a little, then came up again to strength.

'I got the conch!'

He shouted.

'I tell you, I got the conch!'

Surprisingly, there was silence now; the tribe were curious to hear what amusing thing he might have to say.

Silence and pause; but in the silence a curious air-noise, close by Ralph's head. He gave it half his attention — and there it was again; a faint 'Zup!' Someone was throwing stones: Roger was dropping them, his one hand still on the lever. Below him, Ralph was a shock of hair and Piggy a bag of fat.

'I got this to say. You're acting like a crowd of kids.'

The booing rose and died again as Piggy lifted the white, magic shell.

'Which is better — to be a pack of painted savages like you are, or to be sensible like Ralph is?'

A great clamour rose among the savages. Piggy shouted again.

'Which is better — to have rules and agree, or to hunt and kill?'

Again the clamour and again — 'Zup!'

Ralph shouted against the noise.

'Which is better, law and rescue, or hunting and breaking things up?'

Now Jack was yelling too and Ralph could no longer make himself heard. Jack had backed right against the tribe and they were a solid mass of menace that bristled with spears. The intention of a charge was forming among them; they were working up to it and the neck would be swept clear. Ralph stood facing them, a little to one side, his spear ready. By him stood Piggy still holding out the talisman, the fragile, shining beauty of the shell. The storm of sound beat at them, an incantation of hatred. High overhead, Roger, with a sense of delirious abandonment, leaned all his weight on the lever.

Ralph heard the great rock long before he saw it. He was aware of a jolt in the earth that came to him through the soles of his feet, and the breaking sound of stones at the top of the cliff. Then the monstrous red thing bounded across the neck and he flung himself flat while the tribe shrieked.

The rock struck Piggy a glancing blow from chin to knee; the conch exploded into a thousand white fragments and ceased to exist. Piggy, saying nothing, with no time for even a grunt, travelled through the air sideways from the rock, turning over as he went. The rock bounded twice and was lost in the forest. Piggy fell forty feet and landed on his back across that square, red rock in the sea. His head opened and stuff came out and turned red. Piggy's arms and legs twitched a bit, like a pig's after it has been killed. Then the sea breathed again in a long slow sigh, the water boiled white and pink over the rock; and when it went, sucking back again, the body of Piggy was gone.

This time the silence was complete. Ralph's lips formed a word but no sound came.

Suddenly Jack bounded out from the tribe and began screaming wildly.

'See? See? That's what you'll get! I meant that! There isn't a tribe for you any more! The conch is gone —'

He ran forward, stooping.

'I'm Chief!'

Viciously, with full intention, he hurled his spear at Ralph. The point tore the skin and flesh over Ralph's ribs, then sheared off and fell in the water. Ralph stumbled, feeling not pain but panic, and the tribe, screaming now like the Chief, began to advance. Another spear, a bent one that would not fly straight, went past his face and one fell from on high where Roger was. The twins lay hidden behind the tribe and the anonymous devil's faces swarmed across the neck. Ralph turned and ran. A great noise as of sea-gulls rose behind him. He obeyed an instinct that he did not know he possessed and swerved over the open space so that the spears went wide.

from *Lord Of The Flies* by William Golding

Reading for Meaning

1 What did Ralph advise the savages to do?

2 Why did Ralph feel a gust of rage against the savages?

3 How do you think 'the silence and the painted anonymity of the group' defeated Ralph?

4 What sign of civilisation did Samneric show as they were grabbed? (Note: Sam and Eric were twins and because they were always together were called Samneric.)

5 'Jack was inspired.' Why?

6 When did Ralph signal that a crisis between himself and Jack was at hand?

7 As the boys faced each other 'panting and furious', what unnerved them?

8 Why did the tribe allow Piggy to speak?

9 What caused the faint 'Zup' noise that Ralph heard?

10 How did Ralph and Piggy appear to Roger as he crouched above them with his hand on the lever of the boulder?

11 What two contrasting ways of living did Piggy present to the savages?

12 What was the talisman that Piggy held out as he and Ralph faced the tribe?

13 How did Roger feel as he 'leaned all his weight on the lever'?

14 What made Ralph aware of the great rock long before he saw it?

15 How did the rock strike Piggy?

16 '. . . the conch exploded into a thousand white fragments and ceased to exist.' What deeper meaning is present in the destruction of the conch shell?

17 What happened to Piggy's body?

18 How did Jack react to the tragedy?

19 How did Ralph escape from the tribe?

20 What do you think we can learn about human nature from this passage?

A Struggle Against the Sea

Charlie Reeve, who tells the story, and his friend Johnno were teenagers when they went to take a lifesaving exam at the local beach. Unfortunately a storm was rapidly approaching.

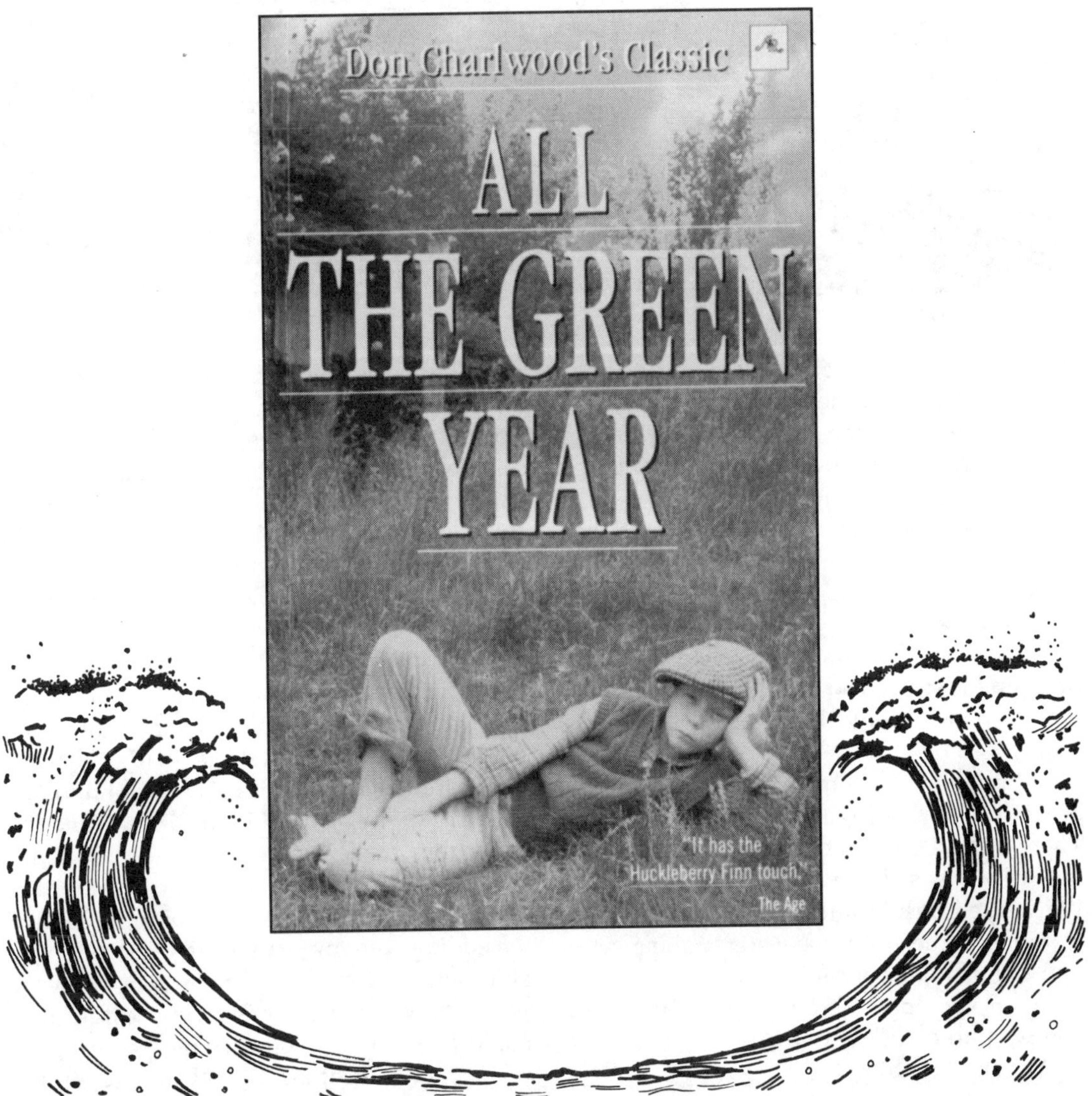

Early in the afternoon the examiner arrived — a tall, hollow-cheeked man wrapped in an overcoat. As there were no other candidates Johnno and I drove alone with him to the beach. The sea was louder now and spray blew occasionally across the L of the pier.

'You're both strong swimmers?'

When Johnno didn't answer I said, 'He's the best in the town.'

The examiner looked at me bleakly. 'But you, you still want to go on with it yourself?'

'Yes,' I said.

There was good reason for this: Johnno was the perfect patient; when he filled his lungs

with air he floated like an inflated beach toy. I knew that if he left school I might never get the opportunity of having him again.

'Very well; get undressed as quickly as you can.'

The dressing shed was deserted and had about it a winter look. It smelt of undisturbed salt deposits, and outside the tea-tree creaked depressingly.

All this was lost on Johnno. He was so at home in the sea and so glad to be out of school that a cyclone would have meant nothing to him.

We put our sweaters on and went on to the beach, our legs stinging in the blown sand. There was no one to be seen except the examiner who was striding up and down the pier. We walked beside him to the end, our eyes watering in the wind, the water making sucking sounds under our feet.

'It's a very poor day indeed. You're sure you want to go on with it?'

'Yes sir,' we said.

'All right, you know the twenty-yard mark — the third bollard on the L. You, Reeve, will swim to a point opposite it, then Johnston will carry out the first method of release followed by the first method of rescue.'

'Yes sir.'

We handed him our sweaters and climbed down on to the landing. The decking was awash and the waves made rushing, slapping sounds round the piles. All this Johnno hardly noticed. He filled his great chest and dived in and began swimming parallel to the L, his feet fluttering rhythmically. I glanced inland at the town as a man might glance if seeing it for the last time, then I dived after him.

The water felt cold enough to stop my heart. Below the surface the depths were silent and hostile, reaching far into darkness. I curved up to the light and saw Johnno well ahead, treading water patiently. The movement of waves was against us as strongly as I had ever felt it.

'First method of release,' cried Johnno.

I lifted my arms in fair imitation of a drowning man and felt them grasped and twisted outward. He turned me on my back, put his hands over my ears and presently I was riding with my head on his chest, all sound shut out, my face clear of the water. Above us was a grey sky, its cloud racing. Under me I could feel Johnno's legs driving powerfully. I relaxed and breathed deeply in preparation for the return.

As we came to the landing the examiner shouted, 'First method of release and first method of rescue, Reeve.'

We swam back together into the oncoming sea and faced each other twenty yards out. Johnno held up his arms and I turned him on to his back. He was unsinkable; even if waves

washed continually over his face, he said nothing. But one thing he couldn't do was control our direction. We ended our run ten feet from the landing.

'All right,' shouted the examiner, 'don't bother to go back to the landing, swim from where you are. Your turn, Johnston — second method of release, second method of rescue.'

Each time Johnno's turn came he attempted to correct my drift, but correcting it completely was beyond him, so we moved slowly down the pier.

Gradually fatigue crept over me, so that I began carrying out each movement automatically, hardly aware sometimes whether Johnno was the patient or the rescuer.

Drifting the way we were, we were beginning to lose protection from the L. Through the corner of my eye I could see the waves coming, and at the last moment would lift Johnno's head and submerge my own.

'Johnston — fourth method of rescue.'

With his mouth near my ear he shouted, 'You okay?'

I heard my own voice answer, 'Okay.'

'Reeve — fourth method of rescue.'

On the last lap I had illusions of relief. The waves seemed less aggressive and the tremendous ache at the back of my neck was easier. The idea came to me that I was not in the water, but lying in bed, vaguely dreaming.

I heard the examiner from a long way off say, 'Good work. Back to the landing and get dressed.'

The landing was no more than fifty yards away, but it seemed beyond reach.

Johnno struck across the lines of waves, his body rising on crests and falling into troughs like a ship. I started after him, but found myself drifting rapidly towards the pier. The idea came to me that it would help to rest awhile by holding one of the piles. I was letting myself drift towards them when I was picked up by a wave and saw I would strike a pile. I dived under the crest, but in a second my head struck hard. As I surfaced in the trough the swirl held me to the pile. Somewhere up above the examiner was shouting, but before I could hear his words the next wave drove me against the pile with a turning motion and I felt mussel shells cut the insides of my arms and legs. In the same instant the pier lifebelt dangled beside me. I lunged at it, pushing my shoulders through it. A third wave swung me again, but when it had gone the two above hauled me on to the rough planking of the pier.

'My God, boy, why didn't you call for help?'

I heard Johnno say then, 'I thought you were just behind me.'

I sat up and saw myriads of small cuts on my arms and legs, done as if with razor-blades. On my forehead a lump was rising.

'Do you feel equal to walking?'

'Yes,' I said uncertainly.

'We'd better go, then — a storm is coming.'

The wind was still from the north-west, but much stronger than before. In the south-west the sky was black, the black clouds advancing quickly. I began to walk between Johnno and the examiner, my body feeling strangely light.

We were about half-way down the pier when the wind suddenly dropped and the air was momentarily still, then it came roaring from the south-west, low cloud flying before it. Inland we saw the trees bend together and branches go flying through the air. The beach was hidden under swirling sand.

'We're for it!' shouted the examiner.

from *All The Green Year* by Don Charlwood

Reading for Meaning

1 When the examiner arrived how did he appear to the boys?
2 'You're both strong swimmers?' Why did the examiner ask this?
3 Why did Charlie, the storyteller, want his friend Johnno for his lifesaving patient?
4 What feelings did Charlie have about the dressing shed?
5 How do we know that the wind was strong on the beach?
6 How did Johnno seem to feel about the bad weather?
7 How did the water feel to Charlie?
8 How did the depths appear to him?
9 'First method of release.' How did Charlie give a fair imitation of a drowning man?'
10 Why was Charlie able to relax and breathe deeply in Johnno's grip?
11 What was the one thing that Johnno couldn't control?
12 How did fatigue gradually begin to affect Charlie?
13 On the last lap, what 'illusions of relief' did Charlie experience?
14 What made Johnno look like a ship?
15 Why did Charlie let himself drift towards the pier?
16 How was Charlie injured when he struck the pier?
17 How was he saved?
18 How did Charlie feel as he began to walk between Johnno and the examiner?
19 What made the examiner shout 'We're for it!'?
20 What creates the interest and excitement in this episode?

The Struggle to Survive an Artillery Barrage

All Quiet on the Western Front is a novel based on the true personal experiences of a young German soldier in the First World War. In this episode, the writer and his friends Katczinsky (Kat) and Kropp are trudging across the battle zone in the early dawn when they are caught in a tremendous artillery barrage.

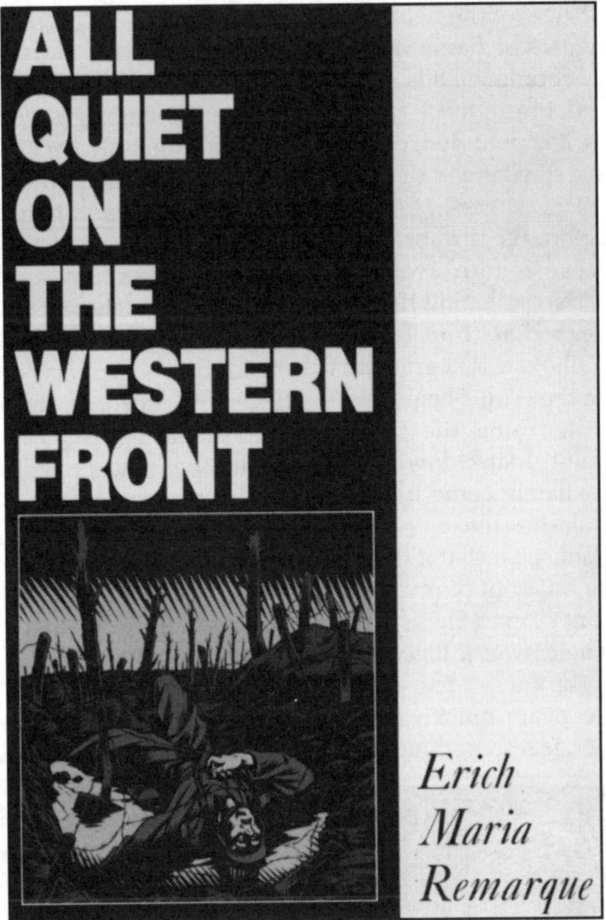

We come to the communication-trench and then to the open fields. The little wood reappears; we know every foot of ground here. There's the cemetery with the mounds and the black crosses.

That moment it breaks out behind us, swells, roars, and thunders. We duck down — a cloud of flame shoots up a hundred yards ahead of us.

The next minute under a second explosion part of the wood rises slowly in the air, three or four trees sail up and then crash to pieces. The shells begin to hiss like safety-valves — heavy fire ——

'Take cover!' yells somebody — 'Cover!'

The fields are flat, the wood is too distant and dangerous — the only cover is the graveyard and the mounds. We stumble across in the dark and as though he had been spat there every man lies glued behind a mound.

Not a moment too soon. The dark goes mad. It heaves and raves. Darknesses blacker than the night rush on us with giant strides, over us and away. The flames of the explosions light up the graveyard.

There is no escape anywhere. By the light of the shells I try to get a view of the fields. They are a surging sea, daggers of flame from the explosions leap up like fountains. It is impossible for anyone to break through it.

The wood vanishes, it is pounded, crushed, torn to pieces. We must stay here in the graveyard.

The earth bursts before us. It rains clods. I feel a smack. My sleeve is torn away by a splinter. I shut my fist. No pain. Still that does not reassure me: wounds don't hurt till afterwards. I feel the arm all over. It is grazed but sound. Now a crack on the skull, I begin to lose consciousness. Like lightning the thought comes to me: Don't faint! I sink down in the black broth and immediately come up to the top again. A splinter slashes into my helmet, but has already travelled so far that it does not go through. I wipe the mud out of my eyes. A hole is torn up in front of me. Shells hardly ever land in the same hole twice, I'll get into it. With one lunge, I shoot as flat as a fish over the ground; there it whistles again, quickly I crouch together, claw for cover, feel something on the left, shove in beside it, it gives way, I groan, the earth leaps, the blast thunders in my ears, I creep under the yielding thing, cover myself with it, draw it over me, it is wood, cloth, cover, cover, miserable cover against the whizzing splinters.

I open my eyes — my fingers grasp a sleeve, an arm. A wounded man? I yell to him — no answer — a dead man. My hand gropes farther, splinters of wood — now I remember again that we are lying in the graveyard.

But the shelling is stronger than everything. It wipes out the sensibilities, I merely crawl still farther under the coffin, it shall protect me, though Death himself lies in it.

Before me gapes the shell-hole. I grasp it with my eyes as with fists. With one leap I must be in it. There, I get a smack in the face, a hand clamps on to my shoulder — has the dead man waked up? — The hand shakes me, I turn my head, in the second of light I stare into the face of Katczinsky, he has his mouth wide open and is yelling. I hear nothing, he rattles me, comes nearer, in a momentary lull his voice reaches me: 'Gas — Gaas — Gaaas Pass it on.'

I grab for my gas-mask. Some distance from me there lies someone. I think of nothing but this: That fellow there must know: Gaaas — Gaaas ——

I call, I lean toward him, I swipe at him with the satchel, he doesn't see — once again, again — he merely ducks — it's a recruit — I look at Kat desperately, he has his mask on — I pull out mine, too, my helmet falls to one side, it slips over my face, I reach the man, his satchel is on the side nearest me, I seize the mask, pull it over his head, he understands, I let go and with a jump drop into the shell-hole.

The dull thud of the gas-shells mingles with the crashes of the high explosives. A bell sounds between the explosions, gongs, and metal clappers warning everyone — Gas — Gas — Gaas.

Someone plumps down behind me, another, I wipe the goggles of my mask clear of the moist breath. It is Kat, Kropp, and someone else. All four of us lie there in heavy, watchful suspense and breathe as lightly as possible.

These first minutes with the mask decide between life and death: is it air-tight? I remember the awful sights in the hospital: the gas patients who in day-long suffocation cough up their burnt lungs in clots.

Cautiously, the mouth applied to the valve, I breathe. The gas still creeps over the ground and sinks into all hollows. Like a big, soft jelly-fish it floats into our shell-hole and lolls there obscenely. I nudge Kat, it is better to crawl out and lie on top than to stay where the gas collects most. But we don't get as far as that; a second bombardment begins. It is no longer as though shells roared; it is the earth itself raging.

With a crash something black bears down on us. It lands close beside us; a coffin thrown up.

I see Kat move and I crawl across. The coffin has hit the fourth man in our hole on his out-stretched arm. He tries to tear off his gas-mask with the other hand. Kropp seizes him just in time, twists the hand sharply behind his back and holds it fast.

Kat and I proceed to free the wounded arm. The coffin lid is loose and bursts open, we are easily able to pull it off, we toss the corpse out, it slides down to the bottom of the shell-hole, then we try to loosen the under-part.

Fortunately the man swoons and Kropp is able to help us. We no longer have to be careful, but work away till the coffin gives with a sigh before the spade that we have dug in under it.

It has grown lighter. Kat takes a piece of the lid, places it under the shattered arm, and we wrap all our bandages round it. For the moment we can do no more.

Inside the gas-mask my head booms and roars — it is nigh bursting. My lungs are tight, they breathe always the same hot, used-up air, the veins on my temples are swollen, I feel I am suffocating.

A grey light filters through to us. I climb out over the edge of the shell-hole. In the dirty twilight lies a leg torn clean off; the boot is quite whole, I take that all in at a glance. Now something stands up a few yards distant. I polish the windows, in my excitement they are immediately dimmed again. I peer through them, the man there no longer wears his mask.

I wait some seconds — he has not collapsed — he looks around and makes a few paces — rattling in my throat I tear my mask off too and fall down, the air streams into me like cold water, my eyes are bursting, the wave sweeps over me and extinguishes me.

* * *

The shelling has ceased, I turn towards the crater and beckon to the others. They take off their masks. We lift up the wounded man, one taking his splintered arm. And so we stumble off hastily.

The graveyard is a mass of wreckage. Coffins and corpses lie strewn about. They have been killed once again; but each of them that was flung up saved one of us.

from *All Quiet on the Western Front* by Erich Maria Remarque

Reading for Meaning

1 What indicates the presence of the cemetery?
2 What sounds do the soldiers hear as the barrage breaks out behind them?
3 As they duck down, what happens ahead of them?
4 What happens to the wood under the second explosion?
5 'Take Cover!' Why is the graveyard their only possible cover?
6 'The dark goes mad.' How does this happen?
7 How do the fields look to the writer by the light of the shells?
8 'The wood vanishes . . .' How does this happen?
9 Explain how the writer is nearly killed three times.
10 Why does the writer fling himself into the hole torn up in front of him?
11 What does the writer use for cover?
12 What warning does Katczinsky yell to the writer?
13 How is the gas warning conveyed to everyone?
14 Why do the 'first minutes with the mask decide between life and death'?
15 What awful sights at the hospital does the writer remember?
16 How does the gas look to the writer as it floats into their shell-hole?
17 How does the fourth man in the hole react when he is hit by a coffin?
18 How do the soldiers give first aid to the wounded man?
19 When does the writer feel it is safe to take off his mask?
20 'I tear my mask off.' How does he feel when he has done this?
21 What tribute does the writer pay to the graveyard?
22 How does this passage help to dispel the belief that war is noble and glorious?

POETRY

POEMS ABOUT STRUGGLE

The Hero

'Jack fell as he'd have wished,' the Mother said.
And folded up the letter that she'd read.
'The Colonel writes so nicely.' Something broke
In the tired voice that quavered to a choke.
She half looked up. 'We mothers are so proud
Of our dead soldiers.' Then her face was bowed.

Quietly the Brother Officer went out.
He'd told the poor old dear some gallant lies
That she would nourish all her days, no doubt.
For while he coughed and mumbled, her weak eyes
Had shone with gentle triumph, brimmed with joy,
Because he'd been so brave, her glorious boy.

He thought how 'Jack', cold-footed, useless swine,
Had panicked down the trench that night the mine
Went up at Wicked Corner*; how he'd tried
To get sent home, and how, at last, he died,
Blown to small bits. And no one seemed to care
Except that lonely woman with white hair.

Siegfried Sassoon

* part of a trench system

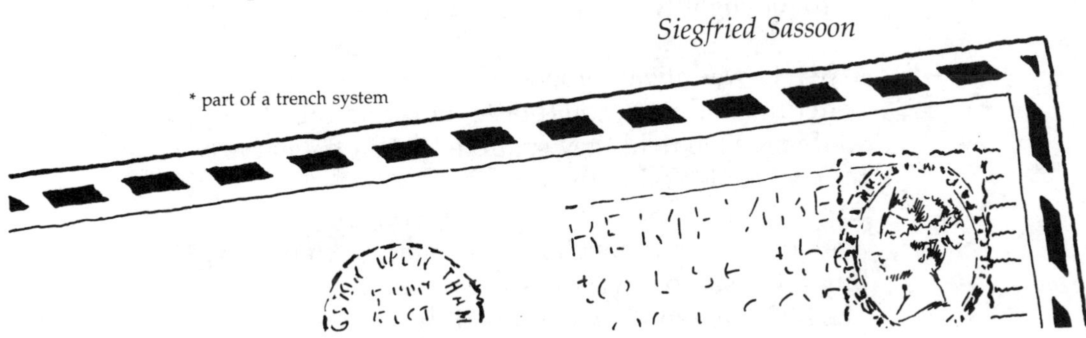

Questions

1 How do you know that the mother thought of her dead son as a hero?
2 What feeling did the Mother have towards 'our dead soldiers'?
3 Why do you think the Brother Officer told the Mother 'some gallant lies'?
4 How did the Mother react to these 'gallant lies'?
5 Why did the Brother Officer think of Jack as a 'cold-footed, useless swine'?
6 What was Jack's fate?
7 What kind of a man was Jack? Give evidence from the poem to support your viewpoint.
8 On what sad note does the poem end?
9 Do you think the title 'The Hero' is appropriate or not? Why?
10 What are your feelings towards the Mother?
11 What is your attitude towards the Brother Officer?
12 What does this poem reveal about war?

The Fifth Sense

A 65-year-old Cypriot Greek shepherd, Nicolis Loizou, was wounded by security forces early today. He was challenged twice; when he failed to answer, troops opened fire. A subsequent hospital examination showed that the man was deaf.
News Item, December 30th, 1957.

Lamps burn all the night
Here, where people must be watched and seen,
And I, a shepherd, Nicolis Loizou,
Wish for the dark, for I have been
Sure-footed in the dark, but now my sight
Stumbles among these beds, scattered white boulders,
As I lean towards my far slumbering house
With the night lying upon my shoulders.

My sight was always good,
Better than others. I could taste wine and bread
And name the field they spattered when the harvest
Broke. I could coil in the red
Scent of the fox out of a maze of wood
And grass. I could touch mist, I could touch breath.
But of my sharp senses I had only four.
The fifth one pinned me to my death.

The soldiers must have called
The word they needed: Halt. Not hearing it,
I was their failure, relaxed against the winter
Sky, the flag of their defeat.
With their five senses they could not have told
That I lacked one, and so they had to shoot.
They would fire at a rainbow if it had
A colour less than they were taught.

Christ said that when one sheep
Was lost, the rest meant nothing any more.
Here in this hospital, where others' breathing
Swings like a lantern in the polished floor
And squeezes those who cannot sleep,
I see how precious each thing is, how dear,
For I may never touch, smell, taste or see
Again, because I could not hear.

Patricia Beer

Questions

1 What is the setting at the beginning of the poem?
2 What image does the shepherd, Nicolis Loizou, use to show us how defective his sight has become?
3 To what does he compare the hospital beds that surround him?
4 What image does he use to show us that the night has become a burden to him?
5 What example of the power of his sense of taste does Nicolis give us?
6 What vivid image does he give us of the acuteness of his sense of smell?
7 How sensitive was his sense of touch?
8 What is the meaning of 'The fifth one pinned me to my death'?
9 Why did the soldiers have to shoot Nicolis?
10 How are we told that the soldiers were ruthlessly dedicated to their training?
11 What is the rhythm of the breathing in the hospital compared to?
12 Why does the shepherd conclude that his defective hearing was the most vital of all his senses?
13 What is the poet's message to the reader?
14 How does the poet create a true-to-life situation?

The Bear

His sullen shaggy-rimmed eyes followed my
  every move,
Slowly gyrating they seemed to mimic the
  movements of his massive head.
Similarly his body rolled unceasingly
From within.
As though each part possessed its own motion
And could think
And move for itself alone.
He had come forward in a lumbering, heavy spurt;
Like a beer barrel rolling down a plank.
The tremendous volume of his blood-red mouth
Yawned
So casually
But with so much menace.
And still the eye held yours.
So that you had to stay.
And then it turned.
Away.
So slowly.
Back
With that same motion
Back
To the bun-strewn
And honey-smelling back of its cage.

Frederick Brown

Questions

1 What scene does the poet present you with at the beginning of the poem?
2 What words of the poet emphasise the bear's size?
3 What comparison does the poet use to tell us how the bear looked as it moved towards him?
4 What features of the bear's mouth does the poet emphasise?
5 What power was present in the bear's eye?
6 What is the poet's purpose in repeating the word 'back'?
7 What contrast can you find in the poem's last two lines?
8 What is the poet's message to the reader in 'The Bear'?
9 Do you think this poem could have been written from the poet's real-life experience? Why?
10 What are your feelings towards the bear?

Out and About, the Lads

pants flapping round legpoles
like denim flags

necks open to the wind
their element

boots the colour of raw liver
boss the pavement

out and about
the lads

voices raised like fists
tattooed with curses

outnumbered rivals
they take in their stride

lampposts and pillarboxes
step aside

out and about
the lads

thick as thieves
and every one a star

Paul uses a knife
you dont feel a thing

Des the best speller
the aerosol king

out and about
the lads

cornered young
they will live their lives in corners

umpteenagers
out on a spree

looking for the likes
of you and me

out and about
the lads

Roger McGough

Questions

1 How do the lads wear their pants?

2 'Boots . . . boss the pavement'. What does this tell us about the lads?

3 What does the poet tell us about the lads' voices?

4 How does the poet convey the impression that the lads dominate everything in the street?

5 How do you know that Paul is an expert with the knife?

6 What is Des's specialty?

7 What is the meaning of 'cornered young/they will live their lives in corners'?

8 What hint of menace is contained in the second last verse?

9 What is the effect of repeating throughout the poem 'out and about the lads'?

10 What does the poet show us about the lads' way of life?

Maladjusted Boys

I have made ten minutes of silence.
I know they are afraid of silence
And the mind's pattern of order.
They gaze at me out of oblique faces
And try to fidget away the bleak thoughts
Simmering in the dark tangle of their minds.
I read their unfriendly eyes, cushion
The confused hatred, stand presumptuously
And pretend not to be afraid.
I keep at them with my eyes,
Will them to work and ride
The storm in a roomful of cold attention.
Here and there faces cringe
And I read a future . . . the dark corner
Of a street hiding the cruel
Thud of a chain or boot.
I see a hunter mask glow on a face
And grimy nailbitten hands bend a ruler
To its limit . . . all this in a room
Yellow with June sun and music
Of birds from a private wood.

Robert Morgan

WRITING

THE WRITER'S IMAGINATION

Novelists depend on imagination to create descriptions that are fascinating for the reader. Look at these passages describing people and places. They have been created by writers from their imagination and they are both fantastic and fascinating.

The Desolate Wind

The air around the second planet of the Frogstar system was stale and unwholesome.

The dank winds that swept continually over its surface swept over salt flats, dried up marshland, tangled and rotting vegetation and the crumbling remains of ruined cities. No life moved across its surface. The ground, like that of many planets in this part of the Galaxy, had long been deserted.

The howl of the wind was desolate enough as it gusted through the old decaying houses of the cities; it was more desolate as it whipped about the bottoms of the tall black towers that swayed uneasily here and there about the surface of this world. At the top of these towers lived colonies of large, scraggy, evil smelling birds, the sole survivors of the civilisation that once lived here.

from *The Restaurant at the End of the Universe* by Douglas Adams

Foggerty

Foggerty wore a long, foul, ragged black overcoat, which seemed to have grown on him. It was secured round the middle with repeatedly knotted string, from which hung various accoutrements, mug, hair-brush, spoon, fly-swat, tin opener. An outsize greasy brown trilby, set low on his forehead, gave him the appearance of having no top to his head, which in fact he hadn't. Son of a long line of camp followers, he had been relieved of his post as lighthouse keeper at the shale rock when he drew the blinds, to 'stop the light shining into the poor sailors' eyes'. The light was closed down, and these days ships have to find their own way on to the rocks.

from *Puckoon* by Spike Milligan

Aliens

A line of tiny animals, if animals they were, came marching down the steps, one behind another. They were four inches high or so and they went on all four feet, although it was plain to see that their front feet were really hands, not feet. They had rat-like faces that were vaguely human, with noses long and pointed. They looked as if they might have scales instead of hide, for their bodies glistened with a rippling motion as they walked. And all of them had tails that looked very much like the coiled-wire tails one finds on certain toys and the tails stuck straight up above them, quivering as they walked.

They came down the steps in single file, in perfect military order, with half a foot or so of spacing between each one of them.

They came down the steps and walked out into the desert in a straight, undeviating line as if they knew exactly where they might be bound. There was something deadly purposeful about them and yet they didn't hurry.

from *The Big Front Yard* by Clifford Simak

Storm at Sea

There was nothing in sight all around the ship but grey waves streaked with white. But they were like no waves Willie had ever seen. They were as tall as apartment houses, marching by majestic and rhythmical; the *Caine* was a little taxicab among them. It was no longer pitching and tossing like a ship ploughing through waves, it was rising and falling on the jagged surface of the sea like a piece of garbage. Flying water filled the air. It was impossible to see whether it was spray or rain, but Willie knew without thinking that it was spray because he tasted salt on his lips.

The ship rolled to starboard and back again, a terrifying sharp roll, but in a familiar rhythm. The tightness in Willie's chest eased. He now noticed the sound that was almost drowning out the voices in the wheelhouse. It was a deep, sorrowful whine coming from nowhere and everywhere, a noise above the crashing of the waves and the creaking of the ship and the roar of the black-smoking stacks. 'Ooooooooo EEEEEEEEEE eeeeeeeeeeeee,' a universal noise as though the sea and the air were in pain, 'Ooo EEEEE, ooooo EEEEEE —'

Willie staggered to the barometer. He gasped. The needle trembled at 29.28.

from *The Caine Mutiny* by Herman Wouk

Robot

For a moment Baley stared curiously at R. Daneel Olivaw. The robot, looking straight ahead, was motionless and unselfconscious under the other's gaze.

Daneel's skin texture was perfect, the individual hairs on head and body had been lovingly and intricately manufactured and placed. The muscle movement under the skin was most realistic. No pains, however extravagant, had been spared. Yet Baley knew, from personal knowledge, that limbs and chest could be split open along invisible seams so that repairs might be made. He knew there was metal and silicon under that realistic skin. He knew a positronic brain, most advanced but only positronic, nestled in the hollow of the skull. He knew that Daneel's 'thoughts' were only short-lived positronic currents flowing along paths rigidly designed and foreordained by the manufacturer.

But what were the signs that would give away to the expert eye that had no foreknowledge? The trifling unnaturalness of Daneel's manner of speech? The unemotional gravity that rested so steadily upon him? The very perfection of his humanity?

from *The Naked Sun* by Isaac Asimov

The Powerful Magician

Iza looked up when an old man, past thirty, hobbled up to her after they were on their way again. He carried neither burden nor weapon, only a long staff to help him walk. His right leg was crippled and smaller than the left, yet he managed to move with surprising agility.

His right shoulder and upper arm were atrophied and the shrivelled arm had been amputated below the elbow. The powerful shoulder and arm, and muscular leg of his fully developed left side made him appear lopsided. His huge cranium was even larger than those of the rest of the clan, and the difficulty of his birth had caused the defect that crippled him for life.

The left side of his face was hideously scarred and his left eye was missing, but his good right eye sparkled with intelligence, and something more. For all his hobbling, he moved with a grace that came from great wisdom and a sureness of his place within the clan. He was Mog-ur, the most powerful magician, most awesome and revered holy man of all the clans. He was convinced that his wasted body was given to him so that he could take his place as intermediary with the spirit world rather than at the head of his clan. In many ways he had more power than any leader, and he knew it.

from *The Clan of the Cave Bear* by Jean M. Auel

The Giant Worm Emerges

Behind them, he heard a hissing — like the wind, like a riptide where there was no water.

'Run!' Jessica screamed. 'Paul, run!'

They ran.

Drumsound boomed beneath their feet. Then they were out of it and into pea gravel. For a time, the running was a relief to muscles that ached from unfamiliar, rhythmless use. Here was action that could be understood. Here was rhythm. But sand and gravel dragged at their feet. And the hissing approach of the worm was storm sound that grew around them.

Jessica stumbled to her knees. All she could think of was the fatigue and the sound and the terror.

Paul dragged her up.

They ran on, hand in hand.

A deep crack stretched its vertical shadow upward into the cliff ahead of them. They sprinted for it, crowded into the narrow hole.

Behind them, the sound of the worm's passage stopped.

Jessica and Paul turned, peered out onto the desert.

Where the dunes began, perhaps fifty metres away at the foot of a rock beach, a silver-grey curve broached from the desert, sending rivers of sand and dust cascading all around. It lifted higher, resolved into a giant, questing mouth. It was a round, black hole with edges glistening in the moonlight.

The mouth snaked toward the narrow crack where Paul and Jessica huddled. Cinnamon yelled in their nostrils. Moonlight flashed from crystal teeth.

Back and forth the great mouth wove.

Paul stilled his breathing.

Jessica crouched staring.

from *Dune* by Frank Herbert

Working with Imagination

Here are some questions that are designed to focus your attention on the ways the writer's imagination has created people, places and situations in the passages you have read.

1 In the imagination of Douglas Adams, what sound and feeling were possessed by the wind that swept across the second planet of the Frogstar system?

2 What words does Douglas Adams use to create a sense of decay?

3 In 'Foggerty', has Spike Milligan used his imagination in providing us with a vivid image of Foggerty's clothing?

4 Why was Foggerty relieved of his post as a lighthouse keeper?

5 In 'Aliens', what is unusual about the behaviour and appearance of Clifford Simak's alien animals?

6 What words has Herman Wouk used to suggest the enormous size of the waves in 'Storm at Sea'?

7 How does Herman Wouk use sound to stimulate the reader's imagination?

8 In 'Robot', how successfully has Isaac Asimov used his imagination to create the character of R. Daneel Olivaw?

9 In 'The Powerful Magician', what contrast in Mo-gur's physical appearance is used by Jean Auel to seize the reader's imagination?

10 In 'The Giant Worm Emerges', how does Frank Herbert use sound to help create a feeling of approaching terror?

11 Why do you think the writer chooses to describe only the mouth of the giant worm in detail?

12 Which passage appeals to your imagination most? Why?

USING YOUR OWN IMAGINATION

Think of the passages you have read as models that will suggest ideas for your imagination. An imaginative piece of writing will need to possess its own special focus. If you have decided to write about a person you must 'see' in your mind the kind of person you are describing. Then use your imagination to make that person different, strange — even fantastic. Foggerty, for example, only really becomes fantastic when we read that his overcoat 'was securèd round the middle with repeatedly knotted string, from which hung various accoutrements, mug, hair-brush, spoon, fly-swat, tin opener'. It is the vividness of Spike Milligan's imagination that makes Foggerty unforgettable. Your aim should be to make your own imaginative descriptions of people, places and situations equally unforgettable.

Choose two of the titles below and write an imaginative paragraph on each.

- The wild landscape of an alien planet
- An unforgettable character
- Aliens
- Terror at sea
- The android
- Future sport
- The wizard
- The monster
- A supernatural experience
- The magical moment

LANGUAGE

UNDERSTANDING SENTENCES

A **sentence** is an arrangement of words that expresses a complete thought or idea. Here is an example of a simple sentence expressing a complete thought.

Jack hurled his spear.

A sentence presents a **subject** and then tells the reader something about it. The subject in the above sentence is 'Jack'. What is said about Jack is that he 'hurled his spear'. This is called the **predicate** of the sentence. Notice that the predicate contains the verb or action word 'hurled'. It will help you to create complete sentences, each containing a complete thought, if you clearly understand that sentences usually contain a subject and a predicate.

Forming Sentences

Here are twelve sentences from the pens of famous novelists. The subjects of the sentences have been separated from their predicates. Recreate each sentence by matching up its subject with its predicate.

Subjects

1 The old man

2 The Grand Trunk Road

3 The unconscious patient

4 Dinner

5 The print of a man's foot

6 Three sailors

7 The shark's dorsal fin

Predicates

cut the glassy water with a hiss.
(*Jaws,* Peter Benchley)

were the barest crew for a cutter.
(*Flying Colours,* C.S. Forester)

were white in her brown face.
(*For Whom the Bell Tolls,* Ernest Hemingway)

were placed in the bear's cave.
(*The Clan of the Cave Bear,* Jean Auel)

vandalised the classroom.
(*The Blackboard Jungle,* Evan Hunter)

gazed from the wall.
(*Nineteen Eighty-Four,* George Orwell)

had been in a motor accident.
(*One Pair of Feet,* Monica Dickens)

8 A weak trickle of steam	(1) was thin and gaunt with deep wrinkles in the back of his neck. (*The Old Man and the Sea*, Ernest Hemingway)
9 Her teeth	(4) was handsomely served at a groaning table. (*Bleak House*, Charles Dickens)
10 The swarm of students	(2) runs straight without crowding India's traffic for fifteen hundred miles. (*Kim*, Rudyard Kipling)
11 The poster with the huge face	(5) was plain to be seen in the sand. (*Robinson Crusoe*, Daniel Defoe)
12 The cave bear's sacred bones	(8) hissed from the engine's outlet valve. (*Puckoon*, Spike Milligan)

Giving a Sentence a Different Subject

Look at this sentence:

- **A shell splinter** slashed my helmet.

Notice that the subject, the shell splinter, performs the action. However, the sentence can be reconstructed to bring a different subject into focus.
For example:

- **My helmet** was slashed by a shell splinter.

In this sentence, 'My helmet' is the new subject.

Give new subjects to each of the following sentences as indicated.

1 Kropp seized the wounded soldier.
The wounded soldier ... was seized by kropp.

2 The sea lashed the pier.
The pier ... was lashed by the sea.

3 The rock struck Piggy a glancing blow.
Piggy was struck a glancing blow by the rock.

4 A tremendous wind whipped up the waves.
The waves ... were whipped up by the tremendous wind.

5 A gust of rage shook Ralph.
Ralph ... was shaken by a gust of rage.

6 A terrific explosion destroyed many trees.
Many trees were destroyed by the terrific explosion.

7 The boys who had turned into savages hunted the pigs.
The pigs were hunted by the boys who had turned into savages.

8 The guns fired at the running troops.
The running troops ... were fired at by the guns.

9 Johnno rescued the drowning victim.
The drowning victim . . .

10 The bullet tore the sleeve of his uniform.
The sleeve of his uniform . . .

Joining Sentences

Use the joining word shown in heavy type to join each pair of sentences below so that they form a complete sentence. Note that sometimes more than one method may be used. Also, you will need to decide whether or not a comma is required. The first sentence has been completed for you.

1 They must keep a signal fire going
A ship appears
Until a ship appears they must keep a signal fire going.

2 I pulled him back into the trench
Another shell was coming over
Because . . .

3 We could still swim across the pool
The water was rough
Although . . .

4 Piggy has the conch
The savages will listen to him
If . . .

5 A cloud of flame shoots up in front of us
We duck down
When . . .

6 The wave flung him against the pier
One boy shouted for help
After . . .

7 He had any breath left in his lungs
Ralph fought gamely
While . . .

8 Gas shells were exploding
They donned their masks
As . . .

9 Johnno saw his mate battling the waves behind him
He could spare a glance
Whenever . . .

10 I struggled
I felt the shells cutting my arms and legs
Until . . .

Changing Sentences from Singular to Plural

Change each of the following sentences from singular to plural. To do this you will need to change all the appropriate words in the sentence from singular to plural. The first example has been done to help you.

1 The swimmer dives through the wave.
The swimmers dive through the waves.

2 The wounded soldier was trapped in his trench.
The wounded soldiers . . .

3 The building goes up in the terrible explosion.
The buildings . . .

4 He puts on his sweater and walks to the dressing shed.
They . . .

5 'Grab him!' yelled the savage who was shaking his fist.
'Grab them!' . . .

6 The tree vanishes as it is pounded and crushed by the bomb.
The trees . . .

Changing Sentences from Plural to Singular

Change each of the following sentences from plural to singular.

1 Our hands were grasping the wounded men.
My hand . . .

2 The spears are raised and the savages shout.
The spear . . .

3 We handed them our towels and kicked off our sandals.
I . . .

4 They remove their masks and are immediately aware of the terrible sights around them.
He . . .

5 They swim forward to meet the booming waves.
I . . .

6 They pause and listen for any hurtling shells.
He . . .

Turning Advertisements into Sentences

Turn each of the following ads into a complete sentence by expanding on the information given. Feel free to use your imagination! The first one has been done for you.

1 Hse 3 bdrms, sea views, close beach and trans. Immac. $250 pw.

If you are thinking of renting, this three bedroom house at $250 per week with sea views will appeal to you because of its immaculate condition and its closeness to both beaches and transport.

2 Unit 2 bdrms, balc, spacious new carpets, BBQ area. $200 pw.

3 Lawns cut/fertilised, reliable, prompt, friendly locals. Free quotes.

4 Shop assistant for bakery. Casual, no exp necessary. Refs required.

5 Ironing Service. Pick up/deliver 24 hr. Exc value.

6 Disco Jo Top music weddings, parties, anything. 12 Yrs Exp. Gd rates.

7 Surfski Raider 2.2 m Must sell. Good cond. One owner $300 ono.

8 Honda Civic, low kms, mech A1 cond, man, air con, runs well $5,500 ono.

9 Dog, Gold Labdr, lost, answers to 'Lucky'. Family pet. Reward.

10 Bargains, house clearance, furn, electrical, lots of exciting goods, browse, no one asked to buy.

GETTING IT RIGHT

COMMON ERRORS

Here are rules that will correct four common errors.

1 Words such as 'unique', 'perfect', 'square', 'circular', 'full', 'empty' should not be used with 'more' and 'most'. For example:

- The examiner has written a most unique book on water safety. (Incorrect)
- The examiner has written a unique book on water safety. (Correct)

2 Make sure you leave out unnecessary words in your sentences. For example:

- Jack ascended up the hill. (Incorrect)
- Jack ascended the hill. (Correct)

3 The word 'either' is used for two people or things. Use 'any one' for more than two. For example:

- Either of these three soldiers can take command. (Incorrect)
- Any one of these three soldiers can take command. (Correct)

4 Make sure that any '-ing' expression you use refers to its proper subject.

- Diving into the water, the waves were huge. (Incorrect)
- Diving into the water, the boy found the waves were huge. (Correct)

Identifying the Common Errors

Correct each of the following sentences and give a reason for each correction.

1. A most perfect day dawned on the island.
2. We descended down the trench before the next explosion.
3. Either of the four boys could easily have wounded Jack.
4. Running along the beach, the sand stung their legs.
5. They crossed over the track at great speed.
6. Try to make the corner of the wall more square.
7. Lying on my back in the water, the rain beat heavily on my face.
8. They lifted up the boxes onto the truck.
9. Either of these six bullets can be used in the gun.
10. Your bracelet's design is more unique than mine.

DRAMA

THINK TANK

To form a 'Think Tank', select from your class an energetic group that is willing to confront, discuss, argue and come up with ideas about resolving some of the issues and problems that we have to live with in the late twentieth century.

Here's how you do it.

1 In your Think Tank you need the following people:

- a chairperson
- a conservationist
- a politician
- a teacher
- a student
- the man or woman in the street
- a priest or minister
- a representative of business
- a scientist
- a doctor
- a pop star
- a journalist

2 Class members should volunteer to adopt the role of each person in the Think Tank. Note that the role of the chairperson is most important. He or she should be energetic and able to control the flow of thought in the Think Tank, cutting short tedious discussion but encouraging original ideas and solutions.

3 The rest of the class should involve themselves by proposing the issue or problem that they want the Think Tank to thrash out. At the end of the session, the class may vote on the solution arrived at by their Think Tank.

4 Any member of the Think Tank has the right to call upon any class member to act as an expert or adviser on an issue or problem for the Think Tank. You may have hidden talents in the class that only your Think Tank can reveal!

Twentieth century issues and problems

1 Increasing violence in our schools
2 AIDS
3 Racism
4 The destruction of rainforests
5 The United States imports 1.6 million dollars worth of petroleum products every day.
6 The world's energy consumption is 80% from non-renewable sources and only 20% from renewable resources. The estimated life of the 80% of non-renewable sources is Oil: 30 years, Natural Gas: 40 years, Coal: 200 years, Uranium: unknown. Note that solar, wind and wave power do not even rate as 1% of energy sources being used at present in the world.
7 It is predicted that the year 2006 will see one billion cars on the world's roads. Where and what is the fuel?
8 The world population explosion
9 The extinction of animal species
10 War as a means of solving the world's problems
11 Third World poverty
12 Global pollution, including the hole in the ozone layer
13 Drug abuse
14 Abortion
15 Street people and homelessness in our cities
16 Marriage and divorce
17 The media and the portrayal of violence
18 The justification or otherwise of space travel
19 Crime and corruption
20 The survival of individuality

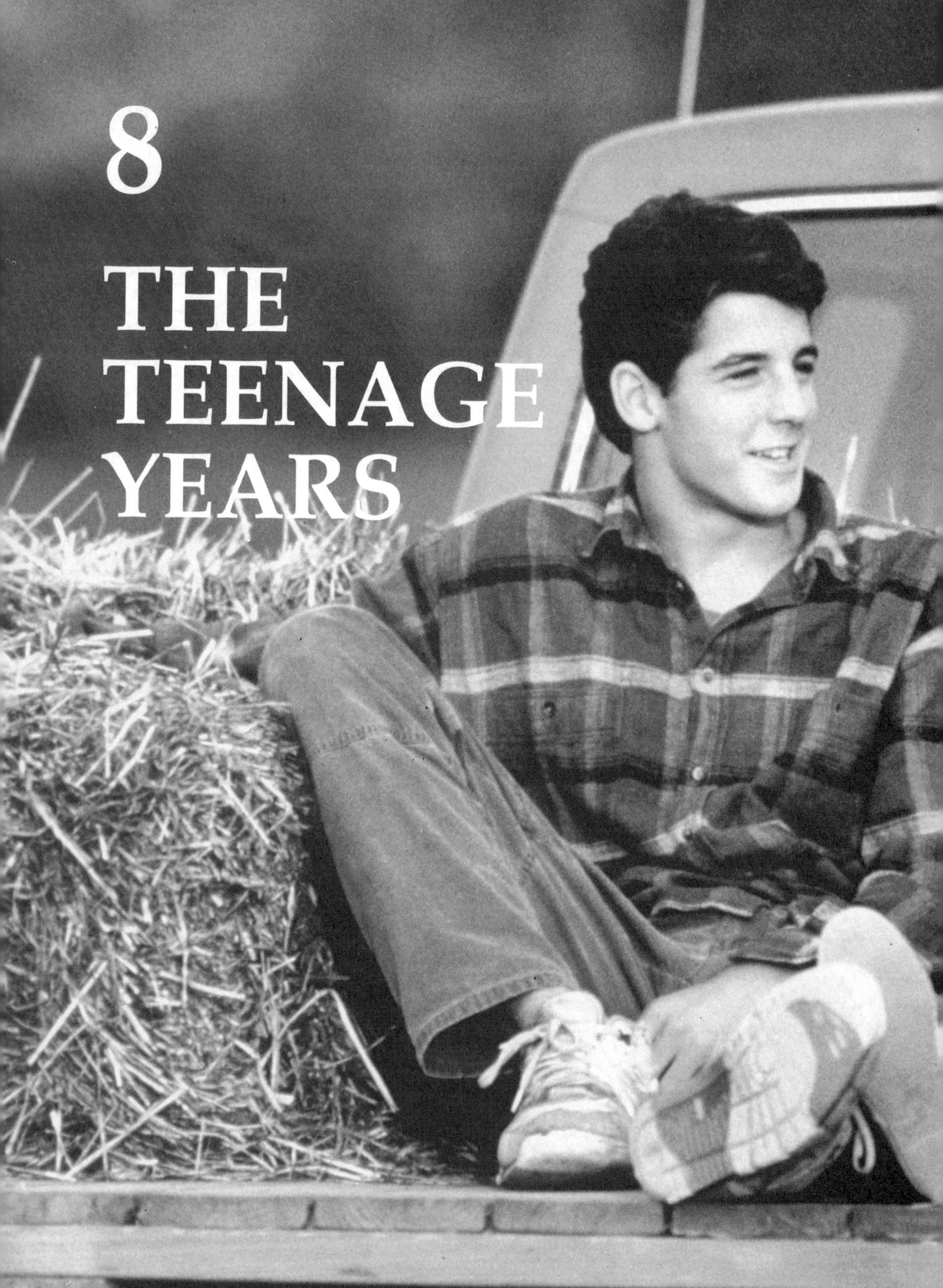

8

THE TEENAGE YEARS

NOVELS

The Pay-back

Pennington turns his creative thinking to an idea for paying back Soggy, the teacher who has so consistently made his life a misery.

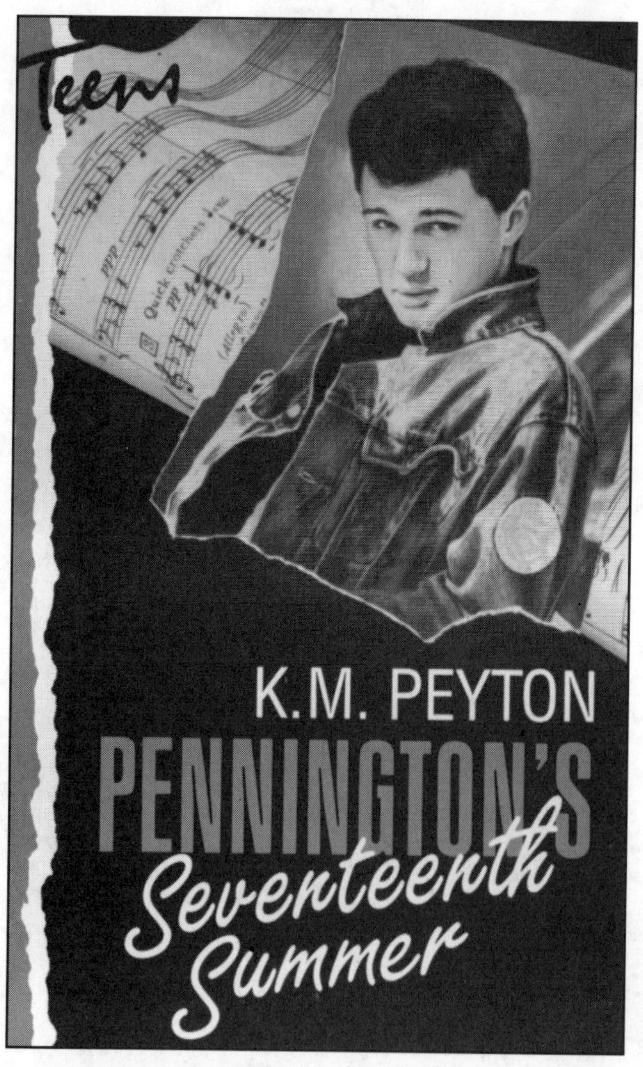

Penn wanted to humiliate Soggy before the whole class, as Soggy had so often done to him. He wanted to burst his pomposity, make him weep. There was nothing bad enough really, but there was a limiting factor: it had to be something that would not interest the police, for Penn had no desire for his three months at Oakhall to be improved into two years at a Borstal. He went into a huddle with Rees and a staunch Soggy-hater called Patterson. Everyone knew what was in the wind, and the class was full of a curious tension that made Miss Harrington say in the staff-room, 'Whatever's got into 5C today? They're in the strangest mood.'

'When Pennington's gone,' said Soggy, 'we might get somewhere with them.'

For his part, he was full of optimism at the way things were looking.

In the dinner-hour Penn screwed a large hook into the ceiling above the class-room door. Rees was hammering a hole into the rim round the bottom of an enormous galvanised bucket which he had taken out of the cleaners' cupboard.

'It's what they do in the *Beano*,' Bates said. 'It'll never work.'

'Oh, won't it?' Penn said grimly.

They had several run-throughs, and Penn marked a chalk cross on the floor just inside the door. And another one a foot or two farther in.

'You must stand there, Rees, to stop him coming any farther. He's got to be on this first chalk mark, or it'll miss him.'

'I've got some rope,' Patterson said. 'I asked Matthews and he gave me some.'

'Did you tell him what it was for?' Penn asked, grinning.

'I said it was for Soggy.'

'Penn, you're not really going to?' Rita Fairweather said. The girls were all pop-eyed and giggling. 'He'll kill you.'

'I don't care what he does,' Penn said recklessly.

'Maxwell and Crombie have made the mixture,' Bates came up to report. ' They've got it in the chemistry lab. Maxwell says he's just adding a smell to it. Herbs, he said, to give it a bouquet. He wants to know, before he hands it over, whether you're going to promise you're taking full responsibility, Penn. He wants it in writing.'

'Yes, if he wants it.'

'Oh, Penn, you're not —' Bates knew he was chicken, but the sight of the mixture had brought the gravity of the operation home to him. He had thought it had all been a joke at the start. But he could see now that Penn was in no mood for jokes.

'What's in it?' the girls wanted to know.

'Soot, liquid manure, oil, blood —'

'Shut up, Bates. It's a secret recipe,' Rees said. 'We don't want everyone to know it.'

Maxwell and Crombie brought it up and everyone stared at it in awe.

'I hope that ruddy hook's strong enough,' Penn said, eyeing the ceiling.

'I must come and see,' Maxwell said. 'This I cannot miss.'

'Soggy has got to walk from 3C to get back here when the last bell goes. It should just give us time to get it fixed. Put the bucket in the cupboard, Maxwell. Patterson, you're to watch for Soggy outside. It would be criminal to waste it on the wrong man. Rees and I will rig it, then I'll operate it, and Rees can stand on the second chalk cross. And everyone else can stand back and cheer.'

'Oh, cripes,' said Bates. He was already pale as a dead leaf.

Penn tested how much weight the hook was up to with a bucket of water. Then he rigged up the pulley system with some more hooks, and fixed the rope on to the bucket. By which time the bell went, and the girls went to Domestic Science, and the boys to Gardening, where they spent most of the lesson looking for the liquid manure which they all knew was in the bucket in their class-room.

Penn, Patterson and Rees got away early and sprinted back to the class-room. By the time the last bell went, the bucket was in place and Penn already had his hand on the pulley rope which ran from the hole in the rim up to another hook at a suitably sharp angle, and down to Penn. The girls came in, cautiously avoiding the chalk marks, and stood in silence. Some of them were pale, and the more chicken characters packed up and went downstairs, unable to face the impending situation. Bates sat in a desk in the farthest corner of the room, looking at the wall. He was trembling, and didn't want anyone to notice.

'All set?' Patterson poked his head in from the corridor.

'Yes.'

'I hope it works after all this,' Rees said, taking up his position.

There was utter silence in the class-room. Twenty-five of them stood as if carved out of stone, watching the door. Penn picked up the rope.

Smeeton said, 'Cripes, Penn, this'll do for you.'

Rees put his head in. 'He's coming!'

It worked all right. Penn had not gone to so much trouble to muff it right at the end. He pulled the rope at exactly the moment Soggy stepped on the chalk mark, and the awful, stinking, filthy black mixture poured out of the bucket with the smooth precision of hot steel from the smelter, its exact target the top of Soggy's head, where the long grey hairs were manfully smoothed across the bald dome. It parted over his crown and ran in glutinous streams down his face and over his ears and down into the back of his collar, then in rivers over the shoulders of his suit, being absorbed, in big globs and splashes, on to his trousers, in a film over his hands and the whole of 3C's English compositions. Penn, giving the rope a final jerk, hoped the bucket would follow up, braining him, but his handiwork had been too good to provide this final satisfaction. He dropped the rope, and stood with his hands in his pockets, taking in the beautiful sight, his face quite grave, composed, and utterly calm.

There was a silence, profound as the dark inside of a tomb. Then one of the girls started to laugh. It was a hysterical laugh, but it was music in Penn's ears. Rees, standing his ground, caught Patterson's eye over Marsh's glistening shoulder, and hiccuped. He turned away. Patterson curled up, leaning against the door jamb, his shoulders heaving, and the bolder girls started to laugh with their usual spluttering and squeaking. Taking courage, even the timid spirits let out horrified giggles, and

in a moment the whole room was in an uproar. Only Penn stood, faintly smiling, never taking his eyes off Soggy's plight.

To give him his due, Soggy remained commendably calm. He put his books on the floor, groped for a handkerchief and wiped his face so that he could see what was going on. When he could see, he saw Penn. When everyone saw him registering, his mind coping, the uproar died down to a silence as tense as the one that preceded it.

'Pennington?' he said, his voice silky.

'Sir?'

'You did this?'

'Yes, sir.'

Soggy turned his head to Smeeton and said, 'Fetch my cane.'

Smeeton fetched it, smiling.

'Come here, Pennington.'

Penn went. He didn't care, for the image of Soggy, dripping with filth, would stay in his mind as a comfort for ever, until the day he died. It was the nicest thing that had ever happened to him and nothing Soggy could do now could take it away.

'Hold out your hand.'

It hurt, but Penn wasn't bothered. Soggy was up to six when Rita Fairweather said, in a strangled voice, 'But, sir! Penn's playing in this music competition tomorrow!'

Nobody, least of all Penn, had remembered the significance of tomorrow. Penn involuntarily took his hand away, and everybody gasped, fascinated by the implications. Soggy paused, blinking. Penn could see the various possibilities chasing themselves through his mind. As he himself was the only one who knew that he wasn't playing in the competition tomorrow, he was more curious than horrified, and relieved, physically, that Rita had stopped Soggy.

But Soggy's reaction was unexpected.

'Hold out your other hand,' he said.

Penn did so, and got another stinging six.

Soggy then said to Rita, very smoothly. 'Pennington is old enough to know that certain courses will incur certain consequences. He is no longer a very small boy, without logic, although one would often think so from the way he behaves.' He then turned to Penn, the malice shining in his eyes, and said, 'I am sorry if you find you are unable to play in the competition tomorrow, Pennington. Very disappointing after all the work you have put in. But I think you will appreciate that I felt bound to equalise — I would not like the punishment to have been as lop-sided as your thinking. I've no doubt that what has happened will be a great disappointment to Mr Crocker, for which you have yourself entirely to blame, not me.' He smiled, transparently delighted that the caning had had a punishment value far and away beyond the simple infliction of physical pain. 'Come and see me on Monday morning, Pennington, in Mr Stack's office, after assembly. Mere caning is not, of course, the end of this.'

from *Pennington's Seventeenth Summer* by K. M. Peyton

Reading for Understanding

1 Why did Penn want to humiliate Soggy in front of the whole class?
2 What limit was there on how far Penn's plan for revenge would go?
3 What effect did the plan for revenge have on 5C?
4 How did they intend to make sure that Soggy stopped at just the right spot?
5 Maxwell, having made up the mixture, seemed preoccupied with what concern?
6 How did Penn test the pulley system for strength?
7 What did the most nervous class members do as the moment of revenge drew close?
8 Why did Bates sit so far away?
9 What was noteworthy about the behaviour of the class members as they waited for Soggy's entrance?
10 The contraption worked almost perfectly. What little aspect deprived Penn of the last bit of satisfaction?
11 'There was a silence, profound as the dark inside of a tomb.' Why is the simile so appropriate here?
12 How does Penn react to the sound of the class laughing at Soggy?
13 Why was Pennington so willing to take the punishment, no matter what it was?
14 What information about the music competition did Penn have that no one else had?
15 Explain how the belief that Penn was to play in a competition next day gave added pleasure to Soggy.
16 What character qualities show up in Soggy, judging from the way he handles this situation? Refer to the passage for evidence to support your statements.
17 What character qualities of Penn stand out throughout this incident? Give evidence from the passage.
18 What conclusions does the class response to Soggy's humiliation lead you to make? Explain your answer.

Visit to Hospital

The Colonel is a remarkable man. On this occasion he is in such pain that he has to be taken to hospital by John and Lorraine.

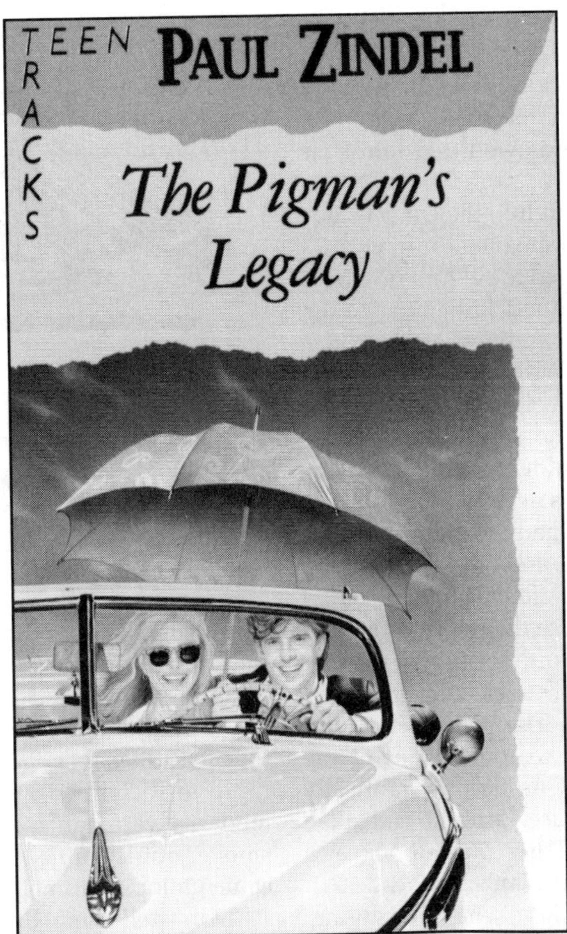

I was just wiping down the windowsills when we heard the Colonel scream out in pain.

'Oh, my God.' Lorraine froze.

I pushed past her and ran up the stairs two steps at a time. 'What is it? What is it?' Lorraine called, now breaking into motion fast behind me. The thumping of my feet on the stairs didn't drown out another scream from the Colonel. And another!

I burst into the Colonel's room. He was bent over in his chair clutching his stomach, moaning deeply, loudly.

'What's the matter?' I cried out.

The Colonel strained to lift his face to me. It was shattered with pain. I didn't know what to do. Lorraine was at my side saying, 'What's the matter? What's wrong?' The Colonel couldn't speak, and I didn't know if I should just run across the street and bang on the door of the convent; or maybe I should just tell Lorraine to run into the middle of the street and stop traffic and say, 'Help! Help!' Finally words began to emerge from the Colonel. He said something about cramps in his stomach. And then I heard very clearly 'Get me to a hospital.'

'Grab him,' I ordered Lorraine. She hesitated. I could see she was frightened. *'Grab him!'* I ordered again, and in a flash we became the old man's crutches once more.

He cried out louder as we lifted him from the chair.

'We've got to get him into the car ,' I said.

'Hurry,' the Colonel moaned, 'hurry!'

Somehow we managed to get him down the stairs. We practically lifted him into the air. We knew it wasn't just indigestion, or something simple like that. We knew it had to be a matter of life and death. Gus was waiting for us at the bottom of the stairs, barking. He jumped up on my shoulders and kept kissing the back of the Colonel's neck as we got him to the side door. That dog had the longest tongue I've ever seen in my life, and I never saw a dog love anyone the way he loved this old guy. I had to move fast to close the door so the dog wouldn't follow us out into the car. In another minute we were in the Studebaker, and I had the key in the ignition. The pistons began to explode again, and as we pulled out of the driveway, I could hear Gus barking frantically now from within the house. Lorraine had taken some Kleenexes out of her pocketbook and was helping dab the old man's forehead.

'It's going to be all right,' she kept saying. 'It's going to be all right.' The old man just kept moaning.

'I need an emergency room,' he wheezed, 'an emergency room.'

'It's all our fault,' Lorraine said.

'You're crazy,' I snapped.

'It's the fudge. You're not supposed to give fudge to anybody who drinks acidophilus milk,' Lorraine moaned.

'I don't even know what acidophilus milk is,' I countered.

The Colonel let out a piercing shriek of pain just as we turned the corner onto Clove Road. A group of Boy Scouts was standing on the corner just shooting the breeze until they heard the scream. Then they all looked up, amazed, as though they had just flunked Advanced Knotting. In another couple of minutes I had the old Studebaker crashing up the emergency ramp to Richmond Hospital. A couple of attendants were right by the entrance sneaking a smoke, but I jammed on the brakes and they came galloping to help us.

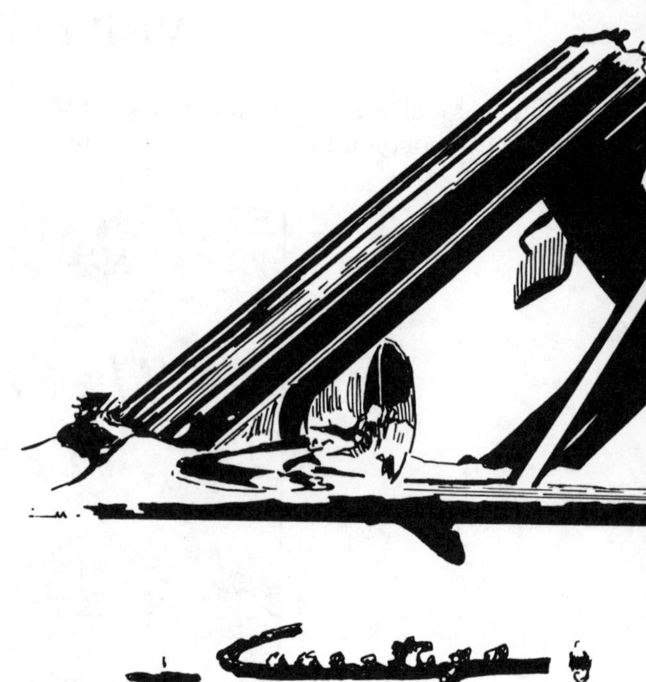

'Don't tell them I'm the Colonel,' the old man said through his pain. 'Don't give them my real name.'

In two shakes of a lamb's tail the attendants had the old guy on a stretcher with wheels and flew him through these automatic doors. Lorraine and I trotted behind, but to our surprise the procession came to a rapid stop in front of an admissions desk.

'What seems to be the problem?' this mean-looking nurse asked us. The Colonel couldn't talk, and you could see he was trying to hold back his anguish, but he still had to cry out in pain. As soon as the mean-looking nurse realised that the old guy wouldn't be doing any

talking, she turned her attention to me, and took up a pen and an information card.

'Name of patient?' she inquired.

'Gus,' Lorraine piped up.

'Gus who?'

'Gus *Bore*,' I invented on the spot.

'What kind of medical insurance does he have?'

'I don't have any,' the old man grunted in an exhale. 'Please help me! Please get me a doctor!'

'Haven't you got Medicare?' the mean nurse pursued.

'Get him to a doctor!' I screamed at her. I wanted to reach out and grab her by the neck and bang her head on the desk. She took a close look at me, and I could see that she knew I meant business. She wanted to know who we were, so we told her we were his grandchildren, and then she ordered us into the waiting room while she had the bozos in white uniforms roll the old man down the hall.

'We want to go with him,' I said.

'That's against hospital rules,' she said, and she sounded so secure about it I figured she wasn't lying. Besides, I knew it was better for her to think we were in the waiting room, because I'm an old hand at sneaking past nurses and going to visit whomever I want in hospitals. I had a cousin once who had his appendix out, and they said there was no visiting after eight o'clock. But I knew how to go up and down the back stairways and walk through the halls as though I was a plainclothes intern. Nobody asks you anything in hospitals if you look as though you belong there.

Lorraine and I decided we'd have to obey orders temporarily because the mean nurse really kept her eyes glued on us. We sat in the horrible waiting room, which had several junk-food machines, a couple of telephones, and these stupid little television sets that you could put a quarter in for an hour's worth of the boob tube.

I got Lorraine and myself hot chocolates with a couple of quarters she had. She just sat on one of the benches sipping it and saying, 'We killed him. We killed him. I know we killed him.'

'He's not dead,' I said.

'He's dying. I just know he's dying.'

'There's a big difference between a stomach ache and dying,' I told her, and then I started to feel sick again myself. Maybe the marble pecan fudge had ptomaine in it, or botulism. After ten minutes I checked with the mean nurse and she told me to just go back and sit down. But I bugged her until she finally admitted the Colonel had been put in examination room number three. I decided to take up watch at the doorway to the waiting room, because from that point I could see all the way down the hall to where the examination rooms were. About a half hour later I saw an attendant roll the Colonel out and start pushing him out of my sight down another hall. A doctor with a stethoscope came out of the room with two nurses behind him, and they all started heading my way. I signalled Lorraine, and we stopped the doctor right in the middle of the hall while the mean nurse kept yelling, 'Get back in the waiting room! Get back in the waiting room!'

'Is he all right?' I asked the doctor.

'We're taking him upstairs now,' the doctor said in a kind, professional voice.

'Can we take him home?' Lorraine asked.

'No. His system has had a terrible shock. We're going to have to run some tests. You're his grandchildren?'

'Yes,' I said.

'Then if you don't mind, please finish filling out the information on him. We're going to have to talk to your mother or father.'

'Yes, sir,' I said, and I was just getting ready to ask him another question when he wiped his nose on his sleeve and dashed off.

The mean-looking nurse seemed delighted. She had an *I-told-you-so* look on her face and Lorraine and I decided we had no other choice than to put down my address for the Colonel and my telephone number. We decided that if the hospital had to call it was better that they call my house, since Lorraine's mother would only think it was a crank and hang up.

'What's his birth date?' the mean nurse wanted to know.

'1906,' I invented.

'Are you sure he has no medical protection whatsoever?'

'I'm not sure,' I said. 'I just don't think so, but I'll check with my mother and father. They were out tonight playing bingo,' I lied, 'and then they were going to a chic cocktail party at the Waldorf-Astoria.' The mean nurse grunted and started slipping another special sheet into the typewriter and began typing. Just then Lorraine nudged me and I turned from the information desk and looked down the hall. I couldn't believe my eyes. There was an old man heading for us like a jogging ghost. He was dressed in a white hospital gown, and had just popped out of the elevator. I don't know why, but I felt he was up to something rather illegal, and I decided to keep saying crazy things to the nurse to distract her. 'Oh, yes, and after the Waldorf-Astoria, they were going to go disco dancing at Studio 54, and then meet for a nightcap at the Plaza Hotel with Jane Fonda and the Archbishop of Canterbury.' The nurse grunted and kept typing and mumbling things like 'We're going to have to have his Social Security number. Who is his private physician? What is his religious preference?'

By this time the old man was practically up to us. He was taking these short rapid steps that made him look like a sandpiper. And he just zoomed by whispering very clearly to us, 'Let's get the 3@!$% out of here!'

Lorraine looked dumbfounded, but I almost burst into laughter because I had never seen a more welcome or a funnier sight. The mean nurse was right in the middle of talking to us when she noticed us move quickly to become

human crutches for this swiftly moving form which she recognised as a patient. She stood up from her desk and began to call after us, 'Where do you *think* you're going? Sir! Sir! Come back here!'

We hit the automatic doors and they flung open. The Studebaker was waiting right where we left it, and like the old pros that we were, within a flash we were in the front seat just as the mean nurse came out the door with a couple of confused attendants and another doctor who looked like a medicinal dwarf. The engine exploded. I threw the car into gear and we peeled rubber down the exit ramp, with a lot of people in white yelling.

'Where are your clothes?' I asked.

'They got 'em, the scavengers,' the old man growled. 'They got 'em!'

'I thought you *wanted* to go to the hospital,' Lorraine reminded him. 'You were in such terrible pain.'

'Yeah, well I'm not now. I just needed a little medicine, not a new home.'

'Right,' I said.

'You betcha,' the old man agreed.

'Back to the house on the double?' I asked him.

He patted my knee again and smiled. 'That's my boy! *That's my boy!*'

from *The Pigman's Legacy* by Paul Zindel

Reading for Understanding

1 What effect did the Colonel's first scream have on the two young people?
2 What actions did John (the boy telling the story) first consider taking?
3 Why did Lorraine hesitate when she was first asked to help support the old man?
4 Why did John have to move quickly to close the door as they left the house?
5 What did Lorraine think had caused the Colonel's agony?
6 What was it that startled the Boy Scouts?
7 Why did the two young people obey the mean nurse's orders?
8 What information did they get from the nursing staff by persistently asking questions?
9 What incident delighted the mean-looking nurse?
10 What was strange about the old man's appearance when they first observed him again?
11 Why did John decide to keep saying crazy things to the nurse?
12 Why did John almost burst into laughter as the old man sneaked by in his escape attempt?
13 What emotions did the mean nurse seem to be experiencing throughout the escape?
14 What evidence is there at the end that the Colonel is completely well again?
15 What qualities of the Colonel's personality are revealed in this passage? Give evidence.
16 What qualities of John's personality does this passage supply evidence for? Refer to the passage in your answer.

The Fishing Lure

A moment's thoughtlessness almost turns into a disaster.

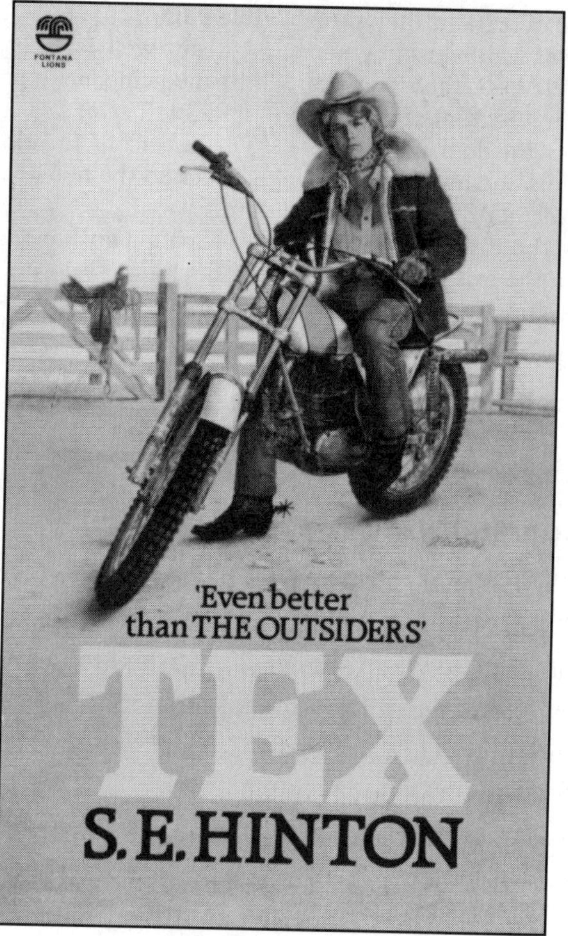

'Even better
than THE OUTSIDERS'
TEX
S.E. HINTON

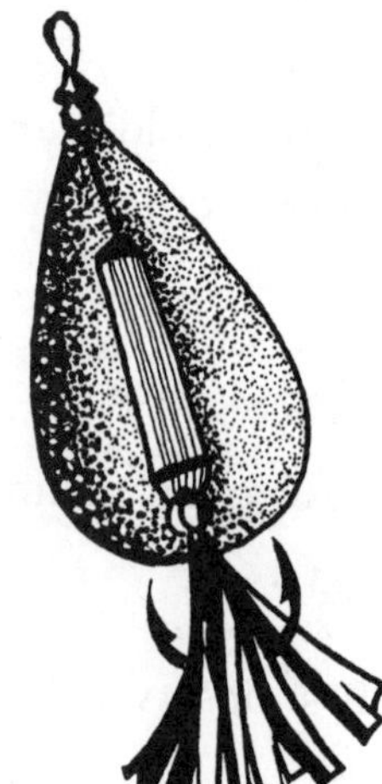

I walked over to the sporting goods store. I meant to look at the guns, but got sidetracked by the fishing stuff. It had been a long time since Mason and me had gone fishing. Maybe if I got us a new lure, he'd want to go again. I like hunting better, myself, but fishing was the only thing Mason really relaxed at.

I looked the lures over, trying to remember what ones he already had, and trying to find one that didn't cost too much. I couldn't believe the way they had gone up in price. Finally I decided on one; it would take what was left of my money, but I hadn't planned on buying anything anyway. Mason could pay for lunch.

Then I went to look at the shotguns. There was no way I could get one, but I liked looking at them. I found a 20-gauge I really liked. I put

the fishing lure in my shirt pocket and picked up the gun to see how it balanced. It seemed a little stock-heavy to me, but maybe that was just sour grapes since I couldn't get it. Good sights on it, though. I sighed and put it down. Duck season was coming up . . . well, Christmas was coming up, too.

I walked around a little more, looking at tennis stuff and skiing stuff and wondering if there were enough people to buy all the stuff in stores. I guess there are, though, or there wouldn't be so many stores. I looked at the water skis. I went water skiing once, and man, I loved it.

Someone tapped me on the shoulder. I turned around and faced a salesman.

'Kid,' he said, 'can you read that sign?'

I looked where he was pointing. 'Shoplifters will be prosecuted.'

'Sure I can read it.'

'Do you know what it means?'

'Yeah. You catch somebody stealing you'll do your best to send 'em to jail.'

'Good. Now come with me.'

I did, not even thinking about asking why. When you're in a strange place you don't think about having control of anything.

I followed him into a back office.

'I got another one, Ed,' he said to a man behind a desk. Ed looked up at me wearily.

'What was it?'

The salesman reached over and pulled the fishing lure out of my pocket. For a second I didn't know what was going on. Then I broke out in a cold, sick sweat. They thought I was stealing it!

'I was going to pay for it,' I said, when I could get my breath. I went from shocked to mad to scared, so quick I couldn't tell which I was feeling. 'I was going to pay for it,' I repeated, trying to keep my voice level. I sounded guilty. I even felt guilty. I must look guilty, too, I thought frantically. All kinds of visions were going through my mind — what would Mason say, what would Pop think, Jamie . . . being put in jail. I couldn't go back to jail!

'They all say that,' Ed nodded.

Say what? I wondered, then I remembered saying, 'I was going to pay for it.'

'I never stole anything in my life!' I said. Borrowing that car hadn't really been stealing. Anyway, I was just twelve when that happened —

'Now that one I never heard before,' Ed said.

I was so scared and sick I was close to crying. They'd never believe me. Nobody'd ever believe me. Pop would disown me. Pop was funny and talkative and loved to laugh and tell stories, but he had never ever said a word about prison or what it was like, just drilled it into us to respect the law. That probably impressed us more than if he had given us a day by day description of it. Anyway, I knew what it was like, sort of. I remembered sitting in that jail cell, listening to somebody beat on the bars down the hall, screaming 'I'm drunk and I'm proud of it!' over and over again and the smell was so bad and the walls got closer and closer and I knew if I had to stay in there I'd go nuts like a caged animal, and beat my head in against the wall, and I was trying to sit real still to keep from doing that when Pop came to get me. From the look on his face I thought I'd go straight from jail to an orphanage. And when we got outside he'd belted me; the only time he'd ever hit either of us.

'I just put it in my pocket for a minute while I looked at a gun,' I said, as steady as possible. The way they were looking at me made me feel like I was the worst kind of trash. Mason, even if he believed me, he'd never live this down. He had such a pride thing about never getting into trouble when he had so many chances to. He had turned very sarcastic on

Johnny once, when Johnny smuggled a carton of Eskimo Pies out of the Safeway store, made him so miserable he couldn't even eat more than one or two.

'Was he out of the store?' Ed asked the salesman. 'Or about to leave the store?'

It was weird, being talked about like you weren't even human.

'He was inside,' the salesman said reluctantly.

'Turn him loose. This time.' He went back to his papers.

The salesman opened his mouth to protest, then snapped at me, 'You heard him, get out.'

Everything had happened so fast I still didn't feel like I could move. 'I was going to pay for it.' I made one more effort to clear myself. 'I got the money to pay for it.' I almost took my billfold out to prove it.

'Kid,' Ed said, 'people come in here, kids with bigger allowances than my salary, and it's just like mountain climbing to them. They take things because they're there. Sometimes we even find merchandise in the trash bins — once they get away with it they're bored with it.'

He glanced up at me, and for a second I felt like he believed me. 'Still want the lure?'

I looked at it, laying there on his desk. A fishing lure was going to make me slightly sick for a long time to come. I shook my head. He escorted me out, but he didn't need to worry. I was never going into the store again.

from *Tex* by S. E. Hinton

Reading for Understanding

1 What was the boy's intention when he first walked towards the sporting goods store?

2 Why was he sidetracked to the fishing gear?

3 What two considerations guided him in the choice of the fishing lure?

4 Identify a positive quality and a negative quality of the shotgun he picked up?

5 What was the boy thinking about when the salesman tapped him on the shoulder?

6 Why didn't he object when the salesman asked him to follow?

7 When does he realise that they believe he is a shoplifter?

8 What emotions does the boy experience when he realises that they believe he is a shoplifter?

9 What evidence is there to tell us that the boy has been in jail before?

10 How had the earlier jail experience been for the boy? Refer to the passage for evidence.

11 'I just put it in my pocket for a minute while I looked at the gun.' What is the boy trying to do at this time to convince the men that he is telling the truth?

12 What fact sways Ed into saying 'Turn him loose?'

13 Why does the boy say 'I got the money to pay for it'?

14 What does the boy determine in his mind as he leaves the shop?

15 Judging from the passage, how important does Mason seem to be in the boy's life? Give evidence.

16 What sort of a person does the main character in this passage seem to be? Give evidence.

POETRY

TEENAGERS IN CONFLICT

The Rebel

When everybody has short hair,
The rebel lets his hair grow long.

When everybody has long hair,
The rebel cuts his hair short.

When everybody talks during the lesson,
The rebel doesn't say a word.

When nobody talks during the lesson,
The rebel creates a disturbance.

When everybody wears a uniform,
The rebel dresses in fantastic clothes.

When everybody wears fantastic clothes,
The rebel dresses soberly.

In the company of dog lovers,
The rebel expresses a preference for cats.

In the company of cat lovers,
The rebel puts in a good word for dogs.

When everybody is praising the sun,
The rebel remarks on the need for rain.

When everybody is greeting the rain,
The rebel regrets the absence of sun.

When everybody goes to the meeting,
The rebel stays at home and reads a book.

When everybody stays at home and reads a book,
The rebel goes to the meeting.

When everybody says, Yes please,
The rebel says, No thank you.

When everybody says, No thank you,
The rebel says, Yes please.

It is very good that we have rebels.
You may not find it very good to be one.

D.J. Enright

Dead Smart One of the Boys

My name . . . Well that don't matter
But I goes to this 'ere school,
And I've got a reputation
For breaking every rule.
The teachers they all hate me,
Every master I annoys,
'Cos I'm a right old criminal —
Dead smart, one of the boys.

The first day at me new school
Me teacher got right shocked,
'Cos straight away I lose me cap —
That's how the lav. got blocked!
And I burns me new school blazer
Hiding gaspers in me pocket,
And I decides, in this 'ere boat,
It's me is gonna rock it.

Next day the form's dead eager
As through the gates they swarm,
And they elects some swotty clot
As captain of the form.
Now so far I've gone easy,
Just sizing up the dump,
But when I sees what that job's worth,
I gives that clot a clump.

So he resigns, and after
I've persuaded all the rest,
I gets elected. Then I starts
To feather my own nest.
I helps with dinner money —
Of course I takes my cut —
The teacher couldn't work it out,

And he promptly done his nut,
So the teachers they all hate me,
Every master I annoys,
'Cos I'm a right old criminal —
Dead smart, one of the boys.

You lot goes to Assembly,
But me, I'm never there.
I sits and has a crafty smoke
Down the — well, you know where.
Then I copies some kid's homework,
And if I gets found out,
I makes him say he copied mine,
Or I punch him on the snout.
So as my innocent years roll by
I'm in on every racket,
And anyone who tries it on,
He quickly cops a packet!

Till in the fourth year I can claim
To be the school's real boss.
And I spends me time in dodging work,
'Cos work, that's a dead loss.
So the teachers, they all hate me,
Every master I annoys,
'Cos I'm a right old criminal —
Dead smart, one of the boys.

Our form gets up a football team,
Of course I wasn't picked.
So when they left the field they found
Their money had been nicked.
But though they're all dead stupid,
They guessed I'd had a go,
So when I tries to talk to them,
They just don't want to know.

Then last week, down the billiard hall,
I joins up with a mob.
And we breaks into some radio shop —
A very crafty job,
Till some dirty copper spots us.
And I'm the one gets caught,
And there's no-one who'll stand by me
Next week when I'm in court.

And you can't help feeling rotten,
When you stand about and wait
For some bloke who'll say 'Hello' to you
But there's no-one who's your mate.
And when the rest all live it up,
There's no-one thinks of me.
But I don't care. When I'm big time
I'll show you — wait and see.

All you teachers, you what hates me,
Every master I annoys,
'Cos I'm a right old criminal . . .
Dead smart . . . One of the boys . . .

William Samson

Questions

1 'I'm a right old criminal'. How does the boy feel about his status at the beginning of the poem?

2 What happened to his school cap on the first day at the new school?

3 How did his school blazer get burnt?

4 Why did the first captain of the form resign?

5 '. . . after/I've persuaded all the rest,/I gets elected'. How do you think he 'persuaded' the others to vote for him?

6 What does the boy do when the others are at Assembly?

7 What attitude does he have to work? Quote a line from the poem to support your answer.

8 What is the first sign that the other students can't stand this boy?

9 Explain why '. . . there's no-one who'll stand by me/Next week when I'm in court'.

10 Are there any signs that this boy's attitude is changing by the end of the poem? Refer to the poem to support your answer.

11 The poem is written from the viewpoint of the delinquent boy. How effective is this?

12 What is your personal response to this poem? Give reasons for your opinion.

Some Days

Some days this school
is a huge concrete sandwich
squeezing me out like jam.

It weighs so much
breathing hurts, my legs freeze
my body is heavy.

On days like that
I carry whole buildings
high on my back.

Other days
the school is a rocket
thrusting right into the sun.

It's yellow and green
freshly painted,
the cabin windows
gleam with laughter.

On days like that
whole buildings support me,
my ladder is pushing
over their rooftops.

Amongst the clouds
I'd need a computer
to count all the bubbles
bursting aloud in my head.

David Harmer

Questions

1 'Some days this school/is a huge concrete sandwich'. Why is the word 'concrete' unusual here? What effect does it have?

2 What impression of school is the poet expressing in the first verse?

3 What evidence of the effect of school on his functioning does the poet offer in the second verse?

4 'The school is a rocket'. What impression of the school is being presented by this image?

5 Why are the colours 'yellow' and 'green' appropriate when they occur?

6 The cabin windows 'gleam with laughter'. Why is 'laughter' an unexpected word here. What effect does this unusual usage have?

7 'Whole buildings support me'. Which earlier line does this line balance? What effect is achieved by this balance?

8 'My ladder is pushing/over their rooftops'. How is the poet feeling on these kinds of days?

9 What do you think the poet means by 'all the bubbles/bursting aloud in my head'?

10 How effectively has the poet conveyed some of his feelings about school? Why?

Truant

Sing a song of sunlight
My pocket's full of sky —
Starling's egg for April
Jay's feather for July.
And here's a thorn bush three bags full
Of drift-white wool.

They call him dunce, and yet he can discern
Each mouse-brown bird,
And call its name and whistle back its call,
And spy among the fern
Delicate movement of a furred
Fugitive creature hiding from the day.
Discovered secrets magnify his play
Into a vocation.

Laughing at education
He knows where the redshank hides her nest, perceives
a reed-patch tremble when a coot lays siege
To water territory.
Nothing escapes his eye:
A ladybird
Slides like a blood-drop down a spear of grass;
The sapphire sparkle of a dragon-fly
Redeems a waste of weeds.
Collecting acorns, telling the beads of the year
On yew tree berries, his mind's too full for speech.

Back in the classroom he can never find
Answers to dusty questions, yet could teach,
  Deeper than knowledge,
  Geometry of twigs
  Scratched on a sunlit wall;
  History in stones,
  Seasons told by the fields' calendar —
  Living languages of Spring and Fall.

Phoebe Hesketh

Questions

1 What does the chorus at the beginning of the poem show us about the world of the truant?

2 'They call him dunce'. Explain the irony in these words.

3 Which of the truant's five senses is shown to be highly developed in the first verse? Give evidence from the poem.

4 'Discovered secrets magnify his play/Into a vocation'. What does the poet mean here?

5 'Laughing at education'. What *is* the truant's attitude to his schooling?

6 According to the poet, what can turn a 'waste of weeds' into something good?

7 Why doesn't the truant speak much? Quote from the poem in giving your answer.

8 The questions asked in the classroom are described as 'dusty' questions? What does the poet mean?

9 What three traditional subjects does the truant have understanding of, according to the last six lines of the poem?

10 Did you enjoy this poem? Why or why not?

One

Only one of me
and nobody can get a second one
from a photocopy machine.

Nobody has the fingerprints I have.
Nobody can cry my tears, or laugh my laugh
or have my expectancy when I wait.

But anybody can mimic my dance with my dog.
Anybody can howl how I sing out of tune.
And mirrors can show me multiplied
many times, say, dressed up in red
or dressed up in grey.

Nobody can get into my clothes for me
or feel my fall for me, or do my running.
Nobody hears my music for me either.

I am just this one.
Nobody else makes the words
I shape with sound, when I talk.

But anybody can act how I stutter in a rage.
Anybody can copy echoes I make.
And mirrors can show me multiplied
many times, say, dressed up in green
or dressed up in blue.

James Berry

WRITING

CAPTURING A HUMOROUS MOMENT

All of us enjoy a piece of genuinely humorous writing. But what is it that enables a writer to capture the humour in a situation? How is it that one writer can bring out the humour, while another writer describing the same situation might fail?

Read through the following passage. Clive James is describing a time when he shared lodgings in London with a young man named Trevor. Trevor has enough money to buy a new mattress which arrives wrapped in a 16-ply brown paper bag. With winter approaching, the insulating qualities of the bag are obvious, so James moves in.

The Man in the Brown Paper Bag

In Trevor's living-room, my suitcase against the wall served as a headboard. Folded clothes made a pillow. Beyond, into the centre of the room, stretched the brown paper bag, forming my bed. Wriggling into it took some time, but once inserted I could settle down in comparative warmth for a long night of turning from one side to the other. It was the hardness of the floor which compelled frequent movement. A lot of this I could do in my sleep, because my body, albeit much abused, was still young and supple, and I have always had Napoleon's gift of falling asleep at will, although unfortunately it has not always been accompanied by his gift of waking up again. The problem resided not in how the hardness of the floor affected my sleep, but in how the noise the paper bag made affected Trevor.

As he lay there in the darkness on his enviably luxurious convertible divan, it was as if, somewhere nearby, a giant packet of crisps was being eaten by one of those cinema patrons who think that they are being unobtrusive if they take only a few crisps at a time and chew them very slowly. When Trevor could bear no more he would switch on his modernistic tubular bedside light, wake me up and tell me to be quiet. Invariably I would discover, upon waking, that my bladder, which was already showing signs of being weakened by the steady inundation of cider, demanded emptying. So I had to get out of the paper bag, go away, pee, come back and get back in, thus creating a double uproar. When Trevor switched his light off again I would lie there trying not to move. Only a dead man or a yoga adept can keep that up for more than twenty minutes. Judging that Trevor was asleep again, I would essay a surreptitious turn to one side, making no more noise than a shy prospective bride unwrapping a lace-trimmed silk nightgown from its tissues. This movement completed, for a long time I would lie there, inhaling and exhaling as shallowly as possible and waiting until the sound of Trevor's steady breathing deepened into the second level of sleep. Only then would I make the necessary full turn on to the other side. A man tearing up a thin telephone directory while wading through dead leaves would have been hard put to be so silent. But if, after these manoeuvres, I dropped off to sleep, it was inevitable that an involuntary shift of weight would sooner or later produce the full effect of a large, empty cardboard box being attacked by a flock of woodpeckers. I can be sure of this because sometimes the noise woke me as well.

from *Falling Towards England* by Clive James

How has Clive James captured the humour of this situation? What 'ingredients' has he made use of? What techniques has he used?

Selection of a humorous incident

Although it may seem obvious, it is important to notice that Clive James is describing a situation that already has a lot of potential humour in it. The very idea of a young man sleeping in a brown paper bag conjures up a set of humorous pictures in our mind. The best humorous writing will have as its starting point a situation that enables the reader to visualise humorous action occurring.

Selection of humorous comparisons

Notice in the Clive James passage how the writer creates humour by the ridiculous comparisons he makes. The sounds of him carefully moving in the paper bag are described as 'a man tearing up a thin telephone directory while wading through dead leaves would have been hard put to be so silent'. The comparison here evokes images that almost compel a smile. What other ridiculous, but graphic, images and comparisons does James use?

YOUR TURN TO CAPTURE HUMOUR

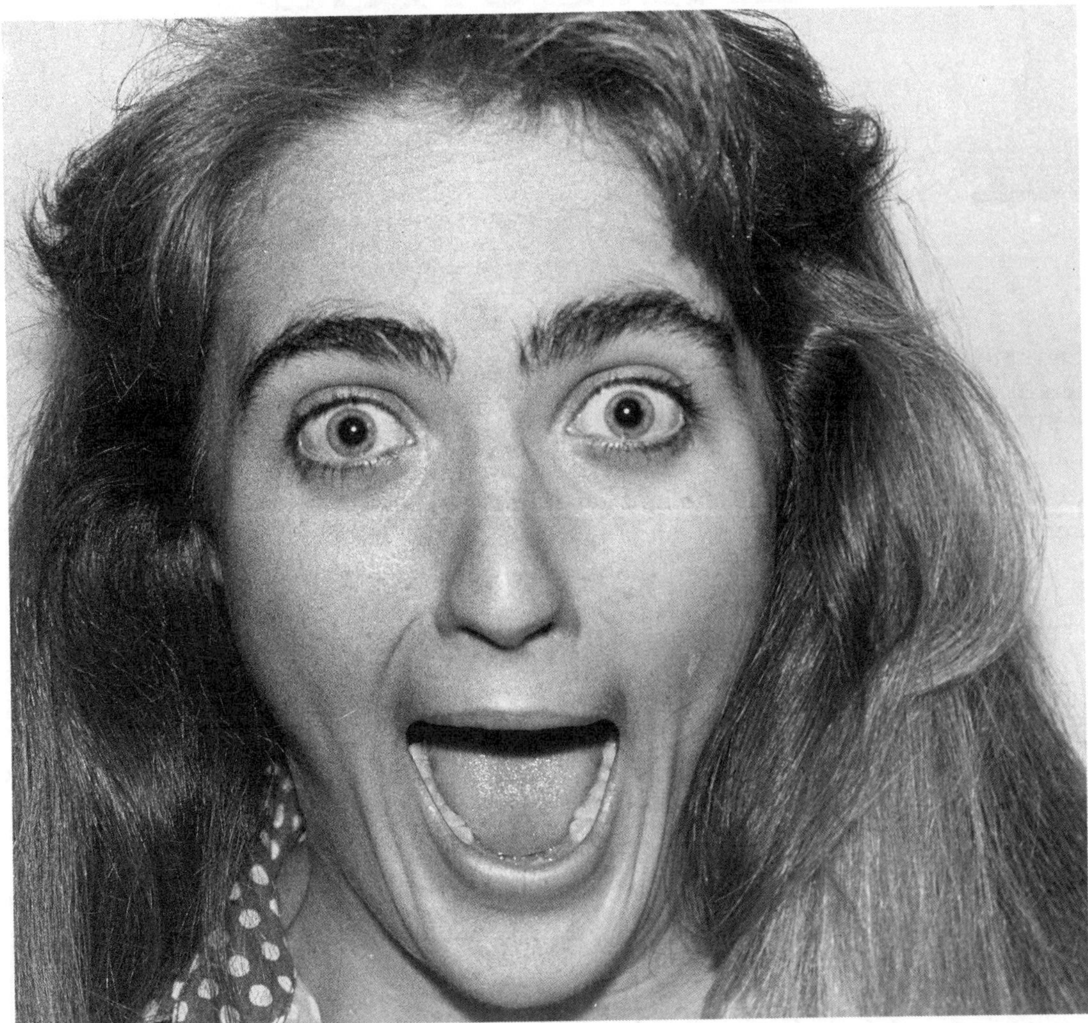

Write two paragraphs of humorous description building from an unusual incident in your life. Try to make use of humorous comparisons and images, and select words that convey energy and fun to the reader. If you are unable to recall a humorous incident, choose one of the following topics.

- The day I lost my bathers!
- An embarrassing sight
- The funniest incident on-stage
- When things go wrong
- Water-bomb fight
- The night our tent fell down
- The party and the swimming pool
- The broken vending machine

LANGUAGE

FIGURATIVE LANGUAGE

Figurative language is the opposite of literal language. The English language has many words and phrases that don't literally mean what they say. Such words and phrases, which often make meaning more vivid, emphatic or dramatic, are called figurative language. Poets and other writers often use figures of speech such as **similes, metaphors, personification, hyperboles** and **idioms** to extend the significance of what they are saying.

SIMILES

Similes are examples of figurative language. They require us to picture one thing as being similar to another, using words such as 'like', 'as' and 'than'. For example:

- His bat was **as steady as a rock.**
- She sang **like an angel.**

Completing the Similes

Complete the following similes by inserting an appropriate word. Try to use popular expressions.

1 as fresh as a ....
2 as strong as an ....
3 as fit as a ....
4 as warm as ....
5 as jumpy as a ....
6 as stubborn as a ....
7 as cunning as a ....
8 as quick as a ....
9 as flat as a ....
10 as full as a ....
11 slower than a ....
12 quieter than a ....
13 weaker than a ....
14 nuttier than a ....
15 braver than a ....
16 heavier than ....
17 colder than ....
18 madder than a ....
19 taller than a ....
20 blinder than a ....

METAPHORS

Metaphors are another form of figurative language. Where the simile asks us to look at one thing as being like another, the metaphor asks us to picture it as *being* the other thing. For example:

- The class raised **a forest of hands** into the air.

Selecting the Metaphor

Choose the word from the brackets that represents a metaphorical use of language.

1 The announcement was greeted by a .... of protest. (howl/storm)
2 The leading yacht .... across the water at great speed. (flew/raced)
3 The speaker looked out at a .... of faces. (sea/lot)
4 A .... of hostility had developed between the two schools. (feeling/wall)
5 Her eyes .... with anger. (blazed/looked)
6 The comic characters .... the show. (enjoyed/stole)
7 .... of laughter swept over the audience. (gales/sounds)
8 She tensed herself as another .... of pain ran through her body. (sensation/wave)
9 The team members showed a .... of courage today. (lot/mountain)
10 The .... of criticism began to destroy their unity. (cancer/severity)

PERSONIFICATION

Personification is a form of metaphor in which an object or idea is likened to a person. For example:

- The sun crept across the sky on leaden feet.

In a verse from the poem 'Drought: A South African Parable', Francis Carey Slater uses personification effectively to describe the coming of rain to break the drought.

The Coming of Rain

Suddenly the drums of the rain are beating,
Over the hills her shining banner comes;
Swiftly the enemy drought is retreating —
Scared by insistent drums.
Painfully and long has the veld been battered,
Smitten and scourged by devils of drought, —
Sweepingly the stubborn foe is shattered
Rain has put him to rout.
Suddenly comes rain with his shining legions,
(Will love come so, bringing peace to earth?)
Suddenly long blasted and barren regions
Wake to the wonder of birth.

Francis Carey Slater

Questions

1 In the first two lines, what is the coming of the rain compared to?
2 What is it about the coming of the rain that makes 'the drums of the rain' an appropriate image?
3 To what human group is the drought compared to in the third line?
4 Who is 'the stubborn foe' in the seventh line?
5 What aspect of the coming of rain do you think 'his shining legions' refers to?
6 What effect does it have to write of rain and drought as though they have human qualities?

HYPERBOLE

Hyperbole is a form of figurative language in which exaggeration is deliberately used, not to mislead but to emphasise a point. For example:

- I'm so hungry I could eat a horse.

Identifying Hyperboles

One of the sentences in each of the following pairs contains an example of hyperbole. Identify the hyperbole in each case. Many of them are common Australian sayings.

1 a Good tradesmen are often hard to find.
b Good tradesmen are as scarce as hen's teeth.

2 a It rained so much it was wet enough to bog a duck.
b Torrential rain pounded the coastal area.

3 a The new batsman didn't make any runs at all.
b The new batsman wasn't worth a crumpet.

4 a The grand piano sounded magnificent after it had been re-tuned.
b She is so hopeless she couldn't find a grand piano in a one-roomed house.

5 a The extra day's study was as helpful as an ashtray on a motorbike.
b After saving for two years Mark bought a new motorbike.

6 a Ray is an incredibly talkative person.
b Ray could talk under water.

7 a Jack studied the town hall clock to see why it wasn't working.
b Jack couldn't tell the time if the town hall clock fell on him.

8 a I was knocked as flat as a pancake.
b I was invited to a breakfast of pancakes and coffee.

9 a The thief must have been lower than a snake's belly.
b The snake slithered across the road just ahead of the car.

10 a After the camp we still had a tonne of food left over.
b The new machine weighed four tonnes.

GETTING IT RIGHT

CONSISTENT VERB TENSES

Changing tenses in writing tends to distract and confuse the reader. For the best effect you need to be consistent. That is, you should not carelessly mix the tenses you are using. For example:

- We **were concerned** at her eating patterns because **she** eats so little. (Incorrect)

The writer has started out in the past tense ('were concerned') and then changed to the present tense ('eats').

- We **were concerned** at her eating patterns because she **ate** so little. (Correct)

Both verbs are now in the same tense, in this case the past tense.

Using Consistent Verbs

Correct the following sentences by making sure that the tense of verbs is consistent throughout.

1. An enormous crocodile rounded the curve of the river and is bearing down on the dog.
2. The weekly appointment at the dentist scares me because I would have to undergo drilling.
3. The bear thought I am after her cubs and she growls menacingly.
4. As he ran along the edge of the lake, he quickly loads his rifle and fires off a shot.
5. She smiles and I smiled back wondering who she is.
6. The sea flattened, the oil slick spreads out, the lifeboat drifted alone and helpless on the ocean.
7. Convenience foods are fast becoming the most popular food because people wanted to save time for other activities.
8. Local surfies resent 'intruders' from other beaches and hassled them at every opportunity.
9. The kangaroo took to the water as the dogs chase him barking.
10. The patrol stopped, the leader approaches the party of refugees slowly, and carefully looks for any sign of danger.

DRAMA

PEOPLE IN CONFLICT

It has been said that conflict is the essence of drama. Without some internal or external struggle, a play tends to be lifeless and insipid.

Frequently, the conflict is external. It will often feature confrontation between two or more participants, and the confrontation can become quite violent and aggressive if the participants do not control their anger.

Read through the following passage from *Twelve Angry Men* by Reginald Rose, a play in which twelve jurors try to decide whether or not a young man is guilty of knifing his father. The extract is taken from the end of Act I. All twelve jurors are in this scene, but only the 3rd juror, 6th juror and 8th juror speak.

Provocation

8th Juror *(To the 5th Juror)* I think this is what happened. The old man heard the fight between the boy and his father a few hours earlier. Then, while lying in bed, he heard a body hit the floor in the boy's apartment, and he heard the woman scream from across the street. He got up, tried to get to the door, heard someone racing down the stairs, and *assumed* it was the the boy.

6th Juror I think that's possible.

3rd Juror *(Shouting furiously)* Assumed? Now listen to me, you people. I've seen all kinds of dishonesty in my day — but this little display takes the cake.

(He turns and strides to the 8th Juror. He waves his hand in the 8th Juror's face.)

You come in here with your sanctimonious talk about slum kids and injustice, and you make up some wild stories, and all of a sudden you start getting through to some of these old ladies in here. Well, you're not getting through to me. I've had enough. *(He turns to the others.)* What's the matter with you people? Every one of you knows this kid is guilty. He's got to burn. We're letting him slip through our fingers here.

8th Juror *(Calmly)* Slip through our fingers? Are you his executioner?

3rd Juror I'm one of 'em.

8th Juror Maybe you'd like to pull the switch.

3rd Juror *(Shouting)* For this kid? You bet I'd like to pull the switch.

8th Juror I'm sorry for you.

3rd Juror *(Backing from the 8th Juror)* Don't start with me now.

8th Juror *(Following the 3rd Juror)* What it must feel like to want to pull the switch.
3rd Juror *(Raging)* Listen, you — shut up!
8th Juror *(Baiting him)* Ever since we walked into this room you've been behaving like a self-appointed public avenger.
3rd Juror I'm telling you now! Shut up!
8th Juror You want to see this boy die because you personally want it, not because of the facts.
3rd Juror *(Roaring)* Shut up!
8th Juror You're a sadist!
3rd Juror Shut up, you son of a bitch! *(He lunges wildly at the 8th Juror.)*

(The 8th Juror holds his ground. The 5th and 6th Jurors grab the 3rd Juror from behind. He strains against the hands, his face dark with rage. The Foreman moves to R of the 8th Juror to restrain him.)

Let me go! I'll kill him! I'll kill him!
8th Juror *(Calmly)* You don't *really* mean you'll kill me, do you?

The 3rd Juror breaks from the 5th and 6th Jurors, stops struggling and stares bitterly at the 8th Juror as —

THE CURTAIN FALLS

Notice in this passage that the 8th Juror is deliberately trying to provoke an angry reaction from the 3rd Juror. Obviously he is successful.

We can learn from this passage some of the things that people do which cause the level of anger in a situation to increase. There are violent physical gestures such as when the 3rd Juror waves his hand in the 8th Juror's face. There is name-calling — 'sadist' and 'son of a bitch'. There are emotive words — 'sanctimonious talk' and 'getting through to some of these old ladies'. The 3rd Juror begins to get louder in volume as he gets angrier. Each of these in some way contributes to the escalation of the anger.

Guidelines for handling anger well

Learning to express anger well becomes particularly important when we look at the social evidence of anger out of control — war, violence, destruction, homicide. These and many other tragic outcomes follow when people fail to manage anger. Many disagreements that could be worked through productively end up being de-railed if one person or the other does not manage his or her anger.

Anger is an important emotion which can be useful in bringing about productive change, but it needs to be managed or it can become very destructive.

Here are some guidelines for managing anger well. Note them, and discuss them in class to clarify any aspects.

1 **Use 'I-statements'** when talking about your feelings of anger, rather than 'you-statements'. 'You-statements' tend to be aggressive and attacking and usually bring a very defensive or counter-attacking response. For example, it is better to say 'I felt very angry when you didn't phone', rather than 'You made me so angry when you didn't phone.'

2 **Avoid name-calling** (e.g. 'idiot', 'liar'). Terms like these usually escalate the anger and make it harder to sort through the disagreement.

3 **Avoid emotive terms and 'buzz words'**. Words like 'always' and 'never' tend to increase defensiveness. For example: 'You always arrive late!' Words like 'stupid' and 'dumb' have a similar effect.

4 **Don't bring up the past**. Anger tends to escalate in unhelpful ways when one person or the other brings up the past. For example: 'And this isn't the first time you've come in late. You did it last weekend, and three times last month, and . . .'

5 **Stay focused on the issue**. Don't bring in other problems or areas of disagreement. This makes it hard to sort things through.

6 **Try to adopt a joint problem-solving perspective**. Ask 'What can we do so this doesn't happen again?'

SOCIAL DRAMA — HANDLING ANGER WELL

Divide the class into groups of three or four students. Then have each group choose one of the situations below and act it out, improvising the dialogue. Make sure that you and all other characters try to practise the guidelines above so that anger is managed well. In order to see the contrast better, one act-out could aim to *break* all the guidelines.

Situations

1 A 16-year-old boy has arrived home at 1:00 am on Sunday morning after being told to be home by midnight. Mum and Dad are angry.
(Characters: mother, father, son)

2 A teacher has set an assignment and required that it be in today. The teacher is angry when two students fail to produce the assignment.
(Characters: Student 1, Student 2, Teacher)

3 A sporting competition has been decided by a poor umpiring decision. There are some angry team members on one side, a referee or umpire and a team member from the winning side on the other. You will need to decide the nature of the sporting contest before you act this one out.
(Characters: referee, member of winning team, 3 members of losing team)

4 A vacant allotment where you and friends congregated is now being fenced off by the owner. You are angry because of the loss and you express your anger at two workmen who are putting up the fencing.
(Characters: you, two workmen)

5 Saturday morning is room-tidying time, but you sneaked out early this morning without cleaning your room. Your parents are angry and are ready to unload on you.
(Characters: you, mother, father)

6 You have worked hard at arranging a party for students from your school. The party was a great success until a few students arrived who had drunk too much. They did some damage and left everyone feeling angry and upset. You decide to confront them at school on Monday.
(Characters: you and a friend, 2 students who were drunk)

7 You have been borrowing floppy disks from your mates to play games on the family computer. Now the computer has a virus and has written it on all the disks your parents have. Your father and mother are very angry as they confront you.
(Characters: you, mother, father)

8 You have a part-time job after school one afternoon a week. You make a mistake during a stock-take and your supervisor expresses anger at you, because the work will have to be re-done.
(Characters: you, supervisor)

ACKNOWLEDGEMENTS

The authors and publishers are grateful to the following for permission to reproduce copyright material:

Poetry and prose

Basil Blackwell Ltd for 'The Pirate' by Huge Chesterman; Bodley Head for the extract from *The Pigman's Legacy* by Paul Zindel; Cambridge University Press for the extract from *Gregory's Girl* by Andrew Bethell; Carcanet Press Ltd for the poem 'The Fifth Sense' from *Collected Poems* by Patricia Beer; John Clarke for the extract from *Daggshead Revisited* by John Clarke; Collins/Angus and Robertson Publishers for 'Dead Smart One of the Boys' by William Samson, for 'Fourteen Men' by Mary Gilmore, for 'Sanctuary' by Judith Wright from *Five Senses*, for the extract from *All the Green Year* by Don Charlwood, and for the extract from *Gallipoli* by Jack Bennett; Bill Condon for his play *Oh No Romeo*; David Harmer for his poem 'Some Days'; David Higham Associates Ltd for the poem 'Ballad of the Landlord' by Langston Hughes,for the extract from *The Lord God Made Them All* by James Herriot and for the poem 'My Mother Saw a Dancing Bear' from *Collected Poems* by Charles Causley; Dobson Books Ltd for the extract from *Survival* by Russell Evans; Berlie Doherty for the poem 'Kieran'; Faber & Faber Ltd for the extract from *The Lord of the Flies* by William Golding; Fremantle Arts Century Press for the extract from *My Place* by Sally Morgan; Hamish Hamilton Children's Books for 'One' by James Barry from *When I Dance*; Houghton Mifflin Australia for the poem 'Death of a Tree' by Jack Davis, and for the poem 'Hypochondria' from *Snakes and Ladders* by Robin Klein and for the poem 'The Black Tracker' from *The First Born* by Jack Davis; John Johnson Ltd for the poem 'Warning' from *Rose in the Afternoon* by Jenny Josephs; Longman Cheshire for 'Enter Without So Much as Knocking' by Bruce Dawe from *Sometimes Gladness*; Murray Pollinger Literary Agent for 'The Hitch-hiker' by Roald Dahl from *The Wonderful Story of Henry Sugar*; Penguin Books Australia Ltd for 'Lucky Lips' from *Round the Twist* by Paul Jennings; Penguin Books Ltd for the poem 'How to Treat House-plants' from *Hot Dog and Other Poems* by Kit Wright (Kestrel Books, 1981) Copyright (c) Kit Wright 1981, for the extract from *Friedrich* by Hans Peter Richter and for the extract from *Animal Farm* by George Orwell; Mr G Sassoon for the poem 'The Hero' by Siegfried Sassoon from *War Poems*; Scott Meredith Literary Agency Inc, 845 Third Avenue, New York, New York 10022. for the extract from *The Ruum* by Arthur Porges reprinted with the permission of the author; Watson, Little Limited Authors Agents for 'The Rebel' by D J Enright from *Rhyme Times Rhyme*, Chatto & Windus 1974; Weldon Publishing for the extract from *They're a Wierd Mob!* by John O'Grady.

Advertisements, photographs, book covers and cartoons

Associated R and R Films for the movie still from *Gallipoli* on p. 183; Auspac Media for the *Garfield* cartoon on p. 30; Copyright United Media Syndicate; Austral International for the photographs on pp. 252, (Sygma) 226, (Camera Press) 86-87, 128-129; Burrows Film Group for the movie stills from *The Man from Snowy River* on pp.175, 176 and 177; Collins/Angus and Robertson Publishers for the cover of *All the Green Year* by Don Charlwood; E C Publications Inc for the extract from *Australian Mad* #299 Nov pp.28-29 Copyright (c) 1990 E C Publications Inc on p. 215; Fremantle Arts Centre Press for the cover of *My Place* by Sally Morgan; Gaffney Licensing Pty Ltd for the *Hagar the Horrible* cartoons on pp. 159, 161, 286; Greenpeace Australia for the advertisment on p.

221; Horizon International for the photograph on p.47; International Photographic Library for the photograph on p. 115; Jolliffe Studios Pty Ltd for the two *On the Rocks* cartoons on pp. 74, 289; Walter Medenbach for the photograph on p. 32; Michael Joseph Ltd for the cover of *The Lord God Made Them All* by James Herriot; Penguin Books Ltd for the cover of *Survival* by Russell Evans and the cover of *The Wonderful Story of Henry Sugar* by Roald Dahl; NASA for the photograph on p. 191; Katherine Praten for the photograph on p. 285; Stock Photos for the photographs on pp. 73, 152, 212, 260-261, 225; Warner Brothers for the *Young Einstein* poster on p. 188.

While every care has been taken to trace and acknowledge copyright, the publishers tender their apologies for any accidental infringement where copyright has proved untraceable. They would be pleased to come to a suitable arrangement with the rightful owner in each case.

Edited by Vivienne Perham
Illustrated by Carol Pelham-Thorman
Cover design and photograph by Jan Schmoeger